THE MOST ILLUSTRIOUS LADIES OF THE ITALIAN RENAISSANCE

Corner House Publishers

SOCIAL SCIENCE REPRINTS

General Editor MAURICE FILLER

Titian. Art Repro. Co.

Caterina Cornaro

Queen of Cyprus.

THE MOST ILLUSTRIOUS LADIES OF THE ITALIAN RENAISSANCE

By CHRISTOPHER HARE AUTHOR OF "A QUEEN OF QUEENS AND THE MAKING OF SPAIN," "DANTE THE WAYFARER," ETC.

CORNER HOUSE PUBLISHERS
WILLIAMSTOWN, MASSACHUSETTS 01267
1972

FIRST PUBLISHED 1907

REPRINTED 1972

BY

CORNER HOUSE PUBLISHERS

Printed in the United States of America

PREFACE

THE Period of the Renaissance has ever been so attractive to the historian that many learned volumes have been written on the subject, and it has been illustrated by much brilliant eloquence. An army of patient students have devoted long years to serious research, in hunting out forgotten treasures buried in foreign libraries, archives, chronicles, diaries, and letters innumerable.

Yet I venture to hope that there may still be room for a modest attempt to bring some of these vast stores of knowledge—more especially as they touch upon woman's life—within reach of those readers who have no leisure for profound and special study.

To them I would dedicate these sketches of some typical women of the Italian Renaissance, which may be regarded as brief appreciations, rather than full and complete biographies.

CONTENTS

CONTENTS

ILLUSTRATIONS

BOOKS AND DOCUMENTS CONSULTED

Archivi Toscani. *Pietro Berti.*

Chronice Fiorentine. *Villani.*

La Vita Italiano nel Cinquecento. Milano. 3 vols.

Istoria d'Italia. *Guicciardini.*

Rime Sacre della famiglia dei Medici. Pub. da *Cionacci.*

Lettere di una Gentildonna Fiorentina del secolo XV. Pub. da *Cesare Guasti.*

Annali d' Italia. *Muratori.*

La Guerra di Ferrara. *Sanuto.*

Relazione di Isabella d'Este con Ludovico Sforza . . . *A. Luzio R. Renier.*

Opere Complete. *Ariosto.*

Le Rime di *Francesco Petrarca.*

Lucrezia Borgia. *F. Gregorovius.* (With original letters and documents.)

Bianca Maria Sforza, Regina dei Romani, Imperatrice di Germania. *F. Calvi.*

Annali Veneti. Archivio Storico Italiano. *D. Malipiero.*

Vita di Caterina Sforza. Dall' Abate *Antonio Burriel.*

Caterina Sforza. *P. Pasolini.*

"Il Cortigiano" del Comte *Baldassare Castiglione.*

Lettere di *Baldassare Castiglione.*

Caterino Cornaro, e il suo Regno. *A. Centilli.*

Rime Spirituali di Vittoria Colonna. Venezia, 1548.

Asolani. *Pietro Bembo.*

BOOKS AND DOCUMENTS CONSULTED

Ricerche intorno a Leonardo da Vinci. *G. Uzielli.*

La Renaissance en Italie et en France, à l'époque de Charles VIII. *M. Eugène Muntz.*

Histoire de la République de Venise. *P. A. Daru.*

Histoire Secrète de la maison de Medicis. *Vaillas.*

Mémoires Historiques sur Naples. *Count Orlaff.*

Les Femmes de la Renaissance. *De Maulde Clavière.*

Vittorin de Feltre. *Benoit.*

Les Origines de la Renaissance en Italie. *Emile Gebhart.*

Louis XII. et Lodovico Sforza. *Louis Pelissier.*

Histoire des Républiques Italiennes. *M. S. de Sismondi.*

Life and Times of Macchiavelli. *Villari.*

History of the Papacy. *Dr. Creighton.*

The Renaissance in Italy. *J. A. Symonds.*

The Civilization of the Renaissance in Italy. *J. Burckhardt.*

Memoirs of the Dukes of Urbino. *James Dennistoun.*

The Renaissance. *W. H. Pater.*

Life of Lorenzo dei Medici. *William Roscoe.*

Life of Leo X. (Dissertation on Lucrezia Borgia.) *William Roscoe.*

Life of Isabella d'Este. *Julia Cartwright.*

Life of Beatrice d'Este. *Julia Cartwright.*

etc. etc.

DAUGHTERS OF THE RENAISSANCE
THEIR LIFE AND SURROUNDINGS.

DAUGHTERS OF THE RENAISSANCE: THEIR LIFE AND SURROUNDINGS.

It has been well said that each country has made to itself a Renaissance after its own image.

In that glorious dawn which succeeded the gloom of the Middle Ages, Italy was the first to awaken. Her clear vision, her intellectual energy, her enthusiasm for art, gave to all Europe the key-note of the future. The secret of her pre-eminence, so willingly accepted by the world, will not be found only in her "favourable situation, her language, her commercial prosperity, her political freedom," when other nations were scarcely emerging from barbarism. We shall rather attribute it to the spirit of intuition, to a nobler conception of man's place in the world, to higher aspirations; in a word, to all that constitutes the true Renaissance.

Italy created that "new spiritual atmosphere of culture and intellectual freedom" which broadened man's horizon, and made all things seem possible to him, in his new-born keen enthusiasm.

In the Middle Ages, scarcely left behind, the ascetic ideal of life taught that beauty and pleasure were deadly perils to the soul, and that ignorance was safer than knowledge. The Renaissance dared to rebel against this mediæval preaching, to set free the reason of man, and to awaken in him a passionate appreciation of the glories of art and nature, and of all the beauty of this living world. The prison doors were thrown open, and in the newly awakened joy of life, the men of the Renaissance raised their eyes from contemplation of the cloister and the grave, and cried aloud in exultation, "It is good for us to be here!"

Then a wonderful thing happened. At this moment of new intellectual birth, of enfranchisement from old prejudices, the beautiful dead past came back, newly revealed, to a generation eager to see, to comprehend all things. The world of classical antiquity, the beauty and strength of ancient Greece and Rome, was a revelation to the far-off sons and daughters of that heroic breed, all unconscious of their glorious heritage. A very fever of enthusiasm was aroused, not alone for the priceless treasures of sculpture in marble and bronze, found beneath the Italian soil, but also for the classics of language and literature, the works of Homer and Plato, of Aristotle and Virgil, of the philosophers and the tragedians of ancient fame. Then came the fall of Constantinople in 1453, and the ruin of the Eastern Empire brought a fresh impulse to the West, in rediscovered treasures and learned exiles.

The religious ideal of the Middle Ages had appealed alike to all—to rich and poor, to the learned and the ignorant; but the cultured spirit of the Renaissance was almost exclusively the possession of those classes who enjoyed wealth and leisure. This mighty intellectual impulse touched women even more deeply than men, for it not only gave them a new independence, but raised them to a high position in social life and the encouragement of art. Sharing the same learned education as the men, they had perhaps in a more marked degree, the passionate love of the beautiful, and the keen desire to collect antique sculptures, paintings, musical instruments, and rare classics brought within their reach by the new wonder of the printing-press.

Thus it comes to pass that in so many a brilliant Court—of Mantua, of Urbino, of Milan, of Naples, of Ferrara, of Asola, and others—we find that a cultured woman is the central figure, who gives harmony to the whole group. So, in making a special study of women in the Italian Renaissance, we find the most typical instances amongst the princesses and great ladies of the day.

Before entering upon individual studies, it will be interesting to consider the conditions of life during the whole period, and to recreate the very atmosphere of that long-past day, to us so strange and remote.

We will attempt to trace the surroundings of an Italian woman of the Renaissance, through the varied scenes of her life, beginning at the hour of her birth. Here, on the threshold, we are met with the knowledge, sharply accentuated in the case of a princess, that too often she is not welcome. Thus we read in a chronicle of Ferrara:

"A daughter was born this day to the Duke. . . . And there were no rejoicings, because every one wished for a boy."

And in the case of a little girl born to Isabella d'Este, we find that the mother would not use the splendid golden cradle with which she had been presented, but put it aside for ten years, until at length the hoped-for son arrived, and it was brought forth in state for his use.

Yet although so vastly inferior to her brothers, a

daughter was of some value as a counter in the game of politics. While she was still an infant, her father would cast an anxious glance towards the neighbouring Courts of Italy, or his ambition might even stretch out as far as Paris, Madrid, or Innsbrück, to consider by what alliance he could best strengthen his position. Then would follow long and shrewd negotiations with some prince who was fortunate enough to possess a son, and in due time, often at a very early age, the little maiden was betrothed—married by proxy—to an unseen bridegroom. In this "marriage for the future" between Vittoria Colonna and Ferrante of Pescara, neither of the children was more than four years old, while in that of Beatrice d'Este, she was five, and Lodovico Sforza, Duke of Bari, was twenty-nine.

When a father's mind was thus set at rest as to the future of his little girl, he had leisure to consider her education. In some cases it was part of the bargain that the child-bride should be brought up in the household of her future husband, that she might enter upon her new life as soon as possible, before she had formed ideas of her own, and could still be moulded to suit the place she had to fill. This was often quite successful, as in the case of Vittoria Colonna, who owed so much of her future distinction to the cultured training of Ferrante's elder sister, Costanza d'Avalos, in the fair isle of Ischia. The children were both sweet-tempered and grew up happily together; indeed Vittoria's devotion to her young husband is a theme of romance.

But in other cases, the plan of bringing up together a future husband and wife has had disastrous consequences, and resulted in mutual dislike; as with Giovanna I. of Naples and Andreas of Hungary, whose tragic story is told later on. There were other dangers, too, with regard to sending a little girl to the Court of her future husband. Sometimes a change of policy or some other cause would break the contract, and then the result was most unfortunate. For instance, Margarita, the daughter of the Emperor Maximilian, was sent to France to be educated as the wife of Charles VIII., but this young king decided to marry, for the sake of her goodly heritage, Anne de Bretagne, who was already betrothed to Maximilian, and poor Margarita was sent back to her father. The result of this cruel insult was a long and devastating war.

An alliance having been arranged for the future, the matter of first importance was the little maiden's education. No longer, as in the Middle Ages, was it governed by Gerson's rule: "All instruction for women should be looked at askance." In the days of the Renaissance this was changed indeed. "A little girl," said Bembo, "ought to learn Latin; it puts the finishing touch to her charms." We can only marvel at the amount of their learning. Music and dancing were taught from earliest childhood; and we hear of a baby-girl performing the most wonderful ballet to entertain a distinguished guest. She would also learn to play the lute and viol, and to sing a canzone to her own accompaniment. It was not unusual for her to talk "with grace and intelligence" at six years old, and by that time she would already have begun her more serious studies. Some distinguished classical scholar would be selected as her tutor, and with him she would certainly learn enough Latin to read Cicero and Virgil, to recite Latin verses, or repeat an oration. She would be taught Greek and Roman history, and would be familiar with Dante, Petrarch, and other Italian poetry, study modern languages to some extent, and in many instances the young girl would learn to read Plato in the original.

In the "Life of Vittorino da Feltre," tutor to the Gonzaga family, we have a delightful account of a great "humanist," who was marvellously successful as a teacher, and carried out a high ideal of education, as it was understood in the days of the Italian Renaissance. We find him in 1420 at Mantua, in the Casa Zoisa, close to the Castello, on the border of the lake. Here a group of high-born youths and maidens were trained in body and mind; taught to live a simple life, to tell the truth, and remember that learning was inseparable from virtue and religion. Their course of study included Latin, Greek, philosophy, mathematics, grammar, logic, music, singing and dancing, varied by outdoor games.

Vittorino had a lofty ideal of a schoolmaster's mission, and inspired his pupils with a passion for learning. He would begin by reading chosen selections from the writings of Virgil, Cicero, Homer and Demosthenes, explaining as he went on; then he would make his class learn passages by heart to form their style. One of his rules was, "First be sure that you have something to say . . . say it simply." He paid special attention to those who were slow to learn, and would take poor scholars without pay, "for the love of God."

In the long summer days he would take his class to the rising ground at Pietole,* the birthplace of Virgil, about two miles south of Mantua; and here, in the

* According to Donatus, Virgil was born at Andes, which a local and very ancient tradition has identified with Pietole.

shady groves, he would tell them the story of Perseus, of Hercules . . . while they rested after their games. His most distinguished girl-pupil was Cecilia Gonzaga, the youngest daughter of his patron, Gian Francesco di Montefeltro, who recited Latin verse and could read Chrysostom at eight years old, at twelve years wrote Greek with "singular purity," and continued her classical studies till she was the marvel of the age. Margherita, her elder sister, married the cultured Leonello d'Este, and he wrote to his wife with regard to Vittorino, "that for virtue, learning, and a rare and excellent way of teaching good manners, this master surpassed all others."

Another princess distinguished for her learning was Ippolyta Maria Sforza, daughter of Francesco, Duke of Milan, and wife of Alfonso of Naples. When Pope Pius II. paid a visit to her father, the little girl was chosen before her elder brothers, to pronounce a Latin oration in honour of his Holiness. It was for Ippolyta that Constantine Lascaris composed the earliest Greek grammar; and in the convent library of Santa Croce, at Rome, there is a transcript by her of Cicero de Senectute, followed by a youthful collection of Latin apophthegms.

It is very curious to notice, in passing, how our feelings have changed of late years towards learning in women. Dennistoun, in his "Dukes of Urbino," written only fifty years ago, remarks that "feminine erudition in professorial chairs" was a "questionable practice." Thus he dismissed the long roll of learned ladies of the Renaissance.

The wonderful little girls of this period seem to have borne all their weight of learning with so light a grace that they had leisure to sit over the embroidery-frame, and produce the most delicate triumphs of needlework. We read of a design of tapestry representing "shepherds and shepherdesses feasting on cherries and walnuts," or "a device of little children on a river bank, with birds flying overhead," worked in gold, silk, and wool; or again of a counterpane with "a cherry-tree and a dame and squire gathering cherries in a basket," and another with a "group of children, their heads meeting in the middle," the whole embroidered with gold thread, on brocade, or with coloured wools.

As the Este children bent over their needle, there was read to them a romance of Spain or Provence, sueh as "I reali di Francia," the last fairy tale of Matteo Boiardo, or a new canzone of Niccolo di Correggio. The Italian girls of the Renaissance were brought up with a love of poetry; Dante, Petrarch, and Ariosto were familiar to them, but above all they had a passion for the drama, and learnt at a very early age to take parts in a classical play. Yet with all this study of books, the training of the body was not neglected, for a high-born maiden's education was not complete unless she could ride boldly, go hunting, and fly a hawk.

Riding was, indeed, an indispensable accomplishment in those days, when most of the long journeys were made on horseback. If a young girl of high degree did not travel much before her marriage, she would certainly have to do so when her betrothal became an actual marriage, and she left her father's home for that of her husband.

At the present time, when with a light heart we set forth on a journey, and accomplish several hundred miles with ease and comfort in a day, it is almost impossible for us to realise what travelling must have been for the ladies of the Renaissance. A sea voyage in a clumsy sailing-ship was a weary matter; it took nearly two months for Queen Caterina to sail from Venice to Cyprus in her gorgeous *Bucentaur;* but a journey by land was infinitely worse. Mule-drawn litters were occasionally used where the roads were possible, but the usual way of travelling on state occasions was on richly caparisoned horses, in splendid dresses, day after day, in all weathers. It is a curious fact that most of the great weddings, described in the following pages, took place in the depth of winter; and the luckless brides had to face heavy snow-storms and tempests, cross rivers in flood, or ride over the Alpine passes in mid-December. We have a very interesting contemporaneous account of the wedding journey of Lucrezia Borgia, when she rode like a queen across Italy from Rome to Ferrara. Her escort numbered about a thousand persons, with a gay young Cardinal, Ippolyto d'Este, at their head. Lucrezia had left Rome in a red silk dress trimmed with ermine, and a plumed hat, riding a white horse with crimson trappings and a golden bridle.

The other costumes were splendid; there were dwarfs and jesters to beguile the way, a company of trumpeters, and hautbois to make martial music, and as the cavalcade noisily crossed the wintry plains, it might well have been taken by a stranger for a travelling circus.

As for the time taken in a journey, we may notice that ambassadors who left England on February 22 reached Rome on May 12.

In the time of the Renaissance we begin to find an interest in travel and a new-born love of Nature, but only in her most smiling aspect. A beautiful sunny day, a soft horizon, scented flowers in a trim garden, the glistening waters of a blue lake—all these things appealed alike to men and women. But for Nature wild and untamed, they had no sympathy; a stormy ocean, bleak mountain-tops were terrible to them, unless, indeed, they were harmonised by some Platonic or ethical thought. Thus when Petrarch had read a passage in Livy, "King Philip ascends Mount Hæmus," it occurred to him that he would climb the Mont Ventoux, near him at Avignon. His feelings on the way were full of awe and anxious alarm. He met an old man who implored him to turn back, but he bravely persevered, and when he had reached the summit he opened the "Confessions of St. Augustine" at the 10th chapter, "And men go forth, and admire lofty mountains and broad seas, and roaring torrents, and the ocean, and course of the stars, and forget their own selves while doing so." Then Petrarch closed the book and read no more.

Here we have the ideal spirit of the Renaissance, which looked upon Nature merely as a setting for the intellectual life.

Returning to the question of travel, not as a luxury but a necessity, as in the case of a young bride's wedding journey, we notice that a train of baggage-mules is usually sent on beforehand with the princess's trousseau. This brings us to the subject of dress, which in the Renaissance attained a sumptuous magnificence, undreamt of before. Having alluded to Lucrezia Borgia, we will describe a few dresses worn at her wedding. The first day she wore a robe of cloth of gold, with underbodice of crimson satin, and over these a mantle slashed on one side with black satin, and trimmed with marten's fur. On her bare neck she wore a string of large pearls with a garnet pendant . . . on her head a gold cap.

Another day she wore a dress with wide sleeves in the French mode, of gold tissue and black satin slashed in stripes, and over that a mantle of woven gold, brocaded in relief, which was open at the side and lined with ermine, as were also the sleeves of her robe. She was riding on a black mule, with furniture of velvet covered with gold, and studded with nails of beaten gold, "a most beautiful and rich sight." On her throat was a collar of diamonds and rubies, and on her head a jewelled cap.

Next day she appeared in a dress of gold thread in the French mode, and a mantle of dark satin with narrow stripes of beaten gold, studded with small gems and trimmed with ermine, on her head a cap bossed with garnets and pearls, and on her neck a jewelled collar.

Her new sister-in-law, Isabella d'Este, wore a robe of green velvet embroidered in gold, and a black velvet mantle trimmed with lynx skin, and the next day a gown of white silver tabi, and her head and neck were decked with pearls. The Duchess of Urbino had a dress of velvet striped with woven gold. Another dress mentioned is of black velvet lined with crimson satin, slashed and bound with lacets of massive gold, and buttoned down the front with ruby studs, her cap being formed of certain gold bars set with precious stones. . . .

These are only a few of the gorgeous costumes described with loving minuteness by the old chroniclers. But it was not only on a special occasion like this, that so much extravagance was displayed. At an earlier date in Florence, a Rucellai bride * had in her trousseau: (1) a white velvet gown richly trimmed with pearls, silk and gold, with open sleeves lined with pure white fur; (2) a dress of zetani, a stuff of very rich thick silk, trimmed with pearls and the sleeves lined with ermine; (3) gown of white damask brocaded with gold flowers, the sleeves trimmed with pearls; (4) one of silk tabi with crimson, gold and brocaded sleeves, and many others; a rich necklet of diamonds, rubies and pearls worth 100,000 gold pieces; a pin for the hair and necklace of pearls with a large pointed diamond; a hood embroidered with pearls; a net for the hair, also worked with pearls; a hood of crimson cloth wrought with pearls; also two caps with silver, pearls and diamonds. . . .

The absence of "massive gold" must have made the dresses of the Florentine bride much more comfortable to wear. It would be easy to fill many pages with such details, but this is enough to give some idea of the unlimited extravagance displayed in the dress of the period. It is only fair to add that the men must have spent quite as much on their own gorgeous Court array.

There was much art needed in wearing those splendid clothes. The young girl had to be taught that the robe must be slightly lifted in front to show the dainty feet, and themantle (the *albernia*) must from time to time be held open with both hands wide in front, "as a peacock spreads his tail."

* Nannini, sister of Lorenzo dei Medici.

A lady's complete costume would consist of a long under garment of fine and costly linen, then a "doublet," a linen bodice to which a white full skirt was sewn. A long-waisted, stiff bodice of stout cloth was worn above this, and by means of lacets or hooks a pair of long, closely-fitting sleeves of rich material could be fastened on, and changed to suit the outer dress. This was a long robe sweeping the ground, tight in the bodice, and sometimes without sleeves, but usually with loose hanging sleeves lined with ermine or some other costly fur. The girdle would be studded with gems on great occasions. Outside this a long mantle (*albernia*) of costly satin or velvet lined with fur, would be worn out-of-doors. The passion for extravagant dress spread to all ranks, and in sober Florence, the grave and careful city fathers sought to check it with the terrors of the law. An account has been preserved in the archives of one "forbidden gown" worn by a certain Donna Francesca.

"A black mantle of raised cloth; the ground is yellow, and over it are woven birds, parrots, butterflies, white and red roses, and many figures in vermilion and green, with pavilions, and dragons, and yellow and black letters, and trees, and many other figures of various colours, the whole lined with cloth in hues of black and vermilion."

It must have been a thankless and fearful task for the censor of dress! An accusation would be lodged against some one for wearing a forbidden number of buttons. "Buttons, say you!" would cry the irate lady. "But where be the button-holes? Nay, these be only harmless bosses. . . ." And so the sumptuary laws would be in vain, as they have ever been against the quick wit of women.

To return from these lower regions of society, to the illustrious lady whose career we are following through life. She was above law, and the chroniclers of her day would exclaim that nothing was too costly or too magnificent to be lavished on her surpassing loveliness.

So far as the bride's dress is concerned, we have certain facts to deal with, but when we come to her personal beauty, it becomes a much more difficult task, for the biographer always deals in superlatives in describing his princess, while her portrait may seem to us much open to criticism. From careful study we can at least learn what was the ideal of beauty in those days. The hair must be thick and long, and if possible fair or golden, as this hue was admired above all others. The forehead smooth and serene, broader than it is high; a good space between the eyes, which should be large and full, the white of the eye faintly blue. The eyebrows must be dark and silky, the skin bright and clear, a delicate colour on the cheeks, the chin round, with the glory of a dimple; a small mouth, the neck white, round and long; the hand also white and plump; and the figure slender and willowy.

False hair was much used by older women, and it was often made of white or yellow silk. Many ladies would pass the whole day in the open air, with the hair spread out in the sun, to bleach it. On her wedding journey a bride would delay the cumbrous procession for a whole day, that she might have her wonderful golden locks washed and fitly cared for. As for the modes of dressing the hair, it would take a volume in itself to do justice to the subject, and would then need the most elaborate illustrations.

Paint was almost universally used and as constantly preached against, but in vain; and in the craze for golden hair, there is very little doubt that the radiant hue was often obtained by artificial means.

When the high-born young bride had successfully accomplished her wedding journey, and had made a splendid entry into the city of her adoption, the next step was to welcome her with magnificent entertainments. In these the princes of the Renaissance specially excelled, shedding on them such artistic splendour and lustre as was unknown to classical or mediæval days. It is very difficult to make a selection, but possibly one of those prepared at Milan for the coming of Beatrice d'Este, is amongst the most interesting.

In this Giôstra, or tournament, the knights wore strange symbolical costumes. Thus a Mantuan troop wore green velvet and gold lace, and carried lances of gold and olive boughs. The Knights of Bologna arrived on a car of triumph drawn by unicorns and stags; then came twelve gallant horsemen in black and gold Moorish dress, with a Moor's head on their helmets and white doves on their sable armour. They were followed by a band of wild Scythians who thundered into the piazza on their Barbary steeds, and then suddenly threw off their disguise, while a Moorish giant came to the front to recite in poetry the praise of the bride. It is with special interest that we find some of the designs on this occasion were by Leonardo da Vinci.

Then tilting matches were carried on during four

days, and the pallium of gold brocade was the reward of the winner. Never was there seen a finer show, and these outdoor entertainments were extremely popular, for all the citizens could enjoy the sight.

Here is the description of a festa at Venice, that fair city which is so marvellously adapted for gay doings. Amidst a number of decorated barks, galleys and gondolas, a raft slowly arrives with figures of Neptune and Minerva, armed with trident and spear, seated on each side of a mimic hill. . . . Neptune began to dance and gambol and throw balls into the air to the sound of drums and tambourines, and then Minerva did the same. Afterwards they both joined hands and danced together. Next Minerva struck the mountain with her spear, and an olive-tree appeared. Neptune did the same with his trident, and a horse jumped out. Then other personages made their appearance on the mount with open books in their hands.

This was interpreted to mean that states are founded on treaties of peace.

The following account of a Miracle-play is given in a letter of Isabella d'Este : "A young angel spoke the argument of the play, quoting the words of Prophets who foretold the Advent of Christ, and the said Prophets appeared speaking their prophecies, translated into Italian verse. Then Mary appeared under a portico supported by eight pillars, and began to repeat some verses from the prophets, and while she spoke, the sky opened, revealing the figure of God the Father surrounded by a choir of angels. No support could be seen either for his feet or those of the angels ; and six seraphs hovered in the air, suspended by chains.

"In the centre of the group was the Archangel Gabriel, to whom God the Father addressed his word, and after receiving his orders Gabriel descended with admirable artifice and stood half-way in the air. Then all of a sudden an infinite number of lights broke out at the feet of the angel choir and hid them in a blaze of glory, which really was a thing worth seeing, and flooded all the sky with radiance. At that moment the Angel Gabriel alighted on the ground, and the iron chain which held him was not seen, so that he seemed to float down on a cloud, till his feet rested on the ground.

"After delivering his message, he returned with the other angels to Heaven, to the sound of singing and music and melody, and there were verses recited by spirits holding lighted torches in their hands, and waving them to and fro, as they stood supported in the air, so that it frightened me to see them. When they had ascended into Heaven, some scenes of the Visitation of St. Elizabeth and St. Joseph were given, in which the heavens opened again, and an angel descended with the same admirable contrivance to manifest the Incarnation." So the festa ended.

But the most interesting of all Renaissance entertainments were the dramatic performances, which were always a great feature in the reception of a bride. Thus Lucrezia Borgia had, during a whole week, the comedies of Plautus acted before her with marvellous interludes; the germ of our modern ballets. One of the best accounts of these is given in a letter of Castiglione. He is describing a play by Cardinal Bernardo Bibbiena, first performed at Urbino, called the Calandra, and afterwards a great favourite with Leo X.

"The scene was laid by a city wall with two great towers, on one of which were bagpipers, on the other trumpeters. . . . Another scene represented a beautiful city, with streets, palaces, churches, towers, all in relief . . . statues, columns, and a brilliant light of torches over all. . . . The interludes were as follows: First, a moresca of Jason, who came dancing on the stage in fine antique armour, with a splendid sword and shield, whilst there suddenly appeared on the other side two bulls vomiting fire, so natural as to deceive some of the spectators. These the good Jason approached, and yoking them to a plough made them draw it. He then sowed the dragon's teeth, and forthwith there sprang up from the stage, antique warriors inimitably managed, who danced a fierce moresco, trying to slay him; and having come on, they each killed the other. After them, Jason again appeared, with the Golden Fleece on his shoulders, dancing admirably.

"In the second interlude there was a lovely car wherein sat Venus with a lighted taper in her hand; it was drawn by two doves which seemed alive, and on them rode a couple of Cupids with bows and quivers . . . preceded and followed by more Cupids dancing a moresco. They set fire to a door, out of which leaped nine gallant men all in flames, who also danced to perfection. . . ." Then followed other interludes, Neptune on his sea-horses, . . . and Juno in her car drawn by peacocks, &c., "of which no description can afford an idea," says the enthusiastic beholder.

Yet if this kind of amusement went on day after day, for five hours or so at a time, preceded by state balls all the afternoon, we can quite understand that even the most cultured lady, such as

Isabella d'Este, was sometimes overcome with "infinite weariness."

When our "illustrious lady" has passed through the ordeal of religious ceremonies and splendid entertainments in connection with her wedding, the next point of interest to consider, will be the home in which she is henceforth to rule. This, of course, would vary greatly, according to the city whither it has pleased Fate to waft her.

In Florence, for instance, in the days of the early Medici, we should see the fair city of to-day as a gloomy mass of battlemented towers, in the midst of densely foliaged trees and tangled undergrowth, encompassed by massive bulwarks and high walls. Where now stands the Piazza di Santa Croce the Arno flowed, passing from the Ponte a Rubicante and the Castle of Altafronte. The corn-market was held where now stands the Loggia of Or San Michele; the tower begun by Giotto was but recently completed, the double dome of Brunellesco was built in 1434; and the Palazza dei Priori stood out in its grim strength, while from its tower, the great bell, the Vacca, summoned the people to elections or sounded the note of war. But the merchant city was growing fast, and each year saw new and splendid palaces rising in its sombre streets, while monasteries and churches kept pace with them.

One of the earliest Medici palaces was in the Via Larga (now Cavour), but both Cosimo and his grandson Lorenzo the Magnificent built delightful villas in the fair country outside Florence, where their families dwelt during most of the year. The Renaissance brought with it a taste for gardens and flowers, fruit-trees and rare shrubs, on which we shall dwell later in describing more fully those of the Este princesses.

The simple severity of Florentine life, in the early part of the fifteenth century, will scarcely give us an ideal presentment of the magnificence found in an Italian palace of the Renaissance. For this we shall have to pass on to a somewhat later date, and seek out the huge square Castello of red brick in the heart of Ferrara, home of the Este princes; the lake-encircled Palazza of the Gonzaga at Mantua; the hill city of classic Urbino; or the far-famed Castello of Pavia, the pride of Milan's dukes. We cannot do better than suffer our choice to fall upon this last.

In the ancient capital of the Lombard kings stands this splendid monument of Renaissance architecture; a great quadrangle flanked by four massive towers. The inner court was surrounded by a double cloister with colonnades of low round arches, while the Gothic windows of the upper loggia and the banqueting-hall were relieved by delicate tracery and shafts of marble, and beautiful mouldings in terra-cotta. The stately palace stood in the midst of exquisite gardens, with avenues of plane-trees, groves of cypress-, mulberry-, orange-, and lemon-trees, myrtle and cystus; broad lawns with fountains of choice design, and dainty pavilions for summer days. In the park beyond, there were artificial lakes, the charm of running water, groups of forest trees, and upland stretches of picturesque wildness which harboured a number of stags and wild deer for the chase.

But the landscape without, "divinely beautiful," as Commines calls it, was not to be compared with the magnificence within the palace walls. Never has that princely lavishness of space been carried to a greater pitch. In the immense ball-room, the banqueting-hall, the vast Sala in which the favourite game of "la Palla" was played, and the whole suite of splendid chambers—the groined ceilings were ablaze with gold and ultramarine in quaint emblem and device—and the frescoed walls were masterpieces of the great artists of the day; Leonardo da Vinci being chief amongst them. The upper chambers were hung with priceless tapestries, and the whole fittings of a room would often be embroidered to match in silk and worsted, and gold and silver thread. These would include hangings for the walls, doors and windows, a baldaquin and counterpane for the bed, and curtains to draw all round it; a coverlet for the low couch, and cushions for the various chairs and benches, which were delicately carved, or of inlaid wood.

There is a most interesting list from an unpublished MS.* of sixty sets of hangings which Valentine Visconti took with her to France, part of the colossal dowry by means of which the daughter of a soldier of fortune found a royal alliance. Amongst these we find:

"Item: A 'chamber' (or set of hangings), the baldaquin worked with a design of angels; the long curtain depending from the tester behind the pillows represents shepherds and shepherdesses feasting on cherries and walnuts; the counterpane, a shepherd and a shepherdess within a park; the whole embroidered with gold thread and coloured wools.

"Item: Wall hangings to match. . . .

"Item: Another chamber with hangings complete with all the Victories of Theseus.

* Madame Duclaux.

"Item: A great tapestry, with the history of the destruction of Troy the Great; green velvet cover for a couch, and chair cushions of green velvet richly emboidered to match.

"Item: A white 'chamber' sown with gladiolus, bed furniture, and all hangings.

"Item: A set of green tapestries with the Fountain of Youth and several personages, with bed hangings, counterpanes, couch-covers, and six wall hangings, all worked very richly with gold, without guards (linen coverings).

"Item: A set of hangings complete of cloth of gold, also another 'chamber' representing a lady playing with a knight at the game of chess."

This would be about a tenth part of one collection. It was not only in palaces that the spirit of the Renaissance had brought such order and beauty into the domestic life of Italy, for when Sir Thomas Hoby, the translator of the "Cortigiano," was entertained as a private gentleman at Salerno, by the Marquis of Capistrano, he says:

"Whithorn and I were had into a chamber hanged with clothe of gold and vellute, wherin were two beddes, thon of silver worke, and the other of vellute, with pillowes, bolsters, and the shetes curiouslie wrought with needle worke."

To appreciate how far England was behind in such matters, it may be interesting to quote a few words from the letter written by Thomas Sackville (Lord Buckhurst) to the Lords of the Privy Council, when he was ordered to entertain the Cardinal de Châtillon at Shene, sixteen years later than Hoby's letter. He had no proper plate or glass or "napery":

"One onlie tester and bedsted not occupied I had, and thos I delivered for the Cardinall him self, and when we cold not by any menes in so shorte a time procure another bedsted for the bushop, I assighned them the bedsted on which my wiefes waiting wemen did lie, and laid them on the ground. Mine own basen and ewer I lent to the Cardinall, and wanted me self . . . ."

To return to Italy. We have a description of a Renaissance bed, raised upon a daïs above a floor of wood mosaic, with a carved canopy of wonderful design and workmanship, supported by four demons of terrible aspect. The furnishing of the chamber would be in keeping, with one or two great carved and painted chests, containing the lady's wedding dowry of rich garments and jewels, and a couch and carved chairs covered with rich tapestry or velvet to match the hangings. On the floor we should find Eastern rugs, and skins of leopard or tiger, and in a secluded corner a reliquary and the image of the Madonna or a saint, before which a lamp would be always kept burning. We read of the jug and ewer being of silver or gold on special occasions, and Infessura tells us how on a certain visit to Rome of the Duchess Leonora of Mantua, every lady in her suite had a washing basin of gold given her by the Cardinal of San Sisto. "Oh, guarda!" he adds, "in such things to spend the treasure of the Church!"

The household and chamber linen, or other material, would be on the same scale of magnificence, for we find such a list as this in the dowry of a noble lady:*

"Item: Seven pairs of sheets of spun silk striped with

* Vittoria Colonna.

gold; twenty pairs of sheets embroidered in different coloured silks; fourteen pairs of Olana (Dutch linen) fringed with gold; . . . two pairs of thin sheets wrought with gold and silk.

"Item: A silk coverlet with stripes of gold; . . . pillow-slips of crimson silk; . . . eighteen counterpanes of silk, one 'alla moresca'; . . . and great stores of splendid bed and table napery, &c."

In the banqueting-hall we should specially notice the immense buffets, or sideboards, ten feet high, loaded with gold and silver plate for use at banquets, with majolica of Urbino and vases from Faenza (called *fayence* in France). On the floor there would be more Eastern rugs; in front of the seats, great mats of embroidered Hungarian leather, and skins of animals killed in the chase or sent from distant lands. The chairs are embossed with gilt, or if of wood, are covered with stamped leather and adorned with clamps of bright metal. Armchairs are sometimes protected with a great carved head, or with a top and curtains, to keep away the draught in those vast apartments, and perhaps stand on either side of the great hearth with its dogs of shining metal, where burn massive trunks of wood, cut in special lengths. Above the fireplace there will rise a magnificent carved overmantel, and in one of the rooms we shall probably find some wonderful clock of copper and brass, with not only a peal of bells, but a complete solar system, showing the movement of all the heavenly bodies, the sun, moon, and stars, as taught by Ptolemy.

As for the library, whether at the villa of Lorenzo dei Medici, at the splendid home at Pavia of the Duke of Milan, or at the cultured and courtly Palace of

Urbino, it would be full of priceless manuscripts, adorned with exquisite miniatures and treasures of classical learning until, as time advanced, the wonder of the printing-press brought the whole learning of the ancient world within the reach of a generous and studious patron. But to do full justice to a splendid library of the Renaissance would require a volume in itself.

With regard to the famous artists and scholars and learned men who were so eagerly welcomed by every cultured princess at her Court, their story will be found in all the chronicles of the period, where women meet with so scant a mention. The kindred subject of intellectual and artistic conversation and of literary coteries is so fully treated later on in the history of Elisabetta Gonzaga and the Court of Urbino, that it will not be needful to touch upon it here.

The ladies of the Renaissance in Italy were not only distinguished in social life and conversation, but were usually great letter-writers, and many quotations from their correspondence are given in the following pages. Fortunately for us, the written word was looked upon with respect in those days, for we are told that of one lady, Isabella d'Este, for instance, nearly two thousand letters have been preserved. It is very interesting to note the difference in handwriting, which betrays many curious secrets. In the sixteenth century it is usually large and free, often very characteristic of the writers. The strokes are delicate and somewhat angular, with many strange contractions and flourishes. The handwriting of Vittoria Colonna, for example, is plain, distinct, and somewhat masculine in style, but slightly nervous and irregular, with various abbreviations and dashes.

"With mine own hand" is a very needful addition, as it was much the custom for a great lady to dictate letters to her secretary, who was often given to embroider on his own account. The following simple little note of Isabella d'Este is an interesting specimen of a dictated letter:

"MY LORD,—I pray you mock not at my letter, and say not that all women are poor things, and ever fearful, for the malignity of others is far greater than my fear and your lordship's mettle. I would have written this letter with my own hand, but the heat is so great that, if it last, we are like to die. The little lad is very well and sends your lordship a kiss, and for my own part, I do ever commend myself to you.

"With sore desire to see your lordship,

"ISABELLA, *with mine own hand.*

"MANTUA, *July 23rd.*"

Here we plainly see that the signature alone was hers; but "it was so hot!"

Every married woman was expected to rule her household well and wisely, according to her rank in life; with magnificence on state occasions, yet with due regard to economy. The young bride of a prince would often find that the expenses of her splendid wedding and reception had been so enormous, as to require careful retrenchment in the Court expenditure or years. Banquets given in honour of distinguished guests would be amongst the most costly items. In the records of Florence we find a detailed account of a series of banquets given on the occasion of a Medici wedding, that of Lorenzo's sister, Giovanna, which lasted from Sunday morning to Tuesday evening. To these all the relations, friends, and the chief citizens were invited, and they sat down five hundred at a time, under great awnings in the Piazza opposite the palace. The cooking was done in the street, by fifty cooks and their helpers. Hither came "quartered bullocks, casks of Greek wine, and as many capons as could hang on a staff borne on the shoulders of two stout peasants; bars of buffalo cheese, turkeys in pairs, barrels of ordinary wine and choice sweet wine, baskets full of pomegranates, hampers of large sea fish, crates of little silver-scaled fish from the Arno, birds, hares, cream cheese packed in fresh green rushes, baskets full of sweetmeats, tarts, and other confectionery prepared in the convents."

With the refreshments there came twenty confectioners, who distributed a profusion of caramels made of pine-seeds. These banquets cost more than 150,000 francs; including "70 bushels of bread, 2800 white loaves, 4000 wafers, 50 barrels of sweet white wine, 1500 pair of poultry, 1500 eggs, 4 calves, 20 large basins of galantine. . . ."

These were public entertainments; but where the company was more select, the extravagance was no less, for the table was idealised with the most fanciful decorations that could be devised. Thus, at a banquet given to welcome the Princess Isabella of Naples, we read of each course being introduced "by some mythological personage. Jason appeared with the golden fleece; Phœbus Apollo brought in a calf stolen from the herds of Admetus; Diana led Actæon in the form of a stag; Atalanta followed with the wild boar of

Calydon; Iris came with a peacock from the car of Juno; and Orpheus carried in the birds whom he had charmed with his lute. Hebe poured out the wines; Vertumnus and Pomona handed round apples and grapes; Thetis and her sea-nymphs brought every variety of fish; and shepherds, crowned with chaplets of ivy, arrived from the hills of Arcady, bearing jars of milk and honey to the festive board."

At a banquet given at Venice in honour of the Duchess of Milan, we hear that the different dishes and confetti were carried in to the sound of trumpets, accompanied by an infinite number of torches. "First of all came figures of the Pope, the Doge, and the Duke of Milan, with their armorial bearings; then St. Mark, the adder and the diamond, and many other objects—all in coloured and gilded sugar, making as many as three hundred in all, together with every variety of cakes and confectionery, and gold and silver drinking-cups, all of which were spread out along the hall, and made a splendid show."

On the marriage of Sigismond, King of Poland, with Bona Sforza, at the Court of Naples, Vittoria Colonna was a guest, and Passari gives a very curious account of the supper which followed. "On quitting the church they sat down to table at six in the evening and began to eat, and left off at five in the morning." There was a stupendous menu, and twenty-seven courses are enumerated. We notice amongst them, Hungary soup ("putaggio Ungarese"), stuffed peacocks, quince pies, thrushes stuffed with bergamott (scented citrons), and "bianco mangiare con mostardo". . . .

This banquet may have had somewhat of a barbaric touch in honour of the Hungarian guests, who possibly spent the night in appreciating the wines of the sunny South after the ladies had retired. It was the usual custom to play at "scartino," or "l'impériale," and other card games, or at chess or backgammon, after dinner; and there appears to have been much gambling. Beatrice d'Este once won three thousand ducats, and we are told she spent it at once.

An interesting book was published in 1543, which throws much light on household expenditure in the days of the Renaissance. It bears the title, "Concerning the Management of a Roman Nobleman's Court." It thus enumerates the members of the house:

Two chief chamberlains.

One general controller of estates, receiving 10 scudi a month.

One chief steward, receiving 10 scudi a month.

Four chaplains, each receiving two scudi a month.

One master of the horse.

One private secretary and assistant secretary.

One auditor and 1 lawyer.

Four Litterati, who among them must know the four principal languages of the world, viz., Hebrew, Greek, Latin, and Italian. Each receiving 100 scudi yearly.

Six gentlemen of the chambers.

One private master of the table.

One chief carver, ten waiting men.

One butler of the pantry, and assistant. One butler of the wines.

Six head grooms. One marketer, with assistant.

A storekeeper, a cellarer, a carver for the serving gentlemen.

A chief cook, under cook, assistant, and a chief sculleryman.

A water-carrier and a sweep.

Last in the list comes a physician, "not because a doctor is not worthy of honour, but in order not to seem to expect any infirmity for his lordship or his household." The physician was required to be not only "learned, faithful, diligent and affectionate," but also, and above all, "fortunate in his profession."

The food in this Roman household cost 4000 scudi (or dollars); 1400 being spent on wine alone. The allowance was a jug holding rather more than a quart of pure wine daily to gentlemen, and the same quantity, diluted by one-third of water, to all the rest.

"Sixteen ounces of beef, mutton or veal allowed for each person.

"Twenty ounces of bread to each person, of more or less fine quality.

"One lb. of cheese to each, monthly; other eatables are all enumerated.

"Four or five large wax candles daily for his lordship. Also an allowance of wax for torches to accompany dishes to table, and to accompany his lordship and gentlemen out-of-doors.

"Wax candles for the altar in the chapel. Tallow candles for use in the house."

It may be well to note here that the ducat of Italy varied in nominal value from about four francs to four shillings of our money; but the coin would buy nearly twelve times the value, in necessaries or luxuries, which that amount represents at the present day in England.

There were other inmates of a great house, not mentioned in the inventory above. The trade with the East had one curious result, in a traffic of slaves, who were much used as domestic servants in Italy, during the fourteenth and fifteenth centuries. In the markets of Venice, of Genoa, or of Naples an able-bodied young woman might be bought at a price varying from six to eighty-seven ducats. We find interesting testimony to this fact in the letters of Alessandra Macinghi to her son Filippo Strozzi, at Naples. She writes:

"AL NOME DI DIO. *A di'* 13 *di Settembre* 1465.

"FIGLIUOL MIO DOLCE,

"I would remind you that we have need of a slave . . . if you give orders to have one bought, let it be a Tartar, as they are the best for hard work, and are simple in their ways. The Russians are more delicate and prettier, but it seems to me that a Tartar would be best. . . . Iddio di male vi guardi.

"Per la tua ALESSANDRA, in Firenze."

De Maulde reminds us that "the mother of Carlo dei Medici was a lovely Circassian girl, bought by the grave and æsthetic Cosimo il Vecchio." A poem of the period tells us that "The loving slaves shook out the dust from their masters' dress every morning, looking fresher and happier than the rose." But when we see, from Madonna Alessandra's letters, how much trouble they often gave, we must look upon this as a poetical licence.

No great household could be without its dwarfs and jesters, and we hear a great deal about them in the life of Isabella d'Este, whose palace at Mantua had a suite of apartments specially built for them. She occasionally gave away a baby dwarf to a friend, as we should a kitten. When Alfonso d'Este was inconsolable for the loss of his wife, a certain Martello, pet dwarf and jester, was lent to him for his comfort. "He could not express the delight which the buffoon had caused him, and esteemed his presence better than the gift of a castle."

But Martello fell ill and died; the poor fool making jokes even on his death-bed. On hearing of the sad event, Francesco, Duke of Mantua, writes:

"Most people can be easily replaced, but Nature will never produce another Martello." This was his elegy written by the bard Pistoia:

"If Martello is in Paradise, he is making all the saints and angels laugh; if he is in hell, Cerberus will forget to bark."

In time of sickness, the first thing which occurred to a friend was to lend the patient a jester or pet dwarf, to keep up his spirits at any cost.

The ladies of the Renaissance had no lack of other pets—their horses, their greyhounds, their falcons; for hunting was a passion with many of them. We read that Isabella d'Este's presence was heralded by the barking of her little dogs, and that she sought far and wide in the convents of Venice for rare Persian and Syrian cats. When a pet animal died it was buried with great solemnity in the gardens of the Castello, and a cypress was planted, or a tombstone inscribed with the name was placed on the grave. All the ladies and gentlemen of the household, and the favourite dogs and cats, joined in the funeral procession, we are told.

Visitors to Lord Pembroke's park at Wilton House will remember the pathetic little cemetery, overshadowed by sombre trees, where the pet dogs have been buried since the days of Queen Elizabeth. The idea may have come from Italy.

While on the subject of pet animals, we must include a wonderful giraffe, which was sent to Florence in 1488, a present from the Soldan of Babylonia to Lorenzo dei Medici. He was seven braccias high, and was led about the streets by two Turks, to the intense delight of the citizens. So great was the curiosity felt about him, even by the nuns, that he had to be taken round to the convents to be inspected. Such a pleasant beast! "It eats everything, poking its head into every peasant's basket, and would take an apple from a child's hand, so gentle is it." It had a stable in the Via Scala, where fires were kept up, for it was much afraid of cold. But, alas! notwithstanding all this affectionate care, the poor giraffe died on January 2, 1489, and "everybody lamented it, for it was such a beautiful animal!"

Beyond the due ordering of her Court and household, many and various were the talents needed by a princess of the Renaissance days. In the absence of her husband she would be called upon suddenly to pilot the ship of state, and form a decision upon important political matters. As a reigning sovereign, Giovanna of Naples showed great presence of mind on various critical occasions, and her defence of her conduct at the Court of Avignon, was a masterly stroke of talent.

Ludovico Sforza could find no more astute and capable ambassador to send to the Signoria of Venice than his Duchess Beatrice, who succeeded admirably in her diplomacy. Again, at a critical moment, when Louis of Orleans was at his gates, and the Duke was seized with sudden and unaccountable panic, it was his wife who came to the rescue with marvellous presence of mind, and took prompt measures for defending the city.

When Francesco, Marchese of Mantua, was a prisoner at Venice, it was his wife Isabella who ruled the state, and by her untiring efforts at length obtained his release. But all these, and many other peaceful incidents, fade into insignificance before the stirring adventures of Caterina Sforza, told in the story of her life. Few women have mounted the ramparts with such mettle as the gallant Madonna of Forli, when she held the Fort of St. Angelo for her husband, or defended her own citadel of Ravaldino.

Italy was very proud of her warrior women; the "virago" is always spoken of with loving admiration. We have an anecdote from Venice, when on a certain Sunday, June 14, 1310, the eve of San Vito's Day, there was an insurrection against the Doge. During the fighting a woman aimed a stone mortar from a window at the standard-bearer of the rebels; it struck his head; bearer and banner fell to the ground. Thereupon panic seized the conspirators; they fled and surrendered.

The heroine, Lucia Rosso, was requested to name her own reward. She only asked that "she might have the right to fly the standard of San Marco from her window on every festa-day; and that the procurators of San Marco would not raise her rent of fifteen ducats, either to her or her successors."

The ladies of Siena were noted for their pluck. In that last heroic siege of 1554 the Gascon general, Blaise de Monluc, pays them this testimony:

"It shall never be, you ladies of Siena, that I will not immortalise your names so long as the Book of Monluc shall live; for in truth you are worthy of immortal praise if ever women were. At the beginning of the noble resolution these people took to defend their liberty, all the ladies of Siena divided themselves into three squadrons; the first led by Signora Forteguerra, who was herself clad in violet, as also those of her train, her attire being cut in the fashion of a nymph, short, and discovering her buskins; the second was the Signora Piccolomini, attired in carnation satin, and her troop in the same livery; the third was the Signora Livia Fausta, apparelled all in white, as also her train, with her white ensign. In their ensigns they had very fine devices. . . . These three squadrons consisted of three thousand ladies, gentlewomen and 'citoyennes'; their arms were picks, shovels, baskets and bavins; and in this equipage they made the muster, and went to begin the fortifications. . . . Never was there so fine a sight. . . ."

We can well believe it, for when did warriors ever go forth in so gay and gallant a spirit, save in dauntless, ardent Siena?

There would be death to face, wounds to bind up, and much patient nursing would fall to the share of these fantastic "nymphs." This leads us to the subject of sickness and medicine in the olden days. We have already seen that the first great requisite for a physician was that he should be "fortunate in his profession." It was also desirable that he should practise astrology, more especially in princely houses, or he would lead but a sorry life. He points to his phials in vain; "against death he has no medicine."

Every woman could brew simples, bind a broken limb, nurse a fever, and dabble a little in medicine. These were some of the most popular drugs: Bark of Indian wood, turpentine, poppy, mustard, myrrh wormwood, lichen, peppermint and aniseed water, Quassia amara, essence of cinnamon, camphor, hops, rue, privet, crocus, marjoram, figs, honey, and much sulphur. Coughs were cured by milk of almonds mixed with sugar and starch, barley sugar, tea of roses and camomile, and infusions of mallow, violet, &c.; in short, most of the favourite French "tisanes" of to-day. Another remedy for a cough was to "take the lungs of a fox and wash it with wine, and dry it in a furnace to a cinder; then powder it and mix well with yolk of egg."

The Sun was supposed to govern the heart and nerves, Jupiter the liver, and Venus the rest of the body.

Complete discord reigned in the scientific world with regard to the treatment of disease; the physicians opposed the surgeons and apothecaries, and such terms as "fool" and "mountebank" were freely bestowed. Paris remained faithful to the traditional and philosophic spirit, while Paracelsus burnt the works of Galen and Avicenna.

"A certain pious author advised that the doors of the medical school should be thrown open freely to women, that they should be taught all that men were taught, indeed, a little more—Greek and Arabic—and that they should then be sent off to the Holy Land to aid in the conversion of the infidels." Did he see from afar the mission of medical women to the Zenanas?

But the ruling principle in illness, with both men and women, was to keep up the patient's spirits. We can quite understand this, when we think of the unhealthy conditions of life, and of that terrible scourge the Plague, which recurred six times between 1348 to the end of the fifteenth century. Fear or melancholy would be a certain precursor of death.

People were strongly impressed with the necessity of keeping in good health; and to this end they were to eat well, to avoid damp, to spend generously without stint or economy, to refrain from melancholy or gloom, not to think of dull, sorrowful things, but to play, ride, and amuse themselves; in short, to be happy. As we have noticed before, on receiving news of a friend's illness, the greatest charity was at once to send a pet dwarf or jester to the sick-room, and do anything to amuse the patient.

The Cardinal d'Este, hearing that his sister Isabella was ill at Mantua, in 1507, sent Ariosto to read his "Orlando Furioso" to the sick lady as he sat by her bedside. Happily she recovered.

We cannot leave the subject of sickness without touching upon that of poison, which was supposed to account for so many deaths, being so difficult of proof in former days. Doubtless, in many cases the suspicion was justified; but in any sudden illness it was always the first cry of ignorance. Our worthy old Fuller, in writing of his special incarnation of evil, Cæsar Borgia, remarks: "He exactly knew the operations of all hot and cold poysons, which would surprise nature on a sudden, and which would weary it out with a long siege; for in truth Italians have poysoning at their fingers end. This Cæsar could contract a 100 toads into one drop, and cunningly infuse the same into any pleasant liquour." There was a notorious poison used in Italy in the seventeenth century, called "aqua tofana," made by a woman of Palermo. Four to six drops was a fatal dose, and it has since been discovered to have been a solution of arsenic.

Closely akin to poisons were the various potions obtained from witches and Egyptians, for securing good luck, or as love philtres, or antidotes to love. These were often used for evil purposes, and bore the name of "selling the devil in bottles." Opium was used to produce delightful dreams; nightshade gave pleasant illusions. Witches were reputed to indulge in midnight orgies, and were constantly consulted by people who wanted to have their fortunes told; they were also believed to bring hail and rain, and to cure diseases by means of amulets and charms.

The boundless ambition of Julius II. was said to spring from the prediction of a sorceress, who had told him to be of good cheer, for he would be elected Pope, and rule the world. Astrology was in high favour, and Savonarola fought in vain against it. The Roman prelates, the great soldiers and sovereign princes, such as Lodovico Sforza and Francesco of Mantua, never moved a step without consulting the stars. The Court astrologer was a man of considerable influence and position, usually a foreigner, and often a Moor or gipsy. His occupation was most lucrative, and a great opening for ambition, as no public ceremony or journey was ever undertaken without his permission. He puts on airs and keeps his clients waiting. If some one sends him a birth date to have his horoscope cast, he sends no reply; "his eyes are weary with gazing into the boundless heavens."

But there are certain risks. As, for instance, when Messer Ambrogia da Rosate, the Duke of Milan's favourite astrologer and physician, after careful study fixed a day for the wedding journey of Bianca Sforza, the bride of the Emperor Maximilian, a terrible storm nearly wrecked the whole party. "Infelice!" was the mildest term applied to the unlucky astrologer; but we may remark, as some slight excuse for him, that the wedding journey, across the Lake of Como and over the passes of the Alps, had to be undertaken in the midst of a severe winter.

We cannot close the story of a woman's life in the days of the Renaissance, without touching on the subject of her religion.

In the earlier days of the period, little girls still went to church every day, and worked chasubles and altar-cloths. At Florence we find Lucrezia dei Medici, a devout woman, given to good works; taking her little son Lorenzo to vespers with her every evening, in the Dominican church of San Paolino. Her "rime sacre," written for her children, are preserved to us, charming in their simplicity, delicate little Christian carols. In the next generation, the great complaint of the learned tutor Poliziano against Lorenzo's wife Clarice, was that she wanted the boy Piero to sing hymns when he should have been learning Greek, and that she interfered with the lessons of the four-year-old Giovanni (afterwards Pope Leo X.) by keeping him to read the Psalter. No great event can take place without the sanction and benediction of the Church. A baptism, a marriage, a funeral—they are each the occasion of a stately and splendid pageant.

The progress of the Renaissance brought a changed outlook in thought and feeling, although in Italy it was not greatly complicated by the religious reform which shook the rest of Europe. Thus an Italian chronicler can write: "At that time, in the furthest part of Germany, the abominable and infamous name of Martin Luther began to be heard."

A new feeling pervaded the whole of intellectual life and "widened the sundering of the Church's claims and the joy of life. St. Augustine's dream of a city of God waxed pale and faint, like a student's midnight taper." The Renaissance, with all its mysticism, was not partial to the dim religious light or shadowed mysteries: it loved clearness, daylight, illumination. For a brief space all Italy was moved by the tremendous question of Savonarola: "Was not the soul the one thing more precious than the sin-stained body? Was it not greater than the living world? Was not the true path to heaven that of sacrifice, and consecration of every thought and every passion to the inner mystic life?"

Like Felix, they heard and trembled, but no mediæval teaching could reach those men and women of the Renaissance, and bring them back to the faith of their forefathers. Yet, if fewer splendid cathedrals were built and not so many convents were endowed as in the earlier days, there was no lack of deep and strong religious feeling. Amongst the writings of Vittoria Colonna we read such words as these:

"With a cable of love and fidelity welded together I fasten my barque to a never-yielding rock, to Christ, the living stone, whereby I may at any time return to port." She was not alone, for Vergerio, the Pope's nuncio in France, writes: "Praise be to God who in our troublous times hath raised up such intelligences —here the Queen of Navarre, of whom I speak; at Ferrara, the lady Renée of France; at Urbino the lady Leonora Gonzaga, with whom I conversed for some hours, and who seemed to me endowed with eminently lofty minds, filled with charity, all on fire with Christ; at Rome the lady Vittoria Colonna—to speak of none but your own sex."

We cannot do better than end with the words of Gebhardt: "The astonishing intellectual freedom with which Italy treated dogma and discipline; the serenity she was able to preserve in face of the great mystery of life and death; the art she devoted to the reconciliation of faith with rationalism; her dallyings with formal heresy, and the audacities of her mystic imagination; the enthusiasm of love, which often carried her up to the loftiest Christian ideal—such was the religion of Italy in the Renaissance."

IN TUSCANY.

NOBLE LADIES OF THE HOUSE OF MEDICI.

LUCREZIA (TORNABUONI) DEI MEDICI, WIFE OF PIERO DEI MEDICI, MOTHER OF LORENZO THE MAGNIFICENT.

CLARICE DEGLI (ORSINI) DEI MEDICI, WIFE OF LORENZO THE MAGNIFICENT.

HISTORICAL SUMMARY.

1430. Birth of Lucrezia Tornabuoni.

1447. Marriage of Piero dei Medici, son of Cosimo, to Lucrezia Tornabuoni.

1448. Birth of Lorenzo dei Medici, January 1.

1451. Alfonso of Naples and the Republic of Venice joïned against Milan and Florence.

1454. Capture of Constantinople by the Turks, who threatened Italy. Under guarantee of the Pope, a league formed between the sovereigns of Naples and Milan, and the Republics of Florence and Venice, to preserve Italy.

1464. Death of Cosimo dei Medici, after a glorious rule of thirty years. Succeeded by his son Piero.

1469. Marriage of Lorenzo, son of Piero, to Clarice Orsini.

1469. State visit of Lorenzo dei Medici to Milan, to the christening of the Duke's son, Gian Galeazzo.

" Death of Piero. His son, Lorenzo the Magnificent, succeeds him.

1472. The Turks first appeared in Italy, at Friuli.

1478. Conspiracy of the Pazzi, who murdered Giuliano dei Medici, brother of Lorenzo, in the Duomo of Florence.

1479. Madonna Clarice dismisses the tutor Poliziano.

1485. Lorenzo dei Medici and Lodovico Sforza of Milan make alliance with Ferdinand, King of Naples, against the Pope. Battle of Lamentana, gained by the Duke of Calabria, son of Ferdinand.

1487. Death of Clarice dei Medici.

1490. Public faith and credit of Florence violated to save Lorenzo dei Medici from bankruptcy.

1492. Death of Lorenzo the Magnificent. He is succeeded by his son Piero, who in 1487 married Alfonsina Orsini.

LUCREZIA (TORNABUONI) DEI MEDICI

LUCREZIA (Tornabuoni) DEI MEDICI, was the wife of Piero dei Medici. As we look upon the portrait, by Sandro Botticelli, of this gracious lady, we see her once more as she lived in those bygone days of the Renaissance; we seem to read her character and pierce the very secret of her soul. The thoughtful brow, the calm steadfast eyes, the firm delicate chin, the sweet placid mouth, even the erect stately bearing, all speak of that noble woman, the mother of Lorenzo the Magnificent, to whom he owed so much.

Lucrezia was one of the Tornabuoni family, those merchant princes of Florence from whose proud energetic stock she seemed to have inherited the more homely virtues, which do not always flourish in a palace. She was a clear-eyed, high-minded woman of business, and ever her son's wisest and most trusted counsellor. Her political insight was keen and just; indeed, there were not wanting those who said that her princely alms, her endowments of poor convents, her dowries to orphan girls, were all so many bids for popularity.

Yet surely in this they wronged her, for her character was deeply religious, and she devoted herself with special care to the pious bringing up of her children. She even wrote hymns for them which are high in the rank of spiritual poems; and one of Lorenzo's earliest memories, was his daily attendance with her at vespers, in the Dominican church of San Paolina, of which his friend, the learned Poliziano, was afterwards curate.

At the same time, Lucrezia had broad views, and a love for literature and art, which we should expect from the sister of that Giovanni Tornabuoni, who commissioned Ghirlandajo to paint the marvellous frescoes in the choir of Santa Maria Novella. Here we find a vivid illustration of the Florentine life, in which Lucrezia herself bore so dignified a part.

In this great series of the Life of the Virgin and of St. John the Baptist, the artist makes the charming anachronism of representing the public and official life of the Tornabuoni, their processions and stately banquets. We recognise them crowding to the temple court, or seated as guests at Herod's feast, with their kinsmen, the partners in the Medici bank, and their learned friends, amongst whom Angelo Poliziano is conspicuous.

But still more picturesque and striking is it to see the young Tornabuoni bride, Giovanna, in her rare jewels and stiff brocaded dress, accompanied by her ladies in rich attire, entering the chamber where the mother of the Virgin lies on her couch, and her friends wish her joy.

Lucrezia dei Medici was herself a patroness of literature also; and to her encouragement we owe the poem "Morgante," rich in description and even pathos, leading the way for Tasso and Ariosto, while in its humour we see a foreshadowing of Cervantes' greater work. The work had grown from verses sung or

LUCREZIA (TORNABUONI) DEI MEDICI

SANDRO BOTTICELLI

recited at the table of the Medici, but Luigi Pulci was overbold for his day, and his great romance was condemned by the Pope, and burnt by Savonarola in the Pyramid of Vanities.

For those troublous times of feud and faction, the story of Madonna Lucrezia was peaceful and uneventful. During most of her married life her father-in-law, Cosimo il Vecchio, was the head of the house of Medici, and with him, the scarlet gown of a Florentine citizen was but a vain symbol of humility for the despotic ruler of the Commune.

Yet on a certain morning of August, in the year 1458, the young wife must have needed all her courage. She was spending the summer with her children in the princely villa of Cafaggiuolo, far beyond Fiesole, amid the slopes of the Apennines, when Piero was summoned to join his father in Florence for a great *coup d'état*, of which the result was more than doubtful. As she watched him ride away beneath the plane-trees, followed by his armed retainers and a motley throng of peasants from the Mugello, devoted to the Medici, her heart must have been heavy with dark misgivings.

In Florence the great bell of the palace tolled, and the piazza was thronged with the excited populace, while on each side was posted an army of horse and foot soldiers. It must have been an anxious moment for Cosimo and Piero within the walls, when the Signoria appeared on their platform outside the palace, the Chancellor read the proposal for the Balla, and the list of the 350 members proposed by the ruling faction. But, to the amazement of the Milanese Podestà, there was no disturbance; the people shouted assent, and the danger of a popular revolution was at an end. Henceforth the power of the Medici was assured.

Cosimo lived six years after this, but broken in health, and his spirit clouded by the loss of his favourite son Giovanni, he appeared but little in public. He was succeeded by his only surviving son Piero, who was inferior to him in every way, and did not inherit his popularity. He was surnamed "Il Gottoso," from his bad health, and showed little talent as a politician. Indeed, he would have been more suited to the quiet life of a merchant, than that of a great ruler and patron of the arts; and the five years of his nominal rule were chiefly spent in retirement, in the Villa Careggi, built by Michelozzi in the most lovely situation, a few miles to the north of Florence. The gardens are still exquisitely beautiful, and we can imagine Mona Lucrezia's leisure spent amidst her books and her flowers, while her more serious thoughts were given to the education of her children, still continued under the guidance of the famous humanist Gentile de' Becchi, and especially to the constant watchful counsel of her sons, Lorenzo and Giuliano, now the practical representatives of the dynasty.

This must have been a gay time for Florence, with these two brilliant youths as masters of the revels; and even in these early days, Macchiavelli attributes to the lad of fifteen, the deliberate design of corrupting the State by pandering to its senses. But Lorenzo, with his keen zest for animal enjoyment, tempered by artistic beauty, was only a type of his city and his age. Constant festivals were the order of the day, from the triumphs and masquerades in the streets to carnival songs, and country dances, and sacred representations.

We read of a great tournament given in the playground of Florence, the vast oblong piazza of Santa Croce, in the year 1467, where Lorenzo was first attracted by Lucrezia Donati, a brilliant, highly cultured girl, of the same family as the wife of Dante. We can still see her beautiful face with its delicate refined features and rippling hair, in a portrait of Andrea Verocchio, and we hear of her later as the bride of Niccolò Ardinghelli. On this occasion the lady gave Lorenzo a wreath of violets, and he promised her in return, a still more splendid tournament.

In the meantime, his mother Lucrezia thought that the time had arrived for a marriage to be arranged for him. There must have been long and anxious consideration on the subject, for Piero does not seem to have been content to wed his son with the daughter of a citizen of Florence; he would choose a lady from some princely house of another State. His choice fell upon the great Orsini family, whose possessions spread from Rome, far and wide, joining those of the Colonna to the east, and extending from the sea to the Apennines.

It was characteristic of her loving caution that Mona Lucrezia herself took the important journey to Rome, that she might make all inquiries on the spot with regard to the young girl's qualifications, other than those of wealth and position. She seems to have been well satisfied with all she heard, and to have convinced herself that Clarice Orsini would be, in behaviour and beauty, a suitable bride for her young hero.

The story of Clarice will be told hereafter. On

Lucrezia's return to Florence she must have been present at the promised tournament, which was publicly announced as being held in honour of the coming marriage. But it is a significant fact that, as an old chronicler tells us, "It was the name of the lady Lucrezia Donati which was on the lips of all the lookers-on and in the heart of Lorenzo, and not that of the Roman bride, Clarice Orsini." It was a gorgeous spectacle. We hear of the ten young men on horseback and the sixty-four on foot, all clad in complete suits of armour, who followed in the procession, with an array of drums and fifes and trumpeters. Young Medici himself wore a surcoat of velvet fringed with gold and adorned by the golden lilies of France upon an azure ground, and a helmet with three blue feathers. His horse was decked out in red and white velvet, embroidered with pearls. The prize was assigned to him, and this is how he modestly mentions the fact in his own memoir:

"That I might do as others, and follow the custom on the Piazza Santa Croce I gave a tournament at great cost and with much magnificence; about ten thousand ducats were spent upon it. I was not a very mighty warrior nor a strong striker, yet to me was assigned the first prize, a helmet inlaid with silver, having a figure of Mars on the crest."

His marriage took place the following year, when he was only nineteen; but he seems to have remained as devoted as ever to his mother. His three sisters were already provided with husbands, the first obligation of a parent in the Italy of those days. Maria was married to Lionetta de' Rossi; Bianca, his favourite, was the wife of Guglielmo Pazzi; and in 1466 the youngest,

Nannina, was married to Bernardo Rucellai. She seems to have been a lively girl with strong religious feelings, and we are told of her strenuous efforts to convert the mercurial Pulci, a constant guest at her father's table, to more devout thought and a stricter life. In his merry jests and in his sonnets, he laughed at sacred things, and although he would recant in his "Confessions," yet it does not appear that Nannina's exhortations had any permanent effect upon his conduct.

Bernardo seems to have been a most desirable husband, if we are to judge from his high character, intellect, refinement, and passionate love for his beautiful gardens. An interesting story is told of him that, under the influence of Lorenzo, who was a champion of the Italian tongue, he refused to write to Erasmus in Latin, much to the embarrassment of his correspondent, who never would learn Italian lest his Latin style should be spoilt.

We next hear of Mona Lucrezia, when her son had gone to Milan, in July 1469, to be godfather to the baby Giovanni Galeazzo. He writes from thence: "I have given to the Duchess a gold necklace with a large diamond, worth about three thousand ducats. In consequence the Duke wishes me to stand for all his future sons."

Lorenzo, indeed, was so much fêted and flattered during his visit, that he was disposed to go beyond his credentials. Piero was willing that his son should take the first place at home, but he kept a strict hold on his foreign relations. He entrusted his wife with the delicate task of warning her son not to act on his own account, as though he were head of the State. "Tell him that while I live, I will not permit that the goslings should lead the geese to drink."

The lesson may have been needed, but the young Lorenzo was learning his part, and preparing for the high position which was so soon to be his. Piero died in December 1469, aged and infirm beyond his years, for he was but fifty-three. He wished for a quiet funeral, and his desire was carried out by his widow and sons. His monument may still be seen in the old sacristy of San Lorenzo, of simple grandeur, the work of Verocchio—an urn of red porphyry with a dark inlaid plaque of green marble and great acanthus leaves round the sides. The urn is fastened by ropes of bronze, and the cords pass behind the tomb to the ceiling of the niche.

After her husband's death, Mona Lucrezia seems to have lived in retirement in her beautiful villa near Florence, with its delightful gardens, full of the choicest flowers and fruit. In the year 1476 we find her little grandson, Piero, then barely five years old, writing to her from the Villa of Cafaggiuolo: "Send us some more ripe figs, I mean those very ripe ones, and send us some peaches with their kernels, and other of those things which you know we like, sweetmeats and tarts and some such little things."

From the somewhat masterful tone of this letter we seem to gather that the small boy had great confidence in the indulgence of his grandmother, who had never spoilt her own children. Although there cannot have been much sympathy between this cultivated woman and her daughter-in-law, Clarice Orsini dei Medici, yet she appears to have been on the most friendly terms with her. Mona Lucrezia kept up an interesting correspondence with the learned Agnolo Poliziano, who writes thus to her on one occasion when tutor to Lorenzo's children, and imprisoned by bad weather in the cold Mugello:

"The only news I can send you is, that we have here such continual rains that it is impossible to quit the house, and the exercises of the country are changed for childish sports within doors. Here I stand by the fireside, in my great coat and slippers, that you might take me for the very figure of Melancholy. Indeed I am the same at all times; for I neither see, nor hear, nor do anything that gives me pleasure, so much am I affected by the thought of our calamities; sleeping and waking they still continue to haunt me. Two days since we were all rejoicing upon hearing that the plague had ceased; now we are depressed on being informed that some symptoms of it yet remain. Were we at Florence we should have some consolation, were it only that of seeing Lorenzo when he returned to his house; but here we are in continual anxiety, and I, for my part, am half dead with solitude and weariness. The plague and the war are incessantly in my mind. I lament past misfortunes and anticipate future evils, and I have no longer at my side my dear Madonna Lucrezia, to whom I might unbosom my cares."

In the allusion to the "calamities" and "troubles" and also in Poliziano's anxiety about Lorenzo, we must understand a reference to the terrible, heart-breaking calamity which overshadowed with gloom the closing years of Mona Lucrezia's life—the murder of her passionately loved son Giuliano. Of this dark stain on the page of history, a brief account will be sufficient in these pages.

In the conspiracy of the Pazzi against the Medici, a shameful plot hatched at Rome, the young and gallant Giuliano, the idol of the populace, fell a victim within the sacred precincts of the Duomo. During the Mass, while the solemn strains of the *Agnus Dei* echoed through the choir, the dagger of the assassin pierced his heart as he stood by the Chapel of the Holy Cross. No circumstance was wanting to aggravate the sacrilege. As the wounded man staggered forwards and fell, he was pierced again and again. Nineteen wounds were found upon his body.

Assailed by a priest, who struck too high and missed, Lorenzo escaped. He had time to draw his sword, his friends rallied round him, and there was a deadly fight in the choir itself, while the terror-stricken Cardinal crouched by the high altar. The fugitives reached the northern sacristy, and, in face of the pursuers, closed the heavy bronze gates of Luca della Robbia.

The plot had failed, for henceforth the power of the Medici was assured, and a fearful vengeance awaited the conspirators in torture and hanging. The whole house of the Pazzi was disqualified from office—their very name was accursed. No citizen might marry a daughter or sister of the condemned, their palaces were looted, their scutcheons were hacked from the walls.

The beloved Giuliano was borne to his grave in San Lorenzo, on Ascension Day, with the pathetic honour of a people's grief. He had been beloved of all, a picturesque and striking personality. Skilled in all athletic pursuits, for which he was so well suited by his tall, magnificent figure, he was also a courteous, refined gentleman, who delighted in music and pictures, and all beautiful things. He wrote poetry, as was the fashion of his day; he could hold his own in the gay witty company at his brother's table; he was a faithful friend and a devoted son and brother.*

With this brief elegy to her youngest son, we will leave the story of the noble Mona Lucrezia dei Medici, well assured that her later years were sweetened and comforted by the unchanging love and respect of Lorenzo the Magnificent, by the duties and wide charities of her high position, and by that keen devotion to learning and literature which outlives all other tastes.

I cannot resist the temptation of inserting two of those "spiritual poems" of Madonna Lucrezia which she wrote for her children. In their charming simplicity and *naïve* devotional feeling they bear a strong resemblance to some of our old English carols.

LAUDA II

Venite Pastori
A veder Gesù, ch' è nato
Nel Presepio ignudo nato,
Più che 'l Sole risplendente.

Venite prestamente
A vedere il bel Messia
Col Giuseppe con Maria
La sua Madre gloriosa.

---

* Giuliano died unmarried, but a posthumous son was born to him, who was adopted by Lorenzo, and subsequently became Pope Clement VII.

Ma non fu si preziosa
    Creatura, nè mai fia;
    Evvi ancora in compagnia
    Solo il bue e l'asinello,

Pezze, fasce, nè mantello
    Non ha' l Signor de' Signori;
    E dal Ciel discendon cori
    Per veder la Deitate.

Quivi vien le Potestate
    Quivi viene è Cherubini
    Le Virtù, è Serafini,
    Con tutta la Gerarchia

E con dolce melodia
    Ringraziandol con disio:
    Gloria in Cielo all' alto Dio
    E in terra pace sia.

O Pastor venite via
    El Signore a visitare
    Vo' sentirate cantare,
    E vedrate il Re di Gloria.

Oggi è il dì della vittoria,
    Che' l nimico fia dolente,
    E li Padri allegramente
    Sentiranno tal novella.

Apparita è una Stella
    Tutto' l Mondo alluminare;
    Venite a ringraziare
    Gesù Christo omnipotente.

Tutte le devote mente
    Contemplando con dolcezza
    Come la divina altezza
    Patir vuol pe' nostri errori.*

---

* To be sung to the tune of "Quando sono in questa Cittade."

LUCREZIA DEI MEDICI

LAUDA IV*

Ecco il Re forte
Ecco il Re forte;
Aprite quelle porte;
O Principe infernale;
Non fate resistenza
Gli è il Re celestiale
Che vien con gran potenza;
Fategli riverenza
Levate via le porte.
Ecco il Re forte! ecco il Re forte!

Chi è questo potente
Che vien con tal vittoria?
Egli è Signor possente
Egli è Signor di Gloria
Avuto ha la vittoria
Egli ha vinto la morte.
Ecco il Re forte! ecco il Re forte!

Egli ha vinto la guerra
Durati gia molt 'anni;
E fa tremar la terra,
Per cavarci d' affanni,
Riempier vuol gli scanni
Per ristorar sua Corte.
Ecco il Re forte! ecco il Re forte . . .

---

* To be sung to the tune of "Ben Venga Maggio."

CLARICE (ORSINI) DEI MEDICI.

THE wife of Lorenzo dei Medici should have had a position unique amidst the ladies of the Renaissance, yet Clarice appears to have been somewhat overweighted by it. She was the daughter of Giacopo Orsini, of the noble and powerful Roman family, whose great possessions spread over half a province, and her mother was of the still more distinguished line of the Bracciano, a sister of the splendid Napoleone. Her uncles were amongst the most influential cardinals in the Curia, and her soldier family was rich in great military captains.

This was the first of the foreign alliances of the Medici, and had many advantages, besides the more obvious one of giving them influence at the Papal Court. The Orsini were traditional enemies of the rival republic of Siena; they could bring a large force into the field, and were in possession of a chain of strongholds which crossed the high road to the south, and would be invaluable in case of home or foreign attacks.

Had Piero chosen a bride for his son in Florence, it would have caused endless jealousy and offence. Lorenzo himself seems to have had very little choice in the matter, but he had seen the lady more than once, and had acquiesced in the choice. She had also met with his mother's approval.

CLARICE DEI MEDICI

Clarice is described as having a tall shapely figure and a delicate white neck, but her carriage was somewhat ungraceful, from a shy habit of bending her head forward. Her face was too round for classical beauty, but she had a pink-and-white colour, and her abundant hair shone with a ruddy glow. We are specially told that her hands were pretty, with long well-shaped fingers. No doubt they were skilled in all the elaborate embroidery and fine needlework of the times, for Clarice does not appear to have been highly educated, according to the Medici standard, in classical learning and philosophy. Yet her stately home at Monte Rotondo, outside the Porta Pia, had been a local centre of Renaissance culture in the previous century, and it was unfortunate for her future happiness that the young girl was dependent on chance visits to her uncle, Cardinal Latino, for any training in art and literature.

One of her earliest letters to Lorenzo has been preserved:

"I HAVE received your letter which has given me great pleasure, and in which you tell me of the tournament where you won the prize. I am glad that you are successful in what gives you pleasure, and that my prayer is heard, for I have no other wish than to see you happy. Give my regards to my father Piero and my mother Lucrezia, and all who are near to you. At the same time I send my regards to you. I have nothing else to say.

"Yours,

"CLARICE DE URSINIS."

Simple words, doubtless written with much thought and anxiety.

The betrothal took place in December 1468, and in the following May Clarice was brought to Florence. The marriage was celebrated on Sunday, June 4, and the festivities lasted for several days. There is a curious little note in the Ricordi of Lorenzo on that date:

"I, Lorenzo, took for wife Clarice, daughter of the Lord Giacopo, or rather she was given to me."

It was doubtless a marriage of state, but there is every reason to believe that a real affection grew up between husband and wife, for there is much simple, tender feeling in the numerous letters preserved, and Lorenzo always treated her with courtesy and kindness.

We have a very full account of the great festivities in Florence at the wedding, which was celebrated with true princely prodigality. The dress of the bride was of the richest white-and-gold brocade, and the splendid horse she rode in the procession, was a gift from the royal stables of Naples. She had other rich presents and great wedding-chests; but it may be mentioned here as a significant fact, that she received no dowry. No doubt the proud house of the Orsini was of opinion that the lady herself was sufficient to bestow on the son of the great banking-house of Florence. The relative position had changed some years later, when her own son Piero married another Orsini, for then a very large dowry was part of the contract.

But, all the same, Clarice was royally welcomed. Pipers and trumpeters, and a gallant train of noble youths and fair maidens bore her company. In the palace of the Via Larga an immense ball-room was made ready to receive the bride, hung with tapestry, adorned with the arms and devices of the Orsini and Medici families, and covered with priceless Eastern carpets. On this occasion the ladies and knights, the old and young, seemed to have dined apart. Clarice and fifty of the younger ladies had the broad balcony above the garden, while the older matrons dined with Madonna Lucrezia in the inner chamber. Round the courtyard were places for seventy of the more grave and reverend citizens, while the hall was given up to all the young gallants. On the ring of tables, costly wine stood in immense vessels of brass.

More than a thousand guests were entertained each day at the Via Larga, and in the house of Carlo dei Medici.

Lorenzo's ingenuity devised the most gorgeous spectacles to amuse the people. There were mimic battles, in which troops of horsemen in armour charged each other, and a fort was built up, to be picturesquely attacked and stoutly defended. There was music and dancing, and probably some of the songs to which the dancers kept time as they sang, were composed by the young poet himself.

We will not dwell further on the details of the banquets, as the full description of a great wedding feast is given in a previous chapter.

Soon after his marriage, the bridegroom went on a journey to Milan, from whence he writes as follows :

"I HAVE arrived here safely and am quite well. This, I believe, will please you better than any other news, if I may judge by my own longings for you and home. Be good company to Piero, Mona Contessina, and Mona Lucrezia, and I will soon come back to you, for it seems a thousand years till I can see you once more. Pray to God for me, and if there is anything you want, let me know before I leave.

"Your own

"LORENZO DEI MEDICI.

"MILAN, *July* 22, 1469."

The death of Piero dei Medici in December of the same year, must have made a difference in the position of his young daughter-in-law. It was a critical time for Lorenzo; but when, on the morrow, he and his brother received the unanimous petition of the citizens "that they would assume the place vacated by their father," the Medici took their stand as "signori naturali," born-lords of Italy. Then, indeed, Clarice became the first lady, I will not say the uncrowned queen, of Florence, for the fact was simply accepted without assertion or ostentation.

A very difficult task was before the young ruler, but he seems to have behaved on the whole with great wisdom and tact. Naturally impatient and hasty, yet his sister Bianca spoke of him in after years, as reconciling the malcontents of his father's rule with infinite patience. The drudgery of that complicated political government must have been sometimes an intolerable burden. He had all the literary and artistic tastes which he might have enjoyed in leisured wealth; he loved the country, and keenly enjoyed the company of men of letters and artists. But most of these pleasures he had to sacrifice to his ruling passion of ambition.

The young bride, fresh from seclusion in the home of her girlhood, must have found it difficult to play her part in this new literary society of Florence.

LORENZO DEI MEDICI

Benozzo Gozzoli

It may have been a welcome change when she had to receive, in March 1471, the Duke of Milan, Galeazzo Sforza, and the Duchess Bona, who came with such a display of wealth and luxury that they brought 2000 persons in their suite. They consisted of 100 men-at-arms and 500 infantry as a guard, fifty running footmen richly dressed in silk and silver, and many noblemen and courtiers and their different retinues. Five hundred couple of dogs, with an immense number of hawks and falcons, completed this astounding show. It is said that this arrogant and pretentious excursion cost Galeazzo 200,000 golden ducats.

It was well for his hosts that this army of retainers was entertained at the public expense. This visit of state was probably made in return for that paid by Lorenzo, two years before, when he stood godfather for the ill-fated baby, Gian Galeazzo, and gave the mother a splendid gold necklace with a great diamond pendant. If she wore it on this occasion, Clarice must have looked at it with a touch of envy.

Grandeur like misery brings strange company, and we cannot but wonder what sympathy there was between these two great ladies. Bona of Savoy, whose youth had been spent with her sister, the Queen of Louis XI., at the French Court, and who for some years had been the wife of such a profligate and cruel man as Galeazzo, must have had far other experiences than the simple Roman girl-wife, whose first baby was barely a month old.

Those men of the Renaissance were often a strange combination. This Duke of Milan, whom chronicles of the day describe as another Nero in his crimes, was a great patron of art and learning, founded a library and collected singers from all Europe to form the choir of his chapel. He is said once to have insisted that his artists, under pain of death, should paint a hall in the Castello of Pavia with portraits of the whole ducal family in a single night.

Such was the visitor of Lorenzo, and we are not surprised to learn that he professed great admiration for the splendid art treasures of the Medici. He was shown the famous statues, vases, intaglios, and gems, the priceless collection of manuscripts and drawings, the paintings of the greatest masters the world has ever seen, and he seems to have had the good taste or the tact to exclaim that, "in comparison with what he had seen, gold and silver lost their value."

Machiavelli speaks with horror of the riot and dissipation of the Milanese guests, but the remark comes somewhat strangely from him that "this was the first time Florence openly disregarded the command not to eat flesh in Lent."

For the entertainment of the visitors, there were three extraordinary public spectacles. First, the Annunciation of the Virgin, then the Ascension of Christ, and lastly the Descent of the Holy Spirit. This was acted in the Church of St. Spirito, and in the unskilled use of many flaring lights, the sacred building caught fire and was entirely destroyed.

The accident was of course ascribed by the people to the wrath of heaven.

During the years which followed, Clarice must have been almost entirely engaged with her family of young children, to whom she was a devoted, if somewhat injudicious mother. Some of these died in infancy, but three sons and four daughters lived to grow up.

These boys were destined to have so great a future that everything connected with their early history is intensely interesting, and fortunately the records of the time give us a very full account of them. The picture of life in the Medici household is very simple and pleasant. Lorenzo was devoted to his children, he was never so happy as in their company, in the villas of Caiano or Careggi; he played with them, rode with them, joined in their music, and even wrote a little play for them to act. But above all he took the keenest interest in their education, a matter on which the unlearned Clarice had quite different ideas, and which seems to have been almost the only cause of discord between them. The renowned and learned Agnolo Poliziano was persuaded by Lorenzo, to whom he owed everything, to undertake the uncongenial task of teaching the Medici children. He accompanied the family away from his beloved Florence, when after the conspiracy of the Pazzi Lorenzo thought it desirable to send them to Pistoia, and afterwards to Cafaggiolo, in the winter. From thence little Piero, the eldest, wrote the most delightful letters to his father in an unsteady childish hand, and chiefly in Latin, which his master left uncorrected.

In 1478, when he was seven years old, he tells his father that he has already learned many verses of Virgil; "and the master makes me decline and examines me every day." Then he adds with pardonable pride: "Also I know the first book of Teodoro by heart, and I think I understand it." He must mean Teodoro Gaza's Greek Grammar.

The child evidently makes good progress, for the following year he writes more easily:

"I wish you would send me some of the best setters that there are. I do not desire anything else. All the company here, everybody, specially asks to be remembered to you, and I also. I pray you to be careful of the pestilence and to bear us in mind, because we are little and have need of you."

In his next letter, on the strength of his Latin, he feels justified in begging for greater favours.

"Nondum venit equulus, magnifice pater" (That little horse has not yet made his appearance). He gives an amusing account of his brothers and sisters: "Giuliano thinks of nothing but laughter; Lucrezia sews, sings and reads; Maddelena knocks her head against the wall, but does not hurt herself; Luisa can already say a few things; Contessina makes a great noise all over the house."

He does not receive the pony, and writes again: "To give a tone to my letters I have always written them in Latin, and yet I have not had the little horse you promised me, so that everybody laughs at me."

Then again later: "I am afraid something must have happened to the horse, because if it had been all right you would have sent it to me as you promised. In case that one cannot come, please send me another."

But at last the pony arrives, and little Piero writes a pretty letter of thanks, promising to be very good.

One of Poliziano's letters about the children is worth quoting in part: "Piero attends to his studies with olerable diligence. We daily make excursions through the neighbourhood, we visit the gardens with which this city abounds, and sometimes look into the library of Maestro Zambino, where I have found some good pieces both in Greek and Latin. Giovanni rides out on horseback, and the people follow him in crowds.

"Raccomandomi a V.M. Pistoii, 31 Augusti, 1478."

This Giovanni, who was only three years old, was the future Pope Leo X. These letters give the sunny outward aspect of life, but beneath, there was a rumbling of thunder, and two lives were very far from happy. Poor Mona Clarice, whose instinct was to spoil her children, and who cared for nothing but their religious education, was at constant feud with this very learned tutor, who was so strict about Latin, and altogether so terribly conscientious about the lessons. To make matters worse, she was clear-eyed enough to see that he despised her for her ignorance. Indeed in his letters to Lorenzo, he complains in no measured language of her interference, "being unlettered and a woman."

"As for Giovanni," he continues, "his mother employs him in reading the Psalter, which I by no means commend. Whilst she abstained from interfering with him, it is astonishing how rapidly he improved: insomuch that he read without assistance."

Then again with regard to Piero when, according to the time-table, he should have been reading his Greek, she called him away to sing hymns.

This divided control had long been a standing grievance between the lady and the tutor, but it came to a climax in that long dull winter of 1478 which, by the desire of Lorenzo, they most unwillingly spent together at the villa of Cafaggiolo, in the cold Mugello. Imprisoned by incessant rain, longing for the various delights of far-distant Florence, and the delightful company of Lorenzo himself, they both became irritable and intolerant. At length Clarice, unable to endure the provocation which she received, compelled the tutor to leave the house, and wrote the following characteristic letter to her husband :

"Magnifice Conjux ec. . . . I shall be glad to escape being made the subject of ridicule in a tale of Franco's as Luigi Pulci was ; nor do I like that Messer Agnolo should threaten that he would remain in the house in spite of me. You will remember I told you that, if it was your will he should stay, I was perfectly contented ; and although I have suffered infinite abuse from him, yet, if it be with your assent, I am patient. But I do not believe it to be so. . . . And the children are all well and have much desire to see you, and still greater have I, who have no other longing than this, having to remain here at this time.

"Sempre a voi mi raccomando. In Cafaggiolo, 28 Maii, 1479."

Lorenzo seems to have quietly acquiesced in the change ; but he gave Poliziano the use of a villa at Fiesole, and their friendship remained unbroken. The banished scholar, no longer worried by opposition or weary teaching, devoted his leisure to a much-admired poem, "Rusticus," in which he sings the praise of his beloved patron.

Of Clarice's three daughters the eldest, Lucrezia, married Jacopo Salviati. We hear of her courage some years later when, cross-questioned by the magistrates of the Republic as to the share she had taken in a conspiracy to restore Piero dei Medici, she boldly replied that he was her brother, and she wished for his success.

Contessina married Piero Ridolfo, and Luisa was engaged to Giovanni dei Medici, but died before the appointed wedding-day. Maddelena seems to have been her mother's favourite, and when a marriage was suggested for her with Franceschetto Cybo, the son of Pope Innocent VIII., there are pathetic letters from Lorenzo, begging that she might be allowed to stay a little longer with her mother, who was in ill-health, and the girl was the very "eye of her head."

This was in 1487, and in March of that year Piero, who was only sixteen, was married by proxy to Alfonsina Orsini, who received a dowry of 12,000 Neapolitan ducats from the head of her noble house. Probably this was the last important event in the life of Clarice, for she died in the following July, not yet forty years of age. She had been dangerously ill, but the end must have come suddenly, for Lorenzo was away from home that week, taking sulphur baths for his gout. It is pleasant to think that the poor mother had her will, and that the dear Maddelena was with her to the end.

Clarice was neither beautiful nor talented, but she was a kind, warm-hearted woman, always ready to befriend those in trouble, and to bring their petitions before her husband, sure of a favourable hearing. Lorenzo mourned for her deeply, and after her death the shadows seemed to gather round his path, and he only survived her a few years.

TWO QUEENS OF NAPLES

PRINCESSES OF THE HOUSE OF ANJOU

GIOVANNA I GIOVANNA II

HISTORICAL SUMMARY

1328. Birth of Giovanna of Anjou.
1341. Petrarch crowned at Rome.
1343. Giovanna I. succeeds her grandfather, King Robert, on the throne of Naples. Already married to Andreas, son of the King of Hungary.
1345. Murder of Andreas, the queen's husband.
1347. Giovanna I. marries Louis of Taranto.
1348. Great plague in Europe. Giovanna I. sells Avignon to Pope Clement VI. She visits Avignon, and pleads her own cause.
1356. Giovanna I. crowned Queen of Sicily.
1362. Death of her husband, Louis of Taranto.
1376. Giovanna marries Otho of Brunswick.
1382. Murder of Giovanna I., Queen of Naples, by her nephew, Charles of Durazzo, after her defeat by the King of Hungary.

1371. Birth of Giovanna II. of Naples.
1382. Charles of Durazzo succeeds to the throne of Naples.
1386. Charles, King of Naples, is murdered.
1399. His son Ladislaus firmly established on the throne of Naples.
1403. Marriage of Giovanna of Naples with Gugliemo, son of the Duke of Austria, Leopold III.
1406. Death of Gugliemo.
1412. Sicily is united to the Kingdom of Aragon.
1413. Ladislaus, King of Naples, takes possession of Rome. Flight of Pope John XXIII.
1414. Giovanna II. succeeds to the throne of Naples on the death of her brother, Ladislaus.
1416. Marriage of Queen Giovanna II. with Jaques de Bourbon, Comte de la Marche.
1421. Giovanna II. summons Alfonso of Aragon to her assistance.
1423. Giovanna II. adopts Louis III. of Anjou as her successor.
1434. Death of Louis of Anjou.
1435. Death of Giovanna II., 2nd February.

GIOVANNA I

. . . "By my troth
I would not be a queen!"

SUCH is our instinctive cry as we read the story of this unfortunate lady. Nowhere do we find in history so close a parallel to the hapless Mary Queen of Scots—in her beauty, her disposition, her many marriages, the sea of troubles which overwhelmed her, and her tragical end. Indeed the resemblance does not end here, for the same bitter controversy has raged ever since as to her character and deserts, the share she had in more than one murder, and the part she played in the drama of her life.

In this slight sketch it will be possible to take a dispassionate view, inclining rather with the poet Boccaccio to the side of mercy and kindly appreciation, for none can deny that, in any case, she was more sinned against than sinning.

All the circumstances of her position were against the poor little princess from the beginning, and it was her fate during life, to suffer from the sins and follies of her nearest relations, while even her own good qualities were fatal to her; for she was trusting where she ought to have been suspicious, and forgiving when sternness was her only chance.

Giovanna was born at Naples in the month of

February 1328. She was the granddaughter of Robert of Taranto, King of Naples, known to fame as "Il buon Rè Roberto," the patron of Boccaccio, the friend of Petrarch, himself a distinguished man of science and letters, a wise monarch, a munificent protector of artists and learned men—one of the most interesting personalities of his day. His father, King Charles II. of Naples, a prince of the house of Anjou, had married Maria, who was heiress to the throne of Hungary, and he succeeded to that kingdom in right of his wife. He must have felt that the union of these two great countries was unwieldy and unnatural, for on his death-bed, he called his sons to his side and divided his dominions, bequeathing to Charles Martel, the elder, the throne of Hungary, and leaving to his younger son Robert, the fair provinces of Naples and Provence. It was in the year 1309 that King Robert entered into possession of his patrimony, just at the earliest dawn of the Renaissance, for Dante and Giotto, Petrarch and Boccaccio, those great forerunners, were all his contemporaries and friends.

He had one son, Charles Duke of Calabria, who married Marie de Valois, sister of Philip of France, and he seems to have been a most accomplished prince, a great favourite with the people of Naples, who gave him the title of "The Illustrious." During two years he held the post of "Captain of the People" at Florence. But he did not long enjoy the honours of his position, for he died young, leaving two infant daughters, Giovanna, the subject of this notice, and a younger sister, Maria.

King Robert, heartbroken at the loss of his only and dearly loved son, raised a splendid monument to his memory in the vast church of Santa Chiara. This beautiful Gothic design was the work of Masuccio II., and has been engraved by Cicognara, as a fine example of the sculpture of the fourteenth century. On a bas-relief—in front of the tomb on which the young prince rests, in his royal robes covered with fleurs-de-lis—he is represented sitting in the midst of the great officers and barons of the kingdom, his feet resting on a wolf, and a lamb drinking at the same fountain, to typify the peace which his reign would have brought.

The bereaved father turned from these ruined hopes to devote himself to the tender care of his orphaned grandchildren, who were still almost babes when they lost their mother. In 1331, when Giovanna was not quite four years old, he proclaimed her heiress to his throne, and all his nobles were assembled with great ceremony, to take the oaths of allegiance to her as Duchess of Calabria. With the title she also inherited all the rights of her father in Naples and Provence.

Poor little motherless duchess, weighted at that early age with functions of state and grandeur, when she should have been playing with her dolls! Still her grandfather may have been justified in this as an act of policy, for in those stormy times sovereignty was nought without pomp and show, and it was needful to secure the loyalty of powerful vassals to the heir of the throne. But the next step taken by "Robert the Wise" was fated to prepare the way for much misfortune and calumny.

Some one was required to take charge of the royal children, and he unfortunately made choice of Philippa the Catenese, a name of dark and tragic repute in the annals of Italy. She was born at Catania in Sicily, the daughter of a poor fisherman, and had entered the service of Violante, the first wife of King Robert, to nurse her infant son Charles. The Queen became so fond of her that she remained at the palace, and gradually rose to a position of great trust and influence, as first maid-of-honour.

Philippa seems to have been a clever, handsome girl, and must have had most attractive qualities, for after the death of her first mistress, she was in still higher favour with the second wife of Robert, Queen Sancha, a lady of high reputation and capacity. The Duke of Calabria, her foster-child, was devoted to her. She married the seneschal of his palace, and became lady of the bedchamber to his wife, and was the first to welcome the baby Giovanna into the world. It was only natural that the favour and affection of the royal family for this woman of the people should give rise to much jealousy and even scandal. Indeed it appeared so incomprehensible in those days that she was accused of being a witch. Orloff speaks of her as "femme intrigante et sans mœurs," but he does not give any sufficient ground for that statement.

Still it was no doubt unwise and impolitic to advance a woman of peasant birth, to a post which must have been eagerly desired by many high-born ladies of the court, and the influence which she gained over the child-duchess caused much ill feeling and evil gossip, and in the end led to her own ruin and destruction.

King Robert the Wise made a yet more fatal mistake, with the most kindly and generous intentions. His fertile realms of Naples and Provence were so much more desirable than the arid wastes of Hungary that the princes of the elder branch had never been satisfied with this division, although it had been ratified by a formal decree of the Pope. So it occurred to the chivalrous gentleman that, if he could make a match between his little heiress and her second cousin, a son of the King of Hungary, it would put an end to all jealous feuds and be a perfect settlement of the family dispute. Negotiations were entered into with impulsive haste, and King Carobert was only too willing to accept such a splendid offer, of a bride with a future kingdom as her dowry, for his second son Andreas.

The boy was only seven years old and Giovanna was five, when this ill-fated marriage took place at Naples with the utmost magnificence. Princely feasts were given to the people, and the rejoicings continued for several days. In distinguished families of that epoch such solemn betrothals, or "marriages for the future," were by no means unusual for political considerations. At that early age, the children of course had no voice in the matter, and the parents had it all their own way.

But in this case, the grievous error was made of bringing up the children together under the same roof, with the knowledge that they were destined for each other. Can we conceive any plan more likely to be fatal to their ultimate happiness? Affection is not usually secured to order, and the very fact that it was expected of them would probably end in mutual dislike. As it happened, the two children were absolutely different in character and tastes.

Full of enthusiasm himself for learning, King Robert devoted great care to the education of his grandchild, who had the best teachers in Italy. All historians agree as to Giovanna's brilliant talent and passion for literature; and an old chronicle says that before she was twelve years old "she was already excelling in understanding, not only every child of her age, but most women of mature years." She must have grown up amid the paintings of Giotto, in Santa Chiara and in the Castel Nuovo, which contained the finest library of the age, and she must have been on intimate terms with Petrarch and Boccaccio when they were at the Court of Naples.

There is a story told of Giotto that when he was at work one summer day, King Robert, who enjoyed his genial company, said to him:

"If I were you I would leave off painting when the weather is so hot."

"So would I if I were King Robert," was the artist's ready reply.

Meantime all this cultured society seems to have been wasted on Andreas. He grew up in the midst of his boorish Hungarian attendants, lazy and ignorant, full of dislike for the Neapolitans he was some day to govern. The King of Hungary, his father, had chosen for his tutor a monk, Fra Roberto, who had a most evil influence over his pupil, and kept him in absolute subjection. Too late the good King became aware of the unfortunate choice which he had made; he foresaw the trouble in store for his darling Giovanna, and he sought to obviate it, by excluding her husband from any share in the government. But this only prepared the way for new dangers, by awaking the rage and jealousy of the Hungarians.

Giovanna's happy childhood soon drew to an end, for at the age of fifteen, she and Andreas began their married life. They were known as the Duke and

Duchess of Calabria, and lived with King Robert and Queen Sancha in the Castel Nuovo, at once a citadel and a magnificent palace, overlooking the lovely Bay of Naples. It must have been a curious household under that princely roof: with the younger sister of Giovanna, the Princess Maria, future Empress of Constantinople, and another Maria, the reputed daughter of Count Aquino, whose wife had been attached to the Court of King Robert—who was, in fact, supposed to be the girl's real father. She was the frail and beautiful lady immortalised by Boccaccio as his "Fiammetta," and the portrait he has left of her, brings her image vividly before us. We are told that he first saw Maria, as he stood leaning against one of the columns of the Church of San Lorenzo.

"Her tresses of a blonde hue, for which it is scarcely possible to find any comparison, shadowed a snow-white forehead, admirable for its well-proportioned width, in the lower portion of which two jet black and infinitely slender brows rise in circling arches, divided from each other by a candid space; and beneath them two lovely eyes, such rogues in their movement that the light flashing from their beauty renders it scarcely possible to be sure what they really are. The slender nose is exactly proportioned to what the perfect beauty of the face requires; the cheeks have no other colour than that of milk which the living blood has just newly tinged, and the vermilion mouth is in appearance that of roses among the whitest lilies; the chin, not protruding but rounded and dimpled in the centre, is poised above the milk-white and straight throat and soft neck" ("Ameta," p. 59).

Boccaccio is said to have written his "Decamerone"

to please this fair Maria, who was afterwards the wife of Robert Count d'Artois.

On the death of her grandfather, the good King Robert, Giovanna became, in 1343, Queen of Naples, Provence, and Piedmont, a goodly heritage. The regency having been refused by the gentle and pious Queen Sancha, a council was appointed to govern during the minority. But Fra Roberto, by his influence over Andreas, set at nought the late king's wishes, and became the ruler and tyrant of Naples. Petrarch, sent on a special mission by Pope Clement, gives a deplorable account of Naples at this time, in a letter to Cardinal Colonna. He speaks of the Court as corrupt, vicious and barbarous, and thus alludes to the ferocious and ignorant ruler, Fra Roberto.

"May heaven rid the soil of Italy of such a pest!—a horrible animal, with bald head and bare feet, short in stature, swollen in person, with worn-out rags, purposely torn to show his naked skin. He not only sets at nought the pitiful supplications of the citizens, but on the ground of his feigned sanctity, treats with scorn the embassy of the Pope."

Giovanna would have kept the poet at her Court, but she was a sovereign only in name, and could but give him the nominal title of her chaplain and almoner. It is important to mention that Petrarch seems to have had a great admiration for her character and talent. He was full of pity for her position, and describes her as "a lamb in the midst of wolves."

Meantime, troubles were thickening around her. The next year her young sister Maria, who had been promised in marriage to Louis King of Hungary, was persuaded to make a clandestine marriage with another cousin, the Duke of Durazzo; a cause of endless misfortune in the future.

Great preparations were made for the coronation of Giovanna, which was to take place on September 20, 1345, and to escape the tropical heat of that August, she and her husband went for change of air to the Celestine monastery at Aversa, about fifteen miles from the capital. They spent some weeks of apparent peace and happiness, in the exquisite gardens of that enchanting spot, when the terrible event occurred, which has ever remained one of the unsolved riddles of history.

It was on the night of September 18, that Andreas was roused by the news that an urgent courier had arrived from Naples. He had scarcely crossed the threshold of his chamber, when he was suddenly attacked by armed men, strangled, and hurled down from a balcony overlooking the garden.

The enemies of the young queen at once accused her of complicity in the murder, yet no proof of her guilt was ever brought forward. It is said that she listened to the awful tale in speechless horror, without a tear; but with regard to this she says in her letter to the King of Hungary: "I have suffered so much anguish for the death of my beloved husband, that, *stunned* by grief, I had well-nigh died of the same wounds."

It seems impossible to believe that a young girl of seventeen, of gentle, mild disposition, should be the cold-blooded assassin of her young husband, the father of her unborn child. We have seen the testimony of Petrarch to her fine character, and Boccaccio says of her: "She was so gracious, gentle, compassionate and kind, that she seemed rather the companion than the queen of those around her."

When the news of this crime reached Naples there was consternation and tumult in the city, and the Hungarians fled in haste. Giovanna returned at once to the Castel Nuovo, where two months afterwards her son was born. Her first step on resuming the government was to give a signed commission to a certain Hugh del Balzo, that he might seek out the murderers of her husband and bring them to judgment. He appears to have lost no time in seizing and putting to the torture some of the chamberlains of Andreas, who, on the rack, were induced to accuse, amongst others, Philippa the Catanese, who held a position of the highest honour with her mistress, her son Count Evoli, and her young granddaughter Sancha, recently married to Count Terlizi.

Giovanna heard nothing of all this, and when Hugh del Balzo asked for an audience, she received him at once within the Castel Nuovo. Availing himself of the authority which the Queen had given him, he summoned all her dearest friends before him and accused them of Andreas' murder. In spite of her anguish and despair, she was helpless to protect them; they were torn from her presence and put to death with atrocious cruelty.

The loss of all whom she loved and trusted at one fell swoop, was a crushing blow from which the young girl never recovered, and from that time her sunny nature was saddened and overcast, and she was never known to have an intimate friend.

Two years later, Giovanna gave much satisfaction to her people by marrying her second cousin, Prince Louis of Taranto, a man of distinguished courage and talent, and so strikingly handsome that he was spoken of as another Phœbus. At this time Louis, King of Hungary, who coveted the crown of Naples for himself, invaded her kingdom on the pretext of avenging his brother's murder. He also laid a solemn accusation against Giovanna before the Roman tribunal of Cola Rienzi, who heard the pleading on both sides, but seems to have been unable or unwilling to pronounce judgment.

Meantime the Hungarian king adopted a horrible device to enlist the sympathy of the multitude. In front of his invading army a black standard was borne, on which was pictured the murder of Andreas, while a train of black-robed mourners followed it in grim procession. Thus escorted, Louis crossed the frontier and arrived at Aversa. Amongst his followers was the husband of Princess Maria, the Duke of Durazzo, who was false and foolish enough to think that if Giovanna were deposed, his wife and children would succeed to the throne. But a far other fate awaited him. The King requested him to point out the scene of the murder, and on his refusal, led the way to the Celestine convent, and on the fatal balcony accused him of complicity, and bid him prepare for death. In vain he protested his innocence and pleaded for mercy ; he was stabbed and cast into the garden below, where he was left unburied.

After this deed of treachery, Louis advanced to Naples and took the city by surprise, but the young Queen was warned in time, and with her household, set sail in three galleys for the coast of Provence. Her fickle subjects, who had failed in courage to defend her, made bitter lamentation over her departure. She landed at Nice and made her way to Avignon, where she demanded of Pope Clement VI. that he and his cardinals should try the justice of her cause. She pleaded in her own person, and the Latin speech which she composed, was said by those who heard her to be "the most marvellous example of a woman's eloquence ever recorded in history."

The Hungarian envoys sent to confront her, seem to have been reduced to silence. Giovanna had a great ovation; she was acquitted with the highest honour and admiration, and the gallant knights of Provence crowded to offer their loyal service. At Avignon she was joined by her sister, the widow of the unfortunate Durazzo, whom she welcomed with tender affection and adopted the orphan children.

In all the annals of history no year has a darker record than that of the Queen's visit to her dominions in Provence, 1348, noted for the coming of the Black Death. It had swept all over Europe, with terror and destruction in its train, and nowhere had its ravages been more fearful than in this city of the exiled Pope, who had actually consecrated the river Rhone for burial of the plague-stricken dead. Laura, the beloved of Petrarch, had fallen a victim to the pestilence soon after the arrival of Giovanna.

After an orgy of horror and bloodshed, the King of Naples was driven away from Naples by the dread of infection, leaving behind a ferocious deputy, Conrad Wolf, whose tyranny and cruelty at length roused the Neapolitans to resistance. They rose against the Hungarians, and sent an abject petition to their queen, promising to deliver her from her enemies if she would consent to return. With a goodly retinue of Provençal nobility, she lost no time in travelling back to her capital, where she was welcomed with enthusiasm, and the Court over which she and her husband presided, soon regained its former magnificence. But while rewarding those who had remained faithful, they showed mercy in the hour of victory, and gave a free pardon to their disloyal subjects.

Enraged at this reverse, the King of Hungary renewed the war, which with varied success and many gallant fights lasted for more than two years, leaving everywhere devastation and misery in its track. Louis of Taranto, who had greatly distinguished himself as a general, at last made the chivalrous offer of ending the struggle by challenging the King of Hungary to single combat. The duel did not take place, but peace was at length concluded in 1353 by the mediation of the Pope, who also granted a Bull for the coronation of Giovanna and her husband. Never were there such rejoicings, and the whole city seemed to have gone wild with exultation. But even in that hour of triumph a new sorrow awaited the unfortunate queen, for on her return home after the coronation, she found her baby-girl, a four-year-old darling, dead in her cradle.

She was destined to be a childless mother, for she had already lost her boy, the son of Andreas; and another daughter, born later, also died in infancy.

Still her life had no lack of outward prosperity, for in 1356 she was offered the throne of Sicily, and crowned with great state at Messina.

But she was soon recalled from her new kingdom by fresh disturbances at home. Louis of Durazzo, the brother of her sister's murdered husband, was defeated, and on his death Giovanna kindly took his orphan son

Charles under her care, little dreaming how her devotion would be repaid.

Three years later she lost her idolised husband, who died of fever, brought on by his own intemperate habits. But she was not very long suffered to remain a widow, for her Ministers felt great anxiety to secure an heir to the kingdom. She was willing to abide by their choice, which fell on Giacomo, the son of the King of Majorca, and for the third time she went through the marriage ceremony. The bridal festivities were held by the lovely Bay of Gaeta, and the Prince of Majorca bore so high a character that once more there seemed to be a prospect of happiness for Giovanna. But within three months, her husband set off on an expedition to Spain to avenge the murder of his father by Pedro of Aragon. He was defeated and taken prisoner, notwithstanding the generous help of Edward the Black Prince. His wife paid an immense ransom for him, but, once free, nothing would deter him from repeating the same rash enterprise, in the course of which he fell a victim to malarious fever.

Again was the poor queen urged to marry by her council, but she had suffered too much, and refused to tempt Providence again by the chances of matrimony. She set herself with great earnestness to the task of ruling her turbulent people, and the following years during which she reigned alone, were the most successful both at home and abroad. With a strong hand, she put down the desperate bands of brigands who infested the high roads, she kept a strict watch on the administration of justice, she gave wise encouragement to commerce, until peace and plenty reigned throughout the land. Her Court was the most brilliant in

Italy, and she was a magnificent patron of learning and art.

She built various churches, amongst others St. Antonio Abate, near the Albergo de' Poveri, with its famous picture of St. Anthony surrounded by angels and saints. But she is best remembered by the Gothic church of L'Incoronata, built to commemorate her coronation and her marriage with Prince Louis of Taranto. She built into it the ancient chapel of King Robert's Palazzo di Giustizia, in which her wedding had taken place, and the frescoes of the school of Giotto give a most curious and interesting representation of incidents in the life of her family.

She also founded and richly endowed the Carthusian Hospital near this church, and one of the paintings in the Chapel del Crocifisso represents the monks doing homage to her. On the beautiful shore of the Mergellina, where Posilippo stretches out into the blue sea, there are still pointed out the picturesque ruins of an unfinished palace, popularly called "della Regina Giovanna." Not far away is the famous tomb of Virgil, where as a child she must have seen the laurel planted by Petrarch, and may even have heard of his interesting visit to the Grotto with her grandfather.

The poet tells us that in his time it was believed to have been formed with magic art by Virgil, and King Robert asked his opinion on the subject. Petrarch replied: "Trusting to the royal humanity, I answered in jest, that I had nowhere read that Virgil was a magician." To this the King, with a nod of assent, confessed that the place showed traces not of magic but of iron: "Non illic magici, sed ferri vestigia confessus est." A very appropriate remark for a man of science in his day.

Queen Giovanna was not suffered to enjoy to the end her peaceful tastes for the intellectual and artistic revival of her day and her works of charity. New misfortunes awaited her. She had become greatly attached to the young Charles of Durazzo, whom she had adopted at the age of twelve, and, after lavishing endless care on his education, granting him every desire of his heart, and fulfilling every whim and fancy he could conceive, she had married him to her favourite niece Margaret. It is possible that life may have been made too smooth for him, as he seems to have been of a restless and ambitious temper; still we cannot explain his conduct, for Giovanna meant him to succeed her on the throne. Instead of remaining to help and protect his benefactress, he actually left her, to fight under the banners of her old enemy, King Louis of Hungary!

Thus forsaken, with fresh troubles arising on every side, the usual remedy was once more pressed upon the poor Queen, and at the age of forty-eight she was induced to take as her fourth husband Otho of Brunswick, Prince of a Guelph family, and about her own age. The choice seems to have been good, for we hear of him as a brave, handsome man, of cultivated taste and kindly disposition, who won the affection of his wife and never failed in his devotion to her. For some years they seem to have reigned in tranquil security, beloved by their people and at peace with the outer world.

But the time came when all Christendom was torn asunder by the conflict between two rival popes:

Urban VI. at Rome and Clement VII. at Avignon. Naples took the side of this last, and Pope Urban, while professing friendship with Queen Giovanna, secretly offered her throne to Charles of Durazzo, at the price of large territorial concessions. The ambitious young prince listened, hesitated, and was lost. He yielded to the shameful temptation, and his first step was to send for his wife and children, who had always lived in the palace of his benefactress and received from her the most devoted affection. Giovanna had received some hint of the conspiracy, but when Margaret asked leave to join her husband, she was treated with the utmost generosity and allowed to set forth on her journey with every honour and respect. It was their first parting and their last farewell, for they met never more.

After this, Charles of Durazzo lost no time, and invaded Italy with a large force of mercenaries, to claim the kingdom of Naples, by right of the Pope's gift. When he reached the capital, he found that Otho of Brunswick had levied an army to protect it, and when fighting began outside the walls, the Queen and her household took refuge in the fortress of the Castel Nuovo and ordered the gates to be closed. But a throng of women and children, and helpless or infirm people crowded before the archway, and with pitiful cries besought protection from the brutal Hungarian soldiery. The tender-hearted Giovanna was deaf to the advice of her companions, and gave orders that the unfortunate creatures should be admitted. This generous deed was fatal, for the store of provisions which should have lasted many months came to an end in a few weeks.

The Queen was in hourly expectation of help from Provence in the way of men and food, and she also trusted to the success of her husband, and held out to the last, although by treachery Durazzo had gained admittance to the city. She had two of her nieces with her, and we are told that the elder one, Agnese of Durazzo, a rich woman, had refused to lend money to help in defending the citadel. When the last extremity of famine was reached, she brought her gold and jewels and laid them at the feet of the Queen, who gently told her that it was now too late.

"A sack of wheat were more precious to us now, my fair niece, than all this treasure!" she sighed.

A desperate battle was fought under the walls of the city, and the brave Otho was wounded and taken prisoner, while his troops were defeated and fled. There was no more hope, and Giovanna was compelled to surrender. Four days later the long-looked-for galleys from Provence, laden with provisions, sailed into the Bay of Naples—alas! too late.

Charles of Durazzo now endeavoured, by persuasion and threats, to induce the unhappy lady to yield her kingdom to him. In full confidence that he would succeed, he permitted her friends from Provence and other loyal nobles to see her. With undaunted spirit she called upon them to witness that she made Louis of Anjou her heir, and that she solemnly revoked all she had ever said in favour of the traitor, who now held her prisoner.

Furious at the failure of his plan, Charles treated her with insult and cruelty, and after eight months of close confinement sent her to the lonely castle of Moro, far away in a deep ravine of the Apennines.

While she lived he would never feel safe, so he caused her to be put to death by some Hungarian soldiers. This was in May 1382, when she was fifty-four years of ago. She was buried in Santa Chiara, amid the tombs of her own people—the most unfortunate of her race. She was well-beloved and long lamented by her subjects, and the legend of her pitiful story still lingers in the land.

"A rare and noble lady," says the poet Boccaccio. "I not only esteem her illustrious and resplendent by conspicuous excellence, but the singular pride of Italy, and such as altogether no other nation has ever seen her equal."

GIOVANNA II., QUEEN OF NAPLES.

THE historian of the Renaissance must not shrink from touching on the darker side of that great movement, which tended to place women on an equal height with men. In earlier medieval days they were more rarely entrusted with absolute power, and in later times they were at least expected to wear a mask of outward decorum. As we have seen, even in this age of licence, there were many great ladies of high and unblemished character, but assertion of such fact was necessary, and it was by no means taken for granted. On the other hand, when they yielded to the temptations which surrounded them, they were wont to cast away all moral restraint, and glory in their shame.

In this second Giovanna of Naples we see a striking instance of a woman swayed only by her desires, whose weakness and vice were unredeemed by any noble qualities, and who brought two centuries of desolation upon her unfortunate country.

Burdened by an evil heritage, she was the only daughter of the traitor, Charles of Durazzo, and her early life was spent at Naples under the loving care of Queen Giovanna I. One of the most striking memories of her childhood must have been that hurried journey, at the age of ten years, to join her father when he was on the point of invading the kingdom of his benefactress, and she cannot have been ignorant of his subsequent murder of that gracious lady. The girl seems to have had neither beauty nor accomplishments, save for the art of dancing, of which she was passionately fond.

Her father did not long enjoy the throne which he had so shamefully usurped, and after his violent death in Hungary, Margaret, his wife, asserted herself as Regent for Ladislaus, the young brother of Giovanna. Many years followed, of ruthless war and perfidious intrigues, in the long struggle between Margaret of Durazzo and her son on one side, and the brave Marie de Blois on the other, fighting for the rights of the boy Louis of Anjou, grandson to the chosen successor of the late Queen. Not until the year 1399 was Ladislaus firmly established in the government, which he disgraced by his crimes.

Meantime the life of his sister Giovanna was spent in strange vicissitudes ; now in a beleaguered fortress, or in the passing shelter of a convent ; in a camp of rough soldiers or amid the dissipation of a profligate Court. She was already thirty-two years of age before, as a political alliance, a husband was found for her—Guglielmo, the son of Leopold III., Duke of Austria. Three years later she became a widow and returned to Naples, where, on the death of her brother Ladislaus, she succeeded to the crown, notwithstanding the shameful notoriety of her evil conduct.

One of her favourites at that time was a man of low birth but imposing presence, Pandolpho Alopo, who, from being her cup-bearer, she promoted to be Grand Seneschal, and whose influence over her was so great that he practically ruled in her name, hated and despised by all. But he was soon to meet with a rival. The famous Condottiere Sforza had entered the service of the late king, and was now commander-in-chief of the army. His real name was Jacopo Attendolo, a peasant of Cotignola, on the plain of Faenza, who enlisted in one of those companies of adventurers always ready to fight for pay under any banner; and rising to high command by his skill and bravery, he received the name of "Sforza," inherited by an illustrious line of princes.

The rivalry of these two favourites caused so many troubles and dissensions, that Giovanna was persuaded to seek protection in marriage with some foreign prince. Her choice fell on Jaques de Bourbon, Comte de la Marche, a distant relation of King Charles of France, who brought a train of French knights with him, and the marriage was celebrated with much splendour. Her husband can scarcely have been ignorant of the lady's reputation, but as he gradually learnt the whole truth with regard to her, his indignation knew no bounds, and he sternly imprisoned her in her own apartments, taking upon himself the absolute government of the realm.

The people of Naples were naturally indignant at this high-handed conduct on the part of a foreigner; and when he further committed the natural imprudence of promoting his French followers to honour and office, a strong conspiracy was formed against him, at the head of which was a young man of great ability, Gianni Carraccioli. A plot was formed by which the Queen was carried off to the Castel Capuana, an ancient fortress of the Suabian rulers of Naples. The people were called upon to rise for her protection, and responding with enthusiasm, the King had barely time to escape with a few friends to the Castel del Ovo, which stands on a rock out in the Bay, and can only be reached by a narrow mole, well fortified by drawbridges. Here he shut himself up, but the place was not provisioned for a siege, and he was forced to surrender on humiliating terms.

He was to content himself with the title of Prince of Tarento, to leave all the sovereign power in the hands of the Queen, and to send away all his French suite and retainers. His position in the palace was now one of constant humiliation, exposed to the scarcely veiled insult of his wife's favourites, and he took no trouble to hide his anger and disgust. Meanwhile Giovanna, who had never forgiven him, only bided her time to get rid of his accusing presence.

One night at supper, there was a dispute in which such strong language was used, that the Prince left the table in a storm of indignation and retired to his own chamber. Carraccioli, who was now highest in favour of all the Queen's parasites, had prepared for this ; by her order the doors were strongly barred, and guarded night and day, and her husband was kept a close prisoner for three years. He must have had ample leisure to repent of the ambition which led him to this fatal city, before he was at length released by the intercession of Pope Martin V.

Broken in health and crushed by misfortune, he went back to his native land ; and resting on the way at Besançon, in a Franciscan convent, by a sudden impulse of religious enthusiasm he joined the Order. Weary of the world which had so betrayed his hopes, he dwelt there for the rest of his life.

Meanwhile Carraccioli, absolute master of Queen Giovanna, under the title of Seneschal, practically ruled the kingdom. With infinite skill, he contrived to get rid of his rivals by giving them some important post away from the Court. The Condottiere Sforza was sent on an expedition to Rome, but all his best-laid plans failed for want of money and supplies, and as the Queen remained blind to the treachery of Carraccioli, Sforza formally renounced her cause and offered his services to Louis of Anjou. Victory would have been assured to them, but that a brilliant stroke of policy occurred to their enemies.

Giovanna appealed to Alfonso, the young king of Aragon and Sicily, and as she could not offer to marry him at her age, she promised that he should be her adopted son, and heir to her kingdom, if he would help her to defend it. The gallant young prince was delighted to accept the splendid offer, and to become the champion of a lady in distress. He lost no time in sending a strong fleet, laden with his picked soldiers, and landed in triumph at Naples in July 1421.

After this, the affairs of the weak and fickle Giovanna, became one tangled mass of intrigues. Sforza is again allured to fight under her banner, then Carraccioli becomes jealous of the influence of Alfonso, and poisons the mind of his mistress against the popular, and possibly vain-glorious young man. She is reminded of the conduct of her own father in a like position, and in a wild panic of fear, she shuts herself up in the fortress of Castel Capuana and summons Sforza to her help. A fierce struggle and much fighting ensues, until at length Alfonso is defeated, his adoption as heir is revoked, and he is compelled to return to Sicily.

At this point there is a most unexpected turn in fortune's wheel. The young Louis of Anjou, whose father and grandfather have fought in vain for the prize during the last forty years, suddenly finds himself chosen as the adopted son and heir of his hereditary foe!

It was at the ancient city of Nola, in the plain of Campania, that Queen Giovanna signed this remarkable treaty, which led later on to the invasion of Italy by the French, and to a European war. But personally she had no reason to regret her choice, for Louis behaved to her with unchanging kindness and devotion to the end of her life. Meantime Carraccioli had been taken prisoner by Alfonso, but he was shortly exchanged for several Spanish prisoners, and returned to his old position of absolute authority. Again there was fighting, this time against the Condottiere Braccio, who had taken Capua and had laid siege to the fortified city of Aquila. It was in the middle of winter that Sforza marched against him into the Abruzzi, but in fording the river Pescara, which was in flood after heavy rain, his horse was carried along by the rapid current and the great general was drowned.

Astrologers had predicted that neither Braccio nor Sforza would long survive each other, and it is possible that this superstitious belief may have had some slight part in the defeat of Braccio shortly after, and his death. This victory of Aquila should have brought peace to the troubled kingdom, but for the perfidy of Giovanna's seneschal, who, becoming jealous of Louis, made secret efforts to bring back Alfonso. He held many important offices which brought him in immense wealth, he had many titles and great possessions but, not satisfied with all this, Carraccioli had the audacity to demand the Principality of Salerno, which was reserved for princes of the blood. To his surprise his mistress refused, whereupon, beside himself with rage, he treated her with the utmost insolence and violence, even going so far as to strike her. The wretched Queen was found in tears by her new lady-in-waiting, Covella Rufo, Duchess of Sessa, who was a deadly enemy of the favourite, and she seized her opportunity.

A warrant was signed for the arrest of Carraccioli, and the Duchess accompanied it with secret orders that he was to be put to death. This was done, after a ball given in honour of his son's wedding, and the weak Giovanna was at first inconsolable when she heard of it, but Covella asserted her power, and for the next three years was the real head of the State. She was a crafty, unprincipled woman, and did all the mischief she could, with her exactions and intrigues. But the end was drawing near. Louis of Anjou died of fever in 1434 and the Queen, broken-hearted at his loss, only survived him a short time.

Thus ended her miserable reign of twenty years, a time of ceaseless unrest, and bitter suffering to her unfortunate people. For the sake of her love to Louis, she bequeathed the kingdom of Naples to his brother Réné, but he never enjoyed the possession of it. Alfonso of Aragon asserted his right to the crown, and seized it by force of arms. The softer climate of Italy and the higher civilisation, seem to have had a special charm for him, as he spent the rest of his life at Naples, leaving his brother Prince Juan to rule in Aragon, and ultimately bequeathing to him all his hereditary possessions in Spain, Sicily and Sardinia, while he left the kingdom of Naples to his illegitimate son Ferdinand. This prince was acknowledged by a special Bull of the Pope, and was the founder of an illustrious race. His daughter Leonora married Ercole, Marquis of Ferrara, and was the mother of the famous Isabella d'Este.

A GROUP OF LOMBARD PRINCESSES.

BEATRICE D'ESTE, DUCHESS OF MILAN.
BIANCA MARIA SFORZA, WIFE OF THE EMPEROR MAXIMILIAN.
ISABELLA D'ESTE, MARCHESA OF MANTUA.
RENÉE OF FRANCE, DUCHESS OF FERRARA.

HISTORICAL SUMMARY.

1472. Birth of Bianca Maria Sforza, at Milan.

1474. Birth of Isabella d'Este, at Ferrara.

1475. Birth of Beatrice d'Este, at Ferrara.

1476. Murder of Galeazzo Maria, Duke of Milan.

1480. Lodovico Sforza (il Moro) usurped the government of Milan in the name of his nephew, Gian Galeazzo.

1482. Pope Sixtus IV. made a league with Venice to despoil the House of Este. War carried on. The Pope withdrew, but Venice continued, until, by the Treaty of Bagnolo, she acquired much Este property.

1484. Death of Sixtus IV.

1485. Lodovico Sforza, for Milan, makes alliance with Florence and Naples against the Pope.

1490. Marriage of Isabella d'Este with Francesco, Marchese of Mantua.

1491. Marriage of Beatrice d'Este with Lodovico Sforza, Duke of Bari.

1492. Pope Alexander VI. (Roderigo Borgia).

1493. Lodovico Sforza, at war with Naples and Florence, invites the King of France, Charles VIII., to invade Italy.

1493. Marriage of Bianca Sforza with the Emperor Maximilian.

1494. Charles VIII. crosses the Alps. Lodovico Sforza joins him at Pavia. Florence, Rome and Naples submit to the French. Death of Gian Galeazzo, young Duke of Naples. His uncle, Lodovico, is crowned Duke of Milan.

1495. Alarmed at the success of Charles VIII., Lodovico forms a league against him, with Venice, Naples, the Emperor Maximilian, &c. Francesco Marchese of Mantua is Captain of the League. The French win the battle of Fornova. They are driven from Italy.

1497. Death of Beatrice d'Este, Duchess of Milan.

1498. Louis XII. of France, successor to Charles VIII., lays claim to Naples, Sicily and Milan.

1499. The French cross the Alps, conquer Milan. Lodovico returns and has a temporary success.

1500. Lodovico, a fugitive, takes refuge at the Court of his niece, the Empress Bianca, at Innsprück. He makes a fresh attack on the French, is defeated and taken prisoner to France.

1503. Pope Julius II. Birth of Federico, son of Isabella d'Este.

1508. Death of Lodovico Sforza in the prison of Loches.

1509. Francesco, husband of Isabella d'Este, made prisoner by the Venetians and kept captive for thirteen months.

1510. Death of Bianca Maria Sforza, wife of Emperor Maximilian.

1511. Maximilian Sforza, son of Beatrice d'Este, becomes Duke of Milan.

1513. Pope Leo X., first Medici Pope.

1515. The French again take Milan, and the young Duke Maximilian is expelled.

1519. Death of Francesco, Marchese of Mantua. Federico succeeds him.

1521. The Pope and Emperor Charles V. combine against the French and drive them from Milan. Francesco Sforza, brother of Maximilian, proclaimed Duke of Milan.

1524. The French, after many defeats in Lombardy, are utterly routed at Pavia, where Francis I. is taken prisoner.

1527. Rome is sacked by the Imperialists, and Pope Clement VII. prisoner in Castello St. Angelo. Ten months of horror.

1528. Marriage of Duke Ercole of Ferrara with Renée of France.

1529. General peace in Italy.

1530. Emperor Charles V. crowned by the Pope at Bologna. Isabella d'Este amongst the guests at Bologna.

1534. Marriage of Francesco, Duke of Milan, to Christina of Denmark. Death of Alfonso, Duke of Ferrara, and of Pope Clement VII.

1535. Death of Francesco, Duke of Milan (son of Beatrice d'Este).

1537. Death of Isabella d'Este, Marchesa of Mantua.

1575. Death of Renée, Duchess of Ferrara.

BEATRICE D'ESTE, DUCHESS OF MILAN.

As we look upon that wonderful frozen image of Beatrice d'Este, in the Certosia of Pavia, the splendid monument of Lodovico's love and sorrow, we seem to pierce somewhat of the mystery of her character.

The ambitious woman who "could not live without a crown," for whose sake more blood was shed, more troubles let loose on her ill-fated land than ever of old for Helen of Troy, becomes for us a delicious, wilful girl who has scarce outpassed her childhood. We see the shapely young head rising from the long rounded throat, the smooth brow with vagrant curls nestling about it, the dainty little nose, the round chin and full soft cheeks, and the sweet mouth closed in the peaceful slumber of an innocent child.

The little feet in their embroidered pattens, once so fond of dancing, peep out from below the stiff brocades which shroud the graceful figure of the beloved Duchess, whose husband had his own effigy carved in marble to rest by her side.

For the moment we forget that insatiable ambition which summoned the hosts of France, with misery and disaster in their train, and we only look with tender pity on the fair young creature, cut off in the heyday of her youth, who so craved for splendour and joy.

BEATRICE D'ESTE

On the noble parentage of Beatrice d'Este we dwell more fully in the story of her more fortunate elder sister, Isabella. Compared to the reigning family of Este—the Rovere, the Sforza, the Medici, and most of the other great families of Italy, were but of mushroom growth ; and this distinction of long descent stood the Dukes of Ferrara in good stead, and did much to preserve their throne in the troublous days, when most of their princely neighbours fell from their high estate.

Our little princess was born on June 29, 1475, into a world which had but a cold welcome for her as a girl, instead of the much-desired heir. She received the name of Beatrice after her aunt, the Queen of Hungary. Her father was Duke Ercole I., one of the most illustrious rulers of Ferrara, distinguished both in peace as a generous patron of art and letters, and in war as a successful general. Her mother was Leonora of Aragon, the daughter of Ferdinand, or, as he is often called, Ferrante, King of Naples. Beatrice was thus born to a heritage of culture on both sides ; and when she was only two years old, she was taken by the Duchess Leonora to the Court of her grandfather at Naples, where she remained for the next eight years. The old king appears to have become so much attached to the bright, intelligent little girl, that he persuaded her mother to leave her behind, when she had to return to Ferrara with her other children, for two sons had followed in quick succession—Alfonso, the heir, and Ferrante, born at Naples.

Meantime war had broken out in Italy, and Duke Ercole having been appointed Captain-General of the armies of Florence, his wife was recalled home to rule his state and city during his absence, thus showing his confidence in her judgment and ability.

It must have been a curious life for the little girl as a spoiled darling of that luxurious Court, all the gayer for the coming of the young Queen Joan of Aragon, Ferrante's second wife. Naples was then in its golden age of literary and artistic glory. There were Tuscan artists, poets, and scholars who found there a congenial home ; the whole coast of that exquisite blue sea, from Santa Lucia to Baiæ, with its orange groves and aloes and palms—was one scene of enchantment, of luxury of indolent enjoyment, and of vice sheltering under a mask of refinement. Amongst the distinguished guests, who came to the Castel Nuovo, was Lorenzo dei Medici, who travelled hither in December 1479, as a bold stroke of diplomacy, to secure the support of the King. He had a friend at Court in the person of the Duchess of Calabria, Ippolyta Sforza, the aunt of little Beatrice.

She may have seen the two allies, as Ferrante called them, pacing up and down the royal terraces between the Vomera and the sea, on the slopes above the Chiaia, that loveliest garden in all Europe. The despot of Florence must have enjoyed his visit in the congenial society he met; and we hear of him as giving magnificent banquets in the palace assigned to his use, releasing galley slaves and dowering poor girls. It was not for nothing that he was called the "Magnificent!" But he had a long, weary time of waiting, while the King went out hunting in the sandy scrub beyond the escarpments of old Cumæ, and kept him in suspense, till at length, at the end of February, peace was concluded, and Lorenzo could return home contented.

The little girl, Beatrice d'Este, was happy at least in

having as companions her cousins, the children of the Duchess Ippolyta; the merry Ferrante, heir to the throne of Naples, and his sister Isabella, who was five years older than herself, and who was destined one day to be her rival. This young girl was already betrothed to the young Duke Gian Galeazzo of Milan, but her marriage did not take place until she was almost eighteen, two years before that of Beatrice, who was still a young child when she first saw her future husband, Lodovico Sforza, the uncle of Gian Galeazzo. He was then Duke of Bari, and being very anxious to secure the friendship of the Duke of Ferrara, he made a formal offer for the hand of Isabella d'Este, who was then a child of six. But she was already promised to the son of Federico, Marchese of Mantua, and the Duke suggests that "he has another daughter at Naples, who is only a year younger, and who has been adopted by the King of Naples as his own child. He will write to his Serene Majesty and ask if he will consent to receive the Signor Lodovico as his kinsman."

Lodovico being quite willing to accept the younger daughter Beatrice, the consent of the King of Naples is obtained, and the child of five years old is betrothed to the handsome and wealthy Duke of Bari, at that time aged twenty-nine. But the little girl remained at Naples with her grandfather for the next five years, and when she returned to her home at Ferrara it was actually with the title of Duchess of Bari, she having reached the age of ten.

With these two young daughters, destined to become great princesses, and to rule Courts of their own, the Duchess must have had a strong stimulus and a definite end in view, with regard to their education. Now, in the year of Beatrice's return, in 1485, there was once more a time of peace and prosperity at Ferrara, after the disastrous war and perilous struggles, when for a time the fate of the dukedom hung in suspense. Art and science, and learning of every kind were cultivated with so much generosity and success, that the University of Ferrara had become the most distinguished in Italy. There was, therefore, no difficulty in obtaining the first scholars of the day, as tutors to the Duke's children.

Battista Guarino of Verona was selected to give a classical foundation to their studies, and with him the little girls learnt to read Cicero and Virgil, and studied the history of Greece and Rome. They were also taught French to some extent, and could enjoy Provençal poetry, but they had the usual difficulty in learning to speak a foreign language fluently, for we find them using interpreters in later years, when a King of France had to be received. Great care was bestowed upon the social arts of music and dancing, in which both the sisters distinguished themselves. As for the poetry and literature of their own land, it came to them naturally as a charming recreation, while they sat at their tapestry in the fairylike gardens of the summer palace, and listened to the most gifted poets of the Renaissance, reciting their latest works. From the example and teaching of their mother, they could not fail to receive a deep religious impression, for she was a pious woman devoted to all good works. As one of her chroniclers remarks; "The illustrious Madonna is high above all other women, and her excellent virtues will open for her without fail the adamant doors of Paradise."

Yet we must not think that Isabella and Beatrice

were always at their studies, for the complete training of a great lady included riding and out-of-door sports. Their father kept a hundred horses of the finest breed obtainable; Barbary horses from the Sultan of Tunis, Spanish jennets and trained palfreys, the very pick of Europe; and their mother had her own splendid greyhounds, which the greatest princesses in Italy would beg for, as a supreme favour. Beatrice was a splendid rider, and always devoted to hunting; indeed, with her gay bright disposition, no amusement came amiss to her. She inherited her father's passionate love for theatrical entertainments of every kind, and also his keen delight in travel, which he liked to indulge in a sumptuous way, as when, in 1484, he went to Venice with his wife, and a suite of seven hundred persons, to stay there in his own magnificent palace on the Grand Canal.

Thus the Este sisters passed a few happy years, surrounded by all the most beautiful works of art, and everything which could contribute to their culture and enjoyment. But all this was drawing to an end, for the young Marquis of Mantua showed himself an eager lover, and would wait no longer for his bride Isabella. In February 1490 the marriage was duly celebrated with great pomp at Ferrara, and the bride departed for her new home at Mantua, leaving Beatrice to await her own wedding, which was somewhat unaccountably delayed.

It is very difficult to form a clear idea of the character of Lodovico Sforza, Il Moro, as he was usually called. He must have been a very striking personality, a wonderful combination of good and evil qualities, and no two historians really agree about him. One will say: "He had a sublime soul and universal capacity. Whatever he did, he surpassed expectation, in the fine arts, in learning, in justice and benevolence. And he had no equal among Italian princes for wisdom and sagacity in public affairs."

Other chroniclers speak of "Il Moro" as an utterly unscrupulous man, a traitor, a murderer, of evil life, and one whose word could never be depended upon by friend or foe. Burckhardt speaks of him as a typical figure of the Italian Renaissance, both in his faults and in his virtues.

He was the fourth son of Francesco Sforza, one of the earliest of those famous Condottieri, captains who commanded bands of mercenaries, and were willing to fight for any state who paid them. This Francesco had married Bianca, daughter of Filippo Maria Visconti, on whose death he made himself Duke of Milan, and reigned there for twenty years. The boy Lodovico was the first son born after his father's elevation, and was brought up with all the advantages of wealth and the wisest culture. His mother, a most capable woman, devoted herself very much to the education of her six sons. "I would have you remember that we have princes to educate, not only scholars," she remarked to one of the learned tutors, who may have grudged the time given to knightly exercises.

It is interesting to notice that her daughter Ippolyta, —afterwards the Duchess of Calabria mentioned at the Court of Naples—shared the studies of her brothers, and on the occasion of a visit from Pope Pius II., it was she who spoke the Latin oration in his honour.

Lodovico was always a great favourite with his father, whose sudden death in 1466 was a great blow to him. His eldest brother, Galeazzo, succeeded to the duchy, and his reign of ten years was one of the utmost magnificence and reckless extravagance. He was cruel and profligate, and his mother, the Duchess Bianca, is said to have died of grief, two years after his accession. "More from sorrow of heart than sickness of body" was the verdict of her physician. Galeazzo married Bona of Savoy, the sister of Louis XI.'s wife, and Lodovico was sent to meet her at Genoa, so that he must have been on good terms with his brother. The murder of Duke Galeazzo in 1476 brought only a change for the worse in the position of his brothers, who were exiled before very long, on strong suspicion of treachery to the young heir, Gian Galeazzo, and the regent, Bona, his mother. She seems to have been "une dame de petit sens," as the historian Commines says, for she encouraged a low-born favourite, and soon became tired of listening to the good advice of her most faithful and able minister, Simonetta. She privately sent for Lodovico, a fatal step, which she had cause bitterly to rue in the days to come.

Lodovico il Moro returned to Milan, where he was formally appointed to the regency with his sister-in-law, and from that time he practically governed the duchy, while before long, the ill-fated Simonetta paid for his fidelity with his life. Lodovico made peace with Florence and paid court to the King of Naples, who at this time accepted an alliance with the Regent of Milan, by permitting the betrothal with his young granddaughter, Beatrice d'Este. Meantime the Duchess Bona showed her "little sense" by leaving everything to her coadjutor, giving up her own time to banquets and dances, in the company of her favourite, who at

BEATRICE D'ESTE, DUCHESS OF MILAN

Leonardo da Vinci

length so presumed on his position, that he was ordered by the Council to leave Milan. With cowardly haste, Tassino made his escape, taking all the money and jewels on which he could lay hand, and the duchess, in her blind rage, gave up everything and fled from the city. She ultimately returned to the French king's court, and her brother-in-law was left sole ruler in Milan.

"Merito e tempore" was the motto he chose, and so far he had indeed proved the truth that, all things come to him who waits. But the end was not yet. At the time of his mother's flight, the young Duke Gian Galeazzo was not quite twelve years old. He had always been a weakly child, and as he became older it was evident that his mind was feeble too. He cared for nothing but boisterous pleasures, and could not apply his attention to anything. Thus, as time passed on, Lodovico's position became more assured than ever, and in everything except the title and outward show, he was the absolute ruler of Milan. During his father's lifetime, Gian had been betrothed to the Princess Isabella of Aragon, and when he had reached the age of twenty the marriage was celebrated; the bride having been first brought from Naples to Milan with the utmost magnificence, although it was a very rough passage to Genoa in the depth of winter. This was in February 1489, but the situation did not change with the young duke's marriage, although his young wife quickly grasped the state of things, and tried to urge him to assert himself, but in vain, for he always foolishly repeated what she advised.

All this time, Lodovico seems to have troubled himself very little about his own engagement to the child

Beatrice, although he had frequent reminders on the subject from Ferrara. As far back as 1485, her portrait had been sent to him, for we find this entry in the archives of Ferrara: "On December 24, Cosimo Turo received four gold florins from the duke, in that he had painted from life the face and bust of the Illustrissima Madonna Beatrice, that it may be sent to Messer Lodovico Maria Sforza, Duca di Bari, consort of the said Beatrice . . . Carlo Contingo bearing it with him."

The Regent of Milan had for years been devoted to his mistress, a certain Cecilia Gallerani, a very beautiful woman, noted for her learning and accomplishments. She had rooms in the Castello of Milan, a palace outside the city, a villa at Cremona, and was treated with honour and respect by the literary and artistic society of which she was the centre. Poets wrote sonnets in her praise as to another Sappho, and Leonardo da Vinci painted her portrait. Lodovico would have married the lady had he dared to risk the consequent jealousies, and also to give mortal offence to the Duke of Ferrara and the King of Naples; but prudence won the day, and he made final arrangements for the long-deferred wedding with Beatrice d'Este.

His first step was to send a magnificent necklace, with a pendant of pearls, emeralds, and rubies, to the young girl, and Cristoforo Romano, the great sculptor, was instructed to carve her bust, which may be seen to-day in the Louvre. The wishes of the Duke and Duchess of Ferrara were carefully consulted, and it was settled that their son Alfonso should join the wedding party, and fetch his own bride, Anna Sforza, from Milan at the same time. We have a very full account of that winter journey from Ferrara to Milan. The weather was bitterly cold, the river Po was frozen for more than a month as far as Brescello, and all the land was white with snow. The bride, with her mother and sister Isabella, who had joined her from Mantua, and all the ladies of her suite, travelled by road until they reached the point where the river was navigable, and here they were met by an ambassador from Lodovico with boats and bucentaurs. A voyage of five days was before them, in which they suffered so much from cold and even hunger, for the supplies were delayed by bad weather, that one lady wrote: "If it had not been for Madonna Camilla, who sent us part of her supper from the other barge, I, for one, should have been a saint in Paradise by this time." Others wept, and even went so far in their wretchedness as to wish themselves dead.

They had started on December 29, and only reached Piacenza, where they had a chance of being warmed and well fed, on January 12. Poor Beatrice must have been rather weather-beaten when she at length arrived at Pavia, and was met in great state by Lodovico and his noble company of knights, who escorted her across the bridge and into the ancient city. He was charmed at first sight with the gay, brilliant young creature of fifteen, with her dark eyes and hair and her sunny smile; whilst she was at once attracted to him by his courtly manners and gentle kindness. As she rode through the city of a hundred towers, the centre of a gorgeous cavalcade, she was cheered with enthusiasm by the populace, who thronged to see her enter the great Castello of Pavia.

Messer Ambrogio, the court physician and astrologer, had selected January 17 as a propitious day for the wedding, which was celebrated in the Visconti chapel. The bride wore a splendid white dress sprinkled with pearls, and shining with jewels, and had her own people round her; her mother and sister, and brother Alfonso, and her uncle the Cardinal Sisismondo. But the great event was to be the triumphal entry into Milan, for which the most sumptuous and extravagant preparations were made. It reads like a fairy tale, the description of that marvellous pageant on the following Sunday, when the bride and her party were met at the gates of the city by Gian Galeazzo, nominally the reigning Duke, and Lodovico, clothed in gold brocade, a magnificent figure amongst his gallant company, preceded by a hundred trumpeters. The streets were hung with costly brocades, and wreathed with ivy, and the armourers' quarter was lined with effigies of warriors in chain armour on horseback, while the heralds made martial music as the bride was lifted from her horse at the great gateway of the Castello, and received by Bona of Savoy, who had returned to her home for the occasion. By her side was her daughter Anna Sforza, who was married the next day to Alfonso d'Este, to the mother's great satisfaction. As for the wedding presents, the festivities, the tournaments, the masques which followed, they were on a scale of unexampled magnificence, and in this brief space it would be impossible to do them justice. But one masquerade of Scythians has a special interest for us, as having been designed by Leonardo da Vinci, who for sixteen years was the court painter of Milan.

The wedding guests, on their departure, having expressed a wish to see the famous Certosa of Pavia, the lordly Lodovico wrote to the prior requesting him to "give them a fitting reception and provide an honourable banquet for the Duchess of Ferrara and her company, which would number about four hundred persons and horses; providing them with a plentiful supply of lampreys."

After her quiet home life, where she had always been rather overshadowed by her sister, the young Beatrice now blossomed out into a great princess, whose slightest wish was gratified almost before she could express it. Nothing was too costly or too beautiful for her service, she lived in an atmosphere of flattery and adulation, where no one had any more serious duty than to please and amuse her, and life seemed to be one long gay holiday. Full of high spirits and the keenest enjoyment of all the new delights which awaited her, she laughed and jested, she danced and sang; she was never tired of playing ball with her gay companions, of riding races with them, and she had a perfect passion for hunting. Her husband looked on with amused interest and pleasure at this bright, merry child, and when he was too much engaged to accompany her, she was constantly attended by one of the Sanseverino brothers, the most distinguished of his courtiers. Of these, Messer Galeazzo, who had married a daughter of Lodovico, was the favourite at court, both for his knightly skill, his wit, and talents. He was a friend of Isabella d'Este, and he writes her the following account of some of her sister's amusements:

February 1491.

"I started at ten o'clock this morning with the duchess and all of her ladies on horseback to go to Cussago . . . and we sang more than twenty-five songs together set for three voices. . . We had a fine fishing expedition, and caught a great quantity of pike, trout, lampreys, crabs . . . and then we dined off them till we could eat no more. Then, to make our meal digest the better, we played ball with great vigour and energy. . . And then we mounted our horses again, and began to let fly some of those good falcons of mine along the river-side, and they killed several birds. By this time it was already four o'clock. We rode out to hunt stags and fawns, and after giving chase to twenty-two and killing two stags and two fawns, we returned home and reached Milan an hour after dark, and presented the result of our day's sport to my lord the Duke of Bari."

Indeed, Lodovico seems to have been so much pleased, that he presented his young wife with the lands and palaces of Cussago, where now only a few fragments are left to recall the beauties of that favourite villa at Visconti. But in the midst of all this gaiety and boundless enjoyment, a dark rumour reached the ear of Beatrice; she first heard the story of Cecilia Gallerani, and of her husband's continued relations with her. It must have been a great shock to the few months' bride, to find that while she was treated as a pampered plaything, Lodovico's confidence and affection were bestowed upon another woman. She behaved with spirit and dignity, bidding her lord take his choice between them, as she would have no divided sway. Meantime, news of this discovery, as of all that befell Beatrice, had been sent to the court of Ferrara, and Lodovico, after an interview with the ambassador of Duke Ercole, became convinced that this scandal must cease. In the following May, Cecilia gave birth to a son, and in July, loaded with splendid presents, she was married to Count Bergami.

We next hear of the Duke and Duchess at Vigevano, the old Lombard town where he was born, and where he spent a fortune on works of irrigation which, as the inscription on the great tower still tells us: "turned the course of rivers and brought flowing streams of water into the dry and barren land. The desert waste became a green and fertile meadow, the wilderness rejoiced and blossomed as the rose."

He had taken much delight in rebuilding the castle, and had laid out beautiful gardens around, and a park which was well stocked with game; but his special pride was a model farm, which forestalled many modern improvements. A French chronicler enumerates with wonder and admiration all that he saw there, of the finest sheep, goats, oxen, and herds of cows tended with skilled attention by labourers specially trained. Great cheeses were made there which were most highly esteemed, and were fit offerings for foreign princes. But the great charm of the place to Beatrice, was the hawking, and hunting the stag or wild boar, in which she would run terrible risks, and was absolutely fearless.

A letter written about this time to her sister is very characteristic. "We are enjoying warm and splendid weather, and every day we go out riding with the dogs and falcons, and my husband and I never come home without having enjoyed ourselves exceedingly in hunting herons and other water-fowl. . . . Game is so plentiful here that hares are to be seen jumping out at every corner. Indeed, the eye cannot take in all that one desires to see, and it is scarcely possible to count up the number of animals which are to be found in this neighbourhood. Nor must I forget to tell you how every day Messer Galeazzo and I, with one or two other courtiers, amuse ourselves playing at ball after dinner. . . . I tell you all this that you may know how well and happy I am, and how kind and affectionate my husband is. . . ." In the next letter we hear about wolf-hunts and narrow escapes; and Isabella is eager to take part in the matter, and show that she has as much courage as her sister.

Meantime the position of Isabella of Arragon, nominally Duchess of Milan, must have been a great contrast to that of her younger cousin Beatrice. Her husband, Gian Galeazzo, was weak and dissipated, and as time went on, his mental deficiency became more marked. He took no part whatever in public affairs, and could scarcely be induced to come to Court. In his fits of savage temper he was even reported to strike his wife, and she, poor lady, who was supposed to have married into such dignity and grandeur, found herself with no real influence of any kind. Still, for a time, the two cousins were apparently the best of friends; they joined in the same sports, and occasionally in wild escapades, such as going to the market-place in disguise, where they nearly got into serious trouble. Then we find them arranging some masque with Turkish costumes, and Beatrice "works at the sewing like any old woman," as her husband remarks with amusement and satisfaction.

Late that autumn, when the young Duchess had a sharp attack of illness, Lodovico was in great distress about her, and showed the utmost devotion, scarcely leaving her chamber night or day. On her recovery, the first thing she did was to drive seven miles into the country, to look on at a boar-hunt, and enjoyed herself immensely. Afterwards she paid a visit *incognita* to Genoa, for change of air from Pavia, which was damp in late autumn.

At this time, Lodovico had asked the King of France to renew his investiture of the Duchy of Genoa, which had been first granted to Francesco Sforza. This Charles VIII. readily agreed to, and in the winter of 1491 he sent an embassy to Milan, which was splendidly entertained; but, after having seen all the magnificence of the Duke of Bari's jewels and other possessions, they were rather disappointed with the presents they themselves received. A few months later, Lodovico sent a return embassy to the French Court, where the nobles from Milan made a great sensation in their gorgeous robes of brocade and cloth of gold. His diplomacy was completely successful, as the King of France entered into close alliance with him.

After this, the christening of Isabella's little son, the Count of Pavia, was celebrated with much festivity, and the young mother seems to have been quite happy and contented for a while, and full of hope for the future.

In this peaceful time, Lodovico devoted much attention to the improvement of the University of Milan as well as that of Pavia; medicine and law were specially encouraged, scholars came from all parts of Europe, and a splendid library was collected and placed at their service. Many great works were executed and much progress was made with the Duomo, while Leonardo da Vinci had full occupation for his various talents. In his early letter to the Duke he says: "In time of peace I believe I can equal any man in constructing public buildings and conducting water from one place to another. I can execute sculpture, whether in marble, bronze, or terra-cotta, and in painting I am the equal of any master, be he who he may. Again, I will undertake to execute the bronze horse, to the immortal glory and honour of the Duke, your father, of blessed memory, and of the illustrious House of Sforza. And if any of the things I have mentioned above should seem to you impossible and impracticable, I will gladly make trial of them in your park, or in any other place that may please your Excellency, to whom I commend myself in humility."

To us, the letter rather breathes of well-justified pride. The great master spent the best years of his life in Milan, amongst congenial friends, happy in his work. The Court of Lodovico and Beatrice was a very galaxy of talent, and, to give only a brief account of the learned men, the poets, the artists, and the musicians, who honoured it with their presence, would take a volume in itself. Perhaps amongst these, after Ariosto who was but a passing guest, Niccola da Correggio the poet, Cristoforo Romano the sculptor and sweet singer, and Atalante and Serafino the musicians, were the most distinguished. As she grew into womanhood, the bright intelligence, the taste and character of the young Princess became more richly cultivated, in a society so stimulating and full of inspiration.

The great event for all Italy in the year 1492, was the death of Pope Innocent VIII. and the election of his successor, Cardinal Borgia, as Alexander VI. But it was some time before the far-reaching effects of this disastrous change were fully realised. Meanwhile that summer was a very happy one for the two sisters,

Isabella and Beatrice, who spent a delightful time together at Pavia, Novaro, and Mortara, hunting the stag, the wolf, and even the wild boar to their hearts' content. A few quotations from the letters of the Marchesa to her husband at Mantua, will give a vivid picture of the chase in those days.

"About four o'clock yesterday, all these lords and ladies rode out with me . . . and had fine sport. White tents were placed on the edge of the forest, and a pergola of green boughs, under which the Duchess and I took our places. . . . One stag of the eight which were found there ran out of the wood, followed by eight of the dogs. Messer Galeazzo galloped after it with a long spear, and killed it before our eyes."

Another day she writes: "We went hunting to-day in the beautiful wooded valley of the Ticino, where all the stags were driven in, so that they were forced to swim the river and ascend the mountains . . . we could watch every movement of the animals as the dogs chased them. . . . Many wild boars and goats were found, but only one bear was killed before our eyes, and one wild goat, which fell to my share. Last of all came a wolf . . . which soon followed its comrades to the slaughter. And so, with much laughter and merriment, we returned home."

On the return to Milan, Isabella seems to have been on the best of terms with the wife of Duke Gian Galeazzo, the Duchess Bona his mother, and his unmarried sister, Madonna Bianca, destined later to become the wife of the Emperor Maximilian. She was shown all the treasures of the Duke of Bari, and could not restrain a feeling of envy at the sight of so much wealth, which she would have had such a talent for spending!

Later in the year, Beatrice had a narrow escape in one of her reckless hunting expeditions, for she suddenly came upon a savage boar which had already wounded several hounds. She boldly attacked him, and he was followed up and slain by her husband and a companion. But the fatigue of that day had been too much for her; she became seriously ill, and her sister, who had left for Genoa, returned to be with her, while her husband showed himself as kind and devoted as ever. One of the chief qualifications for the sick room, seems to have been the faculty of amusing the patient. In letters of this period we are constantly reminded that depression of mind is a fatal sign, to be overcome at any cost by merry talk and the antics of dwarfs and jesters.

In the following January, a son was born to the young Duchess of Bari, and the event was hailed with the most extraordinary rejoicings and public festivities. For a whole week the bells rang out a "gloria" from every church tower, stately processions passed through the streets of the city, with solemn thanksgivings in the Duomo and feasts to the people. The most splendid gifts were presented to the mother, and extravagance unheard of before, even in that sumptuous Court, was shown on the costly decoration of the chamber, where Beatrice received visits and congratulations. Within a few days, a daughter had been born to Isabella of Aragon, the Duchess of Milan, and the two ladies went together in state, to return thanks at Santa Maria with the Duchess of Ferrara. Their costumes are minutely described to Isabella d'Este by her maid of honour.

"The Duchess of Bari had a lovely vest of gold brocade worked in red and blue silk, and a blue silk mantle trimmed with long-haired fur, and her hair coiled as usual in a silken net. She was covered with jewels." A few days later she appeared in a rose-coloured riding-habit and a large jewel in her silk hat, when she rode a gaily-caparisoned black horse. At the next entertainment the young princess wore a feather of rubies in her hair, and a dress of crimson satin embroidered with her favourite pattern of knots and compasses, and also trimmed with many ribbons. Then again we hear of a new robe of gold-striped cloth worn with a crimson vest laced with fine silver thread.

These gorgeous dresses are worthy of mention, as they emphasise the extreme importance attached to the birth of the young prince. It was a matter of general remark that royal honours were paid to this infant, which the little Count of Pavia had never received. Isabella was furious, and her mind was filled with the darkest suspicions, until she could endure her anxiety no longer, and wrote to her father, Alfonso of Aragon, pouring out the whole story of her wrongs. Unfortunately her fears were well grounded, for the birth of their son had awakened in the Duke and Duchess of Bari an eager ambition to make him heir to the ducal crown, and from that time there was a marked change in the policy of Lodovico. He was no longer content with the reality of power and the title of Regent, but aimed at being recognised throughout Italy as the Duke of Milan.

The letter of Isabella met with warm sympathy at Naples from her father, who would have openly taken her part at once, but the old King of Naples advised delay, and suggested underhand means for achieving the ruin of Lodovico, while outwardly he remained on friendly terms. It was plot against plot, for Il Moro lost no time in strengthening his alliance with the new Pope, and proposed to include in the league, the Venetian Republic, Mantua and Ferrara. He also wished to gain over to his side Maximilian, son of the Emperor Frederick III., and sent an ambassador to suggest that he should take as his bride Bianca Sforza, his niece, with an enormous dowry. He was also to ask for the investiture of Milan, which the Visconti dukes had received, but which their Sforza successors had felt too confident in a popular election and their own power, to apply for. If Lodovico could obtain this, he would be the legal Duke of Milan, and his nephew the usurper. Maximilian privately agreed to everything, and continued his negotiations with Charles VIII. of France, who needed very little encouragement to make any alliance which would further his designs on Naples, and the Treaty of Senlis was concluded between them.

Lodovico, with his wife and infant son, had been paying a visit to Ferrara, where they were entertained with the splendid entertainments and theatrical displays which Duke Ercole knew how to do so well, and he was on his way home, when a special envoy reached him with the news, having ridden 600 miles from Senlis in six days. This decided the Duke, and he resolved to throw in his lot with the French King against Naples. For the present all was to be kept secret, and he did not even venture to go in person to Venice for fear of rousing suspicion; he therefore most astutely arranged that his wife should travel with her mother, as though bent on pleasant travel, and that she should act as his ambassador with the Doge and Signoria. No expense was spared for Beatrice to make a good impression; she had ten chariots and fifty mules laden with baggage in her train, and her dresses and jewels were beyond all description. This was her first entrance into the political world, and she played her part well.

A splendid reception was given by the Republic, with the striking decorations to which Venice lends herself so charmingly; and when the bucentaurs of the guests passed S. Clemente, the air was filled with the thunder of artillery from the galleys, the arsenal, from every side at once. It must indeed have been a splendid sight, as Beatrice remarks in her letters—Venice in her glory, with every palace on the Grand Canal hung with rich Oriental draperies, the blue waters crowded with gondolas all decked in gay colours, the Doge and the Senators in their stately array, and the charm of a summer day over all. The visitors were taken to the Este Palace, which was magnificently decorated to receive them, and the next day, the young Duchess was received by the Signoria in the Doge's Sala del Collegio. Here she made an able speech, and set forth that as Regent of Milan her husband was in high esteem with both Germany and France, that he had received news of the French King's designs, and wished to consult them as to his action. She also touched on other matters, and, at a second interview, she pointed out that Lodovico had the treasure, the fortresses, and the army of Lombardy at his disposal.

The Senators were much charmed with this young girl of eighteen and with her courage and eloquence, but they did not commit themselves to anything very definite. She wrote a full account of this to her husband, and also told him of all the grand entertainments provided for her, which she thoroughly enjoyed, as well as the admiration which she received.

That was an eventful year, for, in October, Beatrice had the great sorrow of losing her mother, the good Duchess Leonora of Ferrara—the first grief she had ever known in her happy life. The following month, there was carried out the compact of marriage for Bianca Maria Sforza with Maximilian, who was now Emperor since his father's death. This was on the usual scale of princely magnificence, and the trousseau alone was valued at 100,000 ducats, and was publicly exhibited.

Early in 1493, the strained situation of affairs in Italy became more complicated by the death of Ferrante, the old King of Naples, and the succession of Alfonso, whose hatred of Lodovico was stronger than any other feeling, and who was willing to make any sacrifice to win over the Pope to his side. Upon this the Duke of Bari threw himself into the French alliance with all his soul and hurried on the invasion of Italy, sending at once as his ambassador, Messer Galeazzo to Charles VIII., who had so often desired to have the gallant knight in his service. Thus did his fatal ambition become the cause of all his country's misery, and, in the end, of his own ruin.

The next year saw the invasion of Italy by the French; the Duke of Orleans being the first to arrive in his own territory of Asti, between Turin and Alexandria, which he inherited from his grandmother Valentina Visconti. Charles VIII. reached Asti early

LUCREZIA CRIVELLI

LEONARDO DA VINCI

in September and was met by Lodovico, and splendidly received by Beatrice, who brought her ladies and musicians with her. His mean appearance must have been rather a shock to her, but he behaved with much courtesy, and his followers were greatly impressed by the beauty and magnificence of the Italian ladies. The French king paid a state visit to Pavia, and had scarcely left before the death of Gian Galeazzo, who had been seriously ill for some time, in the watchful care of his mother and wife. There was later a suspicion of poison, but without serious foundation. Lodovico lost no time in sending for the promised investiture from the Emperor Maximilian, and a few days later was publicly proclaimed Lord of Milan, and rode through the city in a mantle of gold brocade. The late duke having been buried with the "greatest pomp and honour," Il Moro hastened to the French camp. He had attained his desire, and reached the summit of his ambition.

The unfortunate Isabella broke down altogether after her husband's death, and refused to be comforted. She had lost everything; and now that her son had been robbed of his inheritance she was indeed friendless and forlorn.

Meantime events made rapid progress; Piero dei Medici in terror, gave up Florence and all her strongholds to the French king without a blow; Siena threw open her gates, and supplied him with money and provisions, and in December, Charles entered Rome and dictated terms of peace to the Pope himself. Still continuing his victorious course, the French king led his army against Naples, from whence Alfonso fled, leaving his son Ferrante in his place. The invader met with little resistance, and on February 22 was crowned, in the Cathedral of Naples, King of the Two Sicilies. The news of these successes filled all Italy with dismay, and Lodovico realised too late what he had done. His reputation was still so high, that he was appealed to on all sides to turn against the foreign conqueror, and save his country from ruin. In that dark hour of danger he was quite willing to act at once, and a league was hastily concluded with Maximilian, the Pope, Venice, Spain, Milan, and other Italian States against France. It was publicly proclaimed in Venice on Palm Sunday, and all the ambassadors formed a stately procession round the Piazza San Marco.

Meantime Milan had been enjoying gay entertainments in honour of the birth of Beatrice's second son, Francesco, and most of the Este family had paid visits of congratulation to her. The Marchesa of Mantua found endless delight in all the treasures of art which her brother-in-law had collected, and found time also to condole with the unhappy Duchess Isabella. It was not until the month of May that the long promised investiture from the Emperor reached Milan, and Lodovico with extraordinary pomp and magnificence, was crowned Duke of Milan, Count of Pavia and Angera, by the Grace of God, and the will of his Majesty Maximilian. He was then clothed in the ducal mantle and cap, and received the sceptre and sword of State, afterwards riding in a brilliant procession to San Ambrogio, to return public thanks. To Beatrice and her husband this was the great day of their lives, when they had reached the very summit of their ambition.

But life has strange contrasts in store for us, and a pinnacle is a dangerous place. Within a week the Duke of Orleans made a sudden night attack on Novaro, the citadel surrendered, and with a strong force he marched on towards the capital. Then a strange thing happened. When the Duke heard the news he lost his presence of mind, and fled to the Castello of Pavia, with his wife and children. It was Beatrice who sent for the nobles and made all arrangements for the defence of the city, with absolute coolness and courage. Fortunately succour was at hand; troops arrived from Venice, and, with their help, the forces of Milan drove the French back to Novaro. Lodovico recovered himself, the promised army arrived from Germany, and the allies could take the field with 25,000 men, under the command of Isabella's husband, the Marchese of Mantua. On July 5 a battle was fought at Fornova, where the French were defeated, but were suffered to make good their retreat through want of discipline amongst the foreign mercenaries in the army of Italy. The Duke of Orleans meanwhile remained a source of anxiety, as he was strongly garrisoned in the fortress of Novaro, within thirty miles of Milan, a constant menace to the neighbourhood. In July he was besieged by the Venetian army, and it was decided to blockade the town rather than make an attempt to take it by assault.

On that broad plain of Lombardy a great review of the whole army was held in August, at which Beatrice was present with her husband, who now sought her company and advice in all his undertakings. By this time the French king was very tired of the war and could get no more supplies of money or soldiers from home, while his wife, Anne de Bretagne, implored him to return. All the combatants were anxious for peace, and in September a great conference was held near the ancient city of Vercelli, a few miles from Novaro. It is very interesting to note that the young Duchess was in attendance with her husband at every meeting, that she had a clear grasp of the whole subject, and, without putting herself unduly forward, was ready at all points, to the wonder of the French commissioners.

At length, after many weary delays, peace was concluded. Louis of Orleans marched out of Novaro with the miserable remnant of his troops; Lodovico's title to Genoa and Savona was admitted; but he had to cancel the immense debt owed him by France, and to pay 50,000 ducats more as a war indemnity, besides other concessions, which must have terribly impoverished his duchy for years. But he was now relieved from anxiety and free to pursue other ambitious plans, for his position in Italy was higher than it had ever been. He was much gratified the following summer of 1496 by a formal visit from the Emperor Maximilian; but it was first arranged that the Duke and Duchess should travel to meet him at Mals, on the frontier of the Tyrol. We have a striking picture of his arrival with a hunting-party, in a grey tunic with the Order of the Golden Fleece, and a lion skin hanging on his side. He treated Lodovico and his wife with the greatest friendliness. They all attended mass together and had wonderful banquets in the woods. Maximilian also held a conference with them and agreed upon a new league, then he rode back with them over the Alps to Bormio, where they had a chamois hunt.

The following month he paid his promised visit to the Duke and Duchess at their country palace of Vivegano. He was much pleased with his reception, and asked that their eldest boy, Ercole, might be called Maximilian after him. This intimacy with the Emperor created some jealousy in Italy; but the renown of Lodovico rose higher than ever; all his designs seemed to be crowned with success, and he believed himself the favourite of fortune.

It was during this time of peace that Leonardo was engaged on his famous fresco of the "Last Supper," in the refectory of the Dominican convent at S. Maria delle Grazie, and the friars would complain to the Duke that he was so slow at his work and had not yet put in the head of Judas. Lodovico was as eager as ever about public works; but he began to find himself much straitened for money, and the people became loud in their complaints of the heavy taxes imposed upon them. He seems to have become somewhat demoralised by all the adulation and flattery which he had received, for we hear rumours of his devotion to one of the ladies-in-waiting, Lucrezia Crivelli, whose portrait he caused to be painted by his great artist. The news of this caused much anxiety at Ferrara, and it is probable that it reached the ears of Beatrice.

But the bright, eager-hearted young princess was not destined to have much more of earthly sorrow or joy, for on January 2, 1497, after she had spent the wintry afternoon in prayer at the Dominican Church of S. Maria delle Grazie, she was taken suddenly ill, a little son was born dead, and, to the grief and dismay of all, she breathed her last. So terrible and unlooked-for a calamity touched the heart of every one, and the mourning for the beautiful, brilliant Duchess of Milan was universal. Cut off thus in her prime, with the world at her feet, her loss has that touch of tender pathos which none can resist. And yet to us, who can read that future which was hidden from her, does it not rather seem that she was snatched from the evil to come—from dark ruin and disaster which would have broken down her proud, brave spirit ? *

Her husband was broken-hearted, and we may well believe that to his bitter grief were added the pangs of remorse for having ever given her cause to grieve. To her sweet memory he caused to be erected that exquisite monument which was described on the opening page, as an enduring memorial for the ages to come, of one so dearly loved.

* Within three short years followed the ruin and downfall of Lodovico, and his sons, more fully dwelt upon in the close of Bianca Sforza's life.

BIANCA MARIA SFORZA, WIFE OF THE EMPEROR MAXIMILIAN.

THE story of Bianca Sforza is interesting to us rather as a striking chronicle of Renaissance life than as a study of individual character.

She had neither the vigour and courage of her half-sister, Catarina, nor the charm and intellect of her young companion, Beatrice d'Este, and although we are told, in the flowery language of the day, that she was, "Bianca di perle, e bella piu che 'l sole," we have no very convincing evidence of her great beauty. Still we are told she had a tall, slim figure and abundance of fair hair, so much admired in her day.

She was born on April 15, 1472, the eldest daughter of Bona of Savoy, Duchess of Milan, and her husband, the Duke Galeazzo Maria Sforza. Of her two brothers —Gian Galeazzo, the ill-fated heir to the duchy, was born in 1469, then followed Ermes—and she had one little sister, two years younger than herself, who was betrothed as an infant to Alfonso, the new-born son of the Duke of Ferrara. Nothing can exceed the magnificence and luxury which surrounded the early years of her life. In the new Castello of the Porta Giovia, the most splendid entertainments, the most costly banquets succeeded each other in the sumptuous Court of Milan, which under this, the second of the Sforza dukes, surpassed all that the old Visconti lords had ever dreamed of.

The chronicles of Milan prove Duke Galeazzo to have been a man of evil life, and of many crimes, but he was a patron of artists and sculptors, whom he kept employed to decorate his palaces; he was the founder of the famous city library, he encouraged musicians and singers, and he took the greatest interest in the professors of the rising University of Pavia. The Duchess Bona, who had been brought up at the Court of Louis XI. with her sister, the king's wife, was reckless in her extravagance, and set a fashion of wearing costly dresses and priceless jewels, such as were rivalled at no other Court in Italy. Very different from her mother-in-law, the good Duchess Bianca, she did not trouble herself much about the education of her children, but being a kind-hearted woman, "of little sense," as one of her biographers remarks, she let them spend their time in pleasure and idleness.

A Milanese historian, Corio, gives us a minute description of the famous visit to Lorenzo dei Medici, which the Duke and Duchess of Milan paid in 1471. There were no less than twelve litters, which could be used as "caretti," but which were carried on mules over the mountains; they had awnings of cloth of gold, and the great feather mattresses laid in them were of cloth of gold or silver, or of crimson satin. The Duke was accompanied by all his great feudatories with their attendants, all the members of his household were dressed in velvet, while some of them had golden collars, and his grooms wore silk adorned with silver.

Besides an army of gorgeous followers, there were fifty led horses and one hundred mules covered with cloth of gold, two thousand other horses, and two hundred mules covered with rich damask to carry the baggage. Five hundred couples of hounds with huntsmen, falcons, and falconers, trumpeters, jesters, players, and musicians, would seem to us rather an encumbrance for a journey over the Apennines, by a steep bridle-path.

But all the pomp and magnificence of which this was a symbol was destined to last but a few years, for when little Bianca was only four years old, Galeazzo's career of tyranny and profligacy was suddenly cut short by his assassination at the door of San Stefano. We are told that Bona had implored her husband not to go forth from the Castello that day, and that three ravens had been seen flying round him, and that as he was entering the church the anthem rang out: "Sic transit gloria mundi."

After his death, the Duchess Bona with the help of her astute minister, Cecco Simonetta, was able to maintain the regency for her son Gian Galeazzo; but after a few years, by her own folly and vanity, which have been spoken of elsewhere, she brought ruin upon her own cause by the unwise recall of Lodovico il Moro, her brother-in-law. Simonetta had duly warned her, for he exclaimed: "Illustrissima Signora, do you know what will be the end of this? My head will be cut off, and ere long you will lose this kingdom."

She must have remembered this prophecy only three years later, on the night of her shameful flight from Milan when, maddened by the treachery of her low-born favourite, Tassino, whom she had loaded with honours, she forsook her home and her children.

Meantime Bianca lived on with her brothers and young sister in the great Castello of Milan, where they had an outward show of grandeur, while their Uncle Lodovico had usurped the government and ruled the duchy with despotic power. Her eldest brother Gian Galeazzo had always been a sickly delicate child, and as years passed it was plain that he was weak in mind also. He could apply his mind to no serious study, and only cared for dogs and horses. On public occasions he was put forward as Duke of Milan with regal pomp ; but for the rest of his time, he only asked to be left to his low pleasures. He had been betrothed in his father's lifetime to Isabella of Aragon, the grand-daughter of Ferdinand, King of Naples, and the marriage was solemnised with much pomp in 1488.

Bianca's hand had been promised to the young Prince of Savoy, and on his early death, she was betrothed in the Duomo of Milan to the eldest son of Matthias Corvinus, King of Hungary. This prince had strong artistic and literary tastes, as we learn that he was the fortunate owner of a rare manuscript by Festus Pompeius, which he had copied for Lodovico, who had promised his father a beautiful painting of the Holy Family by Leonardo da Vinci. This prince also ordered an exquisite organ to be made by the famous Lorenzo da Pavia. But again Bianca was unfortunate in her matrimonial engagements, for when King Matthias died, in 1490, his son was deprived of his crown, and, in consequence, the proposed alliance with Milan was broken off, and he lost his bride also.

Meantime many things had happened, of which the young princess was a passive spectator. Her uncle Lodovico had taken to himself a young wife, the gay

Beatrice d'Este, whose brother Alfonso had come with her from Ferrara to fetch his own promised bride, Anna Sforza, the only sister of Bianca. Her mother, Bona, had returned to Milan on this occasion, and with her elder daughter by her side, took a prominent part in the State reception. They were also great personages during the splendid entertainments, which were continued for a whole week. But though we hear little about Bianca, it must have been a trial to lose her only sister, whose sweet temper and gentle disposition are often mentioned. The parting would have been sadder still had they known that, after a few short years of quiet happiness, Anna would be lost indeed to them by an early death on the birth of her first child. "She was very beautiful and very charming, and there is little to tell about her because she lived so short a time," says an old chronicler.

The coming of Beatrice d'Este must have added fresh life and gaiety to the life of Bianca, who was much at the Court with her other ladies and joined in many of the hunting excursions. But we never find her mentioned as adding any brightness to the party, and her feeling was no doubt one of jealousy towards this Princess, three years younger than herself, who had so much more brilliant a position. Her uncle Lodovico appears to have looked upon her as a useful counter in the game of politics, for, when he sent his ambassadors to France in 1492, we find him offering her hand to the young King of Scotland, James IV. But this came to nothing, and we find Madonna Bianca mentioned on various State occasions, such as the visit of Isabella d'Este and the stately procession to return thanks for the birth of Beatrice's boy.

So far she has always been a spectator ; but the time was approaching when she was to take the place of honour in her turn. In 1493, when Bianca had reached the mature age of twenty-one, her uncle the Duke of Bari was anxious to promote a close alliance with the Emperor and his son Maximilian by any means in his power. This prince, who was now thirty-nine years of age, was a widower and had recently been deprived of his promised bride, Anne de Bretagne, by the King of France. Lodovico sent his envoy, Erasmo Brasca, with private instructions to offer the hand of Bianca Maria Sforza, his niece, with the immense dowry of 400,000 ducats, to the King of the Romans in exchange for the renewed investiture of Milan. Maximilian was tempted by the offer and willing to agree to it, but he stipulated that it should be kept secret for the present. His father, the Emperor Frederick III., was still alive, but not expected to recover. In the month of June following he sent a special messenger from his castle of Gmunden, to ask for the hand of Madonna Bianca Maria Sforza, sister of Gian Galeazzo, Duke of Milan, while at the same time he promised Lodovico the investiture of the duchy for himself. In August, on his father's death, Maximilian became Emperor, and announced his purpose of sending ambassadors to celebrate his marriage and bring the Lady Bianca to Innsbruck.

This despatch gave the greatest satisfaction at Milan, and the mother of the expectant bride was especially delighted at so splendid an alliance. The wedding was settled to take place by proxy at the end of November, and the most splendid preparations were set on foot at once. The Court was in mourning for the Duchess of

Ferrara, the mother of Beatrice, but that was to be laid aside for the occasion. The trousseau of the bride was to be on the most magnificent scale, worthy of an empress, and was to include a great store of fine linen, sumptuous bed-hangings, carpets, mirrors, and gold and silver plate. Nor was this all, for the chronicler of Bianca tells us of gorgeous horse-trappings and saddles, and also of unique altar-cloths and ornaments for a chapel, all this besides the most splendid dresses and priceless jewels. Bianca must have felt that if her day had been long in coming, such grandeur would indeed make up for the delay.

On the 7th of November the two chosen ambassadors from the Emperor, or, as he was still called, the King of the Romans, not having yet received the imperial crown, reached Milan, and were met by the Regent and his nephew, the Duke of Milan, at the Porta Orientale, and taken with all honour to the Castello. They were feasted and made much of, and received splendid presents while they awaited the wedding-day, which was fixed for the 30th of November. The city was decorated with rich tapestry and armorial bearings, and brocades, and myrtle boughs, while on the triumphal arch, in front of the Castello, was placed the great clay model of Leonardo's statue of Francesco Sforza on horseback. The imperial bride looked her best that day, as she rode through the city in her triumphal car drawn by four white horses.

She wore a vest of crimson satin, embroidered with gold thread and covered with jewels; her train was of great length, and the sleeves of her dress looked like two wings. The Duchess Beatrice sat on one side and the Duchess Isabella, wife of Gian Galeazzo, on the other. Next, there came chariots with all the ambassadors of various princes, and Lodovico and his nephew on horseback. Then followed ten chariots with the noblest maidens in Milan, and the ladies of the bride, all wearing the same livery, with tan-coloured camoras and mantles of bright green satin. The streets were crowded with men and women, and so hung with colours and green boughs that it rather looked like May than November. The ceremony was performed by the Archbishop of Milan, "to the sound of organ-music, flutes, and trumpets, and the singing of the exquisite choir voices." The Princess Bianca stood before the altar with the ambassadors of the Emperor, and after the marriage service was concluded the splendid imperial crown was placed on her "bare head," as Calvi tells us, by the Archbishop, assisted by the Bishop of Brixen, who had given her the ring.

Then the great procession passed down the Duomo, the train and the sleeves of the bride being supported by great nobles; and they all rode through the streets, a baldacchino of white damask, lined with ermine, being carried over the head of the newly-made queen. All the ambassadors agreed that they had never seen so magnificent a sight, and the illuminations and festivities which followed for two days and nights were on the same scale. Duchess Bona is said to have wept for joy at her daughter's great promotion, and almost forgot all her past troubles in the triumph of the hour.

Three days later, Bianca set forth on her journey to Innsbruck with a great company, the ambassadors of Maximilian, her brother Ermes, and, fortunately for us, amongst her retinue was the envoy from Milan, Erasmo Brasca, whose letters give us a full account of the journey and much that happened afterwards. All the Court of Milan accompanied the travellers as far as Como, where they were conducted to the cathedral for a solemn service of thanksgiving. The next day the bride said farewell to her mother and all her family, and with a gala show of decorated barges, to the sound of triumphant music, the gaily-dressed company crossed the blue waters of the lake, as far as Bellagio. Here they rested for the night, and were hospitably entertained at the castle, continuing their journey next morning. But now their troubles began, for they had not proceeded far up the lake when the sky was darkened, and a sudden storm came on with so much violence that the festal barges were scattered in all directions. The ladies, in terror, sobbed aloud, and fell on their knees to pray for mercy; most of the courtiers were quite as much alarmed, and even the boatmen were full of dismay.

The chief indignation of Messer Erasmo was directed against the duke's favourite astrologer and physician, Ambrogia da Rosate, without whose advice nothing was ever undertaken. "Infelice" is the mildest term the poor envoy uses, and he declares there was a "vento indiavolato a Bellagio." However, after tossing about all day, the queen was able to put back to the shore, and make another start next morning, and on December 8 the wedding-party boldly adventured to cross the passes of the Alps. At the present day a traveller would hesitate to ride across the Stelvio Pass with its excellent road at that season, and when we remember that a rough mule-track was then the only way across the mountains, we cannot wonder that these great ladies, who so often took their wedding journeys in the dead of winter, had to suffer great hardships.

"Those fearful cruel mountains" were indeed terrible, and one lady-in-waiting, Madonna Michela, had to be left behind at Gravedona, utterly exhausted, while the others were so loud in their complaints that poor Bianca made an angry appeal to Erasmo, who wrote thus to Milan: "Our gracious lady bears herself well on the whole, but she constantly complains that I deceive her, for each morning when she mounts her horse I tell her that she will not find the path so rough that day, and then by ill-fate, lo! it is worse than ever."

It was not until Christmas Eve that the poor weather-beaten travellers at length found themselves in safety at Innsbruck, to discover, to Bianca's cruel disappointment, that Maximilian was not there to receive her. The ambassador was still more troubled, and wrote at once to the laggard bridegroom at Vienna to inform him of their arrival. Meantime the Archduchess Sigismond of Austria did her best to entertain the neglected bride with balls and parties, which made her quite happy, and she wrote long letters to Milan telling how the ladies had been wearing fancy dresses, à la Tedesca, and à la Lombarda; and how the painter who had travelled from home with her, Ambrogio de Predis, had painted a portrait of Madonna Barbara. She did not realise the gravity of the situation, but poor Brasca, quite distracted with anxiety, set out for Vienna at once on receiving permission to do so, taking with him this very singular epistle from the bride: "Serenissimo Re e Signore mio, I find myself under such obligations towards your Majesty, that I am quite dazed at the love you manifest for me. I could not if I tried express the joy which floods my soul. Being unable to testify to it sufficiently in writing, I send Messer Erasmus Brasca to speak on my behalf; and I beseech your Majesty to believe him, and I commend myself to you.

"Innspruck. XXVJ. Decembris. 1493.

"Maiestatis Vestra Serva.

"Bianca Maria. manu propria."

The ambassador was determined to do his duty manfully, and not return alone. Maximilian received him with marked friendliness, invited him to entertainments, and spoke in flattering terms of the Sforza family; but he said nothing about going to Innsbruck, and the unhappy Brasca became more and more distressed. Two months had passed away before the imperial procession set forth, and Bianca having no reluctance to travel part way, the final and long-hoped-for meeting took place at Ala on March 9. "To the confusion of all our enemies!" cries Brasca, in his letter to his master at Milan.

Bianca's married life had not begun in a very propitious manner, and this triumph of diplomacy was not a great success for her. She had always been childish and foolish, and her husband compared her unfavourably with his first wife, Marie de Bourgogne; telling Brasca that his mistress was quite as fair but not so wise as that lady. Still he behaved kindly to his bride at first, and bestowed upon her splendid robes for her coronation when she had a fancy to appear in German fashion. Then she took a passionate liking for one of the maids-of-honour, Violante Caimi, who seems to have been as unwise as her mistress, and made mischief by her intrigues. When Bianca had the opportunity she would be wildly extravagant, as when the city of Cologne made her a wedding-present of 2000 florins she actually managed to spend it in one day. This came to the ears of Maximilian, who expressed his annoyance to her, and she lost her temper.

The result of all this was that her husband soon became tired of her, and would leave her for weeks together at Innsbruck, in the gloomy old castle with its vast walls, where she had nothing to relieve her dulness, and would look back with longing to the gay sunny palaces at Milan and Pavia. Before the end of the year she had fresh cause for trouble in the news which reached her of her brother Gian Galeazzo's death. She also received letters from her mother, who spoke in very bitter terms of the conduct of Lodovico in assuming the duchy, but many of these were suppressed by her secretary, Il Cotta, who on more than one occasion owns, with frank impudence, that he has burnt a certain letter.

Meantime, Lodovico had never received the promised investiture of Milan, and he sent a special envoy, Maffeo Pirovano, to press the matter. The poor man travelled in the winter, and met with many adventures; floods and terrible storms, and highwaymen in the streets of Cologne, but he at length arrived at Antwerp, where he was to meet the emperor, who made a great impression upon him. He writes: "Il Serenissimo Re has the most noble presence of body, as well as the highest qualities of soul and mind; and, to judge from outward signs, there is no doubt of his wisdom and loyalty . . . and, if his dealings seem slow and lingering, there are two difficulties . . . want of money, and the small confidence he can place in his ministers."

The Empress Bianca was very glad to see a friend from her dear Milan, and had much talk with him. She gave him many messages and commissions when he went home. He was to take her condolences to her mother and the widowed Isabella, and he was to ask all her family to send their portraits.

She wrote specially to the young Duchess Beatrice, asking her for silks and powders and scents, and, above all, a bunch of heron's plumes. She also wanted some pearls which were in possession of Catarina Sforza, and she sent a private message to Lodovico begging that he would persuade Il Re Serenissimo, the Emperor, to pay a visit to Italy, "but do not say that it is I who wish it."

Bianca frequently wrote to the Duke of Milan, asking her uncle to send her jewels or perfumes, or on one occasion a special white brocaded velvet for a dress, for these were all the things she cared for. The news of Beatrice's sudden death in 1497 must have grieved even her shallow nature, for she had a kindly disposition. In the after years, when Lodovico's troubles came upon him, when all his ambitious hopes had failed and he was cast down from his high estate, the wife of Maximilian was his best friend. But it was little she could do for him, as she never had any real influence with her husband, and she could only give the unfortunate duke, an outcast and an exile, hospitable welcome in her castle at Innsbruck, when he fled there in September 1499. It must have been a painful meeting for him with the faithful Erasmo Brasca, who still lived on at the Court of Bianca, devoted to her service until his death in 1501.

It was while Il Moro was ill with an attack of asthma, in the emperor's gloomy castle, that the fatal news reached him of the treachery of the man he had so absolutely trusted, the Governor of the Castello of Milan, where he had left all his priceless treasures. It was well garrisoned and supplied with provisions and ammunition, but Bernardino da Corte surrendered it to the enemy for a share of the plunder. Lodovico remained silent for some minutes, unable to grasp the full horror of what had befallen him. His great captain, Galeazzo, sat speechless by his side, till his master turned to him and said, "Never since the day of Judas has there been so black a traitor as Bernardino." And after that he kept silence for the whole day.

But as time passed on his indomitable spirit revived, and he adopted a new motto: "I will beat the drum in winter and dance all the summer," with the device of a tambourine. A famous preacher of Verona wrote to him, drawing a moral from his fall, and preaching justice to him; and this gave him an opportunity of putting forth an address to the world at large, justifying his conduct. What a good Christian he had always been, hearing so many masses, giving so much in alms! Who had a greater love for justice than himself? and he proceeds to explain a few doubtful matters. He had only desired peace and prosperity for his people, who were dear to him as his own children. Finally he calls upon his subjects to place him once more on the throne of his forefathers.

Some old friends respond to his call, and, joining him at Innsbruck, tell him of the awful state of Milan under the French, and assure him that his return is eagerly desired. On this the Duke makes a fresh effort. Maximilian is induced to supply him with all he can raise in the way of money and soldiers, he finds means to raise a force of mercenaries, and even appeals to the King of England and to the Turks. On January 24 he took his last leave of his niece, and set forth on the disastrous expedition which closed in ruin and despair.

We may imagine how sadly Bianca watched, from afar, his last struggle and defeat, his hopeless and lingering captivity in the dungeons of Loches, where he ate his heart out like a caged lion, until his final release by death in the month of May 1508. The empress had never ceased her efforts to help her unfortunate uncle, and Maximilian interceded in vain with the French king for his release. His two young sons found a home at Innsbruck when all else had failed, those idolised children of the Duchess Beatrice, born to so princely a fortune and such splendid hopes. It must have been a sad and gloomy life for them, brought up in that uncultured Court in the midst of boorish barons, who disliked the more gently-nurtured Italians, of whom so many had taken refuge in their exile at Innsbruck, and amongst them the gallant Galeazzo. The elder brother, Maximilian, was the god-son of the emperor, who in later years took up arms on his behalf. But their best friend was always the empress, and it must have been a great loss to them when she died, from the lingering disease from which she had suffered for years, on December 31, 1510, saddened by the evil fate of all she loved.

The Empress Bianca Maria Sforza, wife of the great

Maximilian, was buried in the ancient church of the Franciscans at Innsbruck. Here a splendid tomb was raised to the memory of the emperor, first of its kind in all Europe, and in the midst of this masterpiece of bronze work, there still meets our view the stately image, robed in the stiff brocades of her lifetime, of his unloved second wife, who pined away in that chill land, far from her sunny Lombard home.

ISABELLA D'ESTE, MARCHESA OF MANTUA.

As we approach the history of this peerless lady, "la prima donna del mondo," we are almost overwhelmed with the amount of information which has been collected with regard to her. In the libraries of Mantua and Milan, of Rome, of Florence, of Turin, &c., a long train of scholars and learned men have devoted years to the study of documents and correspondence connected with her, and have died ere the task was completed.

Of her own letters more than two thousand have been preserved, and her whole splendid career, from 1474 to 1539, is spread out before us in a flood of dazzling light.

We see her in the most intimate privacy of her family from childhood to age; we trace her relations towards every distinguished person of her time, crowned head, or artist, or man of letters—learning what they said, and what she said and thought—we follow in each step of her frequent travels, so keenly enjoyed; and we are even admitted to her toilet, and informed on what occasion she wore her crimson satin with gold and silver embroidery, her violet velvet with gold acorns, or her priceless mantle made of eighty of the finest sables.

Surrounded from her childhood by all that was beautiful, she was early distinguished by her cultured taste in music and art, her proficiency in classical studies, and her marvellous charm. It was her singular good fortune that, brought up in the very heart of the Renaissance, the small and passing incidents of her every-day life, are to us memorials of a classic age when the gods of Parnassus walked with men. Her march through life is a triumphal progress. Ever the "cynosure of neighbouring eyes" for her beauty and talent, poets write endless sonnets in her praise, adulation surrounds her on every side, until from her equal height she would advise the greatest masters in their own craft; witness some forty or fifty letters to a Bellini or a Perugino, with minute descriptions as to how they were to paint the picture for her.

Such magnificent audacity takes away one's breath!

Isabella has all that she desires, she has but to hear of the discovery of an antique, of a work of art, a priceless gem, a rare MS., an Aldine edition, a silver lute, a choice inlaid organ—any new and beautiful thing—but she straightway requests that it be sent to her, or if that be not possible, that another still more precious be procured for her. She would be outdone by no one, and nothing short of perfection would content her. Her supremacy was not alone artistic and intellectual. This lady of Mantua was the mirror of fashion for every Court in Europe. Stately princesses contest for early news of her gorgeous costumes, and humbly plead for the design of a sleeve, or the pattern of a new rosette.

We seem to read her very soul in those letters of hers; always so beautifully expressed, with infinite tact and delicacy. She ever knew how to say the right thing; whether to deprecate the wrath of a pope, or hostile king, who distrusted her husband's policy; whether to condole with a friend on the loss of a wife or a kingdom; to arrange a diplomatic marriage, or lend her pet dwarf to lighten the tedium of a sick bed; to plead for a cardinal's hat for her son, or beg for a Persian kitten.

The Marchesa d'Este was beyond praise in most o the relations of life; a pious and high-minded woman, and yet it was not safe to rely upon her too far. Dearly as she loved her friends and kindred, yet when they were utterly and hopelessly forsaken by fortune, she turned away from them with a sigh, to welcome their enemies with a smile. A true daughter of the light-hearted Renaissance, when their splendid palaces were looted, she was always ready to enrich herself with their spoils; but when they came as suppliants to her gates, she would receive them with princely generosity if her own safety were secured.

In the striking words of her last and most comprehensive biographer: "Like others of her age she knew no regrets and felt no remorse, but lived wholly in the present, throwing herself with all the might of her strong vitality into the business or enjoyment of the hour, forgetful of the past and careless of the future." *

Having thus introduced Isabella d'Este with this slight sketch and appreciation of her character, we turn to a short account of the events which are chiefly remarkable in her life.

She was born in the palace of Ferrara on May 18,

* Mrs. Ady.

1474. Her father, Duke Ercole, was the descendant of that illustrious house of Este which had reigned for more than two hundred years over the fertile plains of Ferrara. Her mother was Leonora, the daughter of King Ferrante of Naples, and the name Isabel, by which her first daughter was baptized, may have been in honour of her kinswoman the great Queen of Spain.

There does not seem to have been great rejoicing on the birth of a daughter, and there was still less when a little sister was born the next year; but when the hoped-for heir to the duchy arrived in due time, there was no lack of enthusiasm and delight in the city. Those were troublous times, and, a few days after the christening of young Alfonso, the duchess and her infant children barely escaped with their lives from a conspiracy of the duke's nephew.

In the following year Isabella took her first journey as far as Naples, where her little sister Beatrice was left behind with the grandfather for the next eight years. Meantime the young princesses, even at that early age, had attracted attention and interest at the neighbouring courts, and, after much negotiation, a public announcement was made on the Piazza, in the heart of old Ferrara, that Madonna Isabella was betrothed to Francesco, son of the Marquis of Mantua, and Madonna Beatrice to the Regent of Milan, Lodovico Sforza.

This was early in 1480, when the elder girl was only six years old, and the following spring, on the Feast of St. George, the patron saint of Ferrara, she made the acquaintance of her future bridegroom, a bright, handsome boy of fourteen. There seem to have been great festivities on the occasion, and immense crowds assembled to see the famous race for the *pallium*, which was won by the horses of the Mantuan guests, who appear to have greatly enjoyed their visit.

Her marriage and future life being thus provided for, the small Isabella had time to go back to her lessons. Born in an atmosphere of cultivation and learning, she seems to have been the delight of her teachers, who were amazed at her "marvellous facility." Latin was her most serious study, and for this she had the most learned tutors, and was reported in later years to speak the language with ease and elegance. Besides her classical studies, she read all the poetry and literature within her reach in various modern languages; she was a good musician, and learnt to play the clavichord and accompany her singing on the lute, and even found time to become proficient in design and embroidery.

The finest works of art and the most beautiful treasures were always in sight, and in the Este Palace she met all the most distinguished men and women of the day. We are told that she grew up a beautiful girl, with regular features, sparkling dark eyes, a brilliant complexion, and thick waves of golden hair. She was not very tall, but she bore herself with stately dignity.

Francesco, who was now Marquis of Mantua since his father's death, pressed on his wedding, which was at last fixed for the month of February 1490, when the bride would be almost sixteen. Nothing can exceed the exquisite taste and beauty of the presents prepared for her to take to her new home, on which artists, goldsmiths, and many of the most skilled craftsmen were engaged for more than a year. The wedding must have been a gorgeous spectacle, and is described by the chroniclers with ardent enthusiasm; also the stately journey to Mantua in a gilded bucentaur, with attendant galleys, which sailed up the Po, and the grand entry into the city, garlanded with flowers and hung with banners, with ambassadors from every state in Italy riding in her train.

But that which must have given most pleasure to the girl-bride was to meet at the foot of the great staircase of the Castello, her husband's sister, Elisabetta, who had recently married the Duke of Milan, and who then, and through life, was her dearest friend.

"There is no one I love like you, except my sister Beatrice," she once wrote to her, and this affection never changed, in sorrow or joy. It must have been a great comfort to Isabella that she was able to keep her sister-in-law with her for the first few months in her new home, where all was so strange to her. Her husband was very much devoted to her, but they cannot have had much in common. He had always shown more taste for outdoor sports than for intellectual pursuits; he was noted for his horses and dogs; yet, if he had not much taste for books, he could be a generous patron to artists and men of letters. He was very proud of Andrea Mantegna, who lived at his Court, and had just finished his series of triumphs for the walls of the Castello.

In the letters of this period we find how much Isabella was missed in her old home. One courtier writes: "Even the tricks and jests of the dwarfs and clowns fail to make us laugh."

She wrote to ask her tutor to send her old Latin books that she might occupy herself with her studies, and she sent presents to her old friends, while her weekly letters to her mother showed devoted affection. Ferrara was at no very great distance, and she was able to pay occasional visits, especially during that first year, when preparations were being made for her sister's wedding. This took place with much magnificence in the Castello of Pavia; but it was in January, and the journey thither in the depth of a severe winter had been a terrible experience for the Duchess Leonora, her two daughters, and their suite.

When the young duchess was well settled at Milan, we read of frequent visits between the sisters; but it was rather a serious matter of expense for Isabella, who needed fine new dresses and jewels for herself and her suite, to do justice to the magnificent reception which she received at Milan. Her ideas of jewels were of the most princely magnificence. We hear of a constant succession of orders for rubies, emeralds, diamond rosettes, engraved amethysts, rosaries of black amber, and gold-enamelled roses, corals and turquoises, and gems unnumbered. If a goldsmith keeps the imperious lady waiting unduly, he will probably find himself in the dungeon of the Castello. What became of her dressmakers we do not hear, but they must have been overwhelmed with the costly variety of Oriental silks and velvets, the priceless brocades and fine linen with which they had to carry out her designs.

But this outward splendour only satisfied one side of her nature. The young marchioness had an insatiable appetite for literature, and she seems to have read all the mediæval romances of her day, in French and Spanish as well as Italian. But this did not interfere with her taste for the classical authors, her study of the Christian Fathers, and her keen love for poetry. With all this she had time to hear sermons and to keep up her friendship with the saintly Dominican nun, the Beata Osanna. In a picture by Bonsignori, she is represented, with three of her ladies, kneeling at the feet of the holy woman.

Isabella also devoted much attention to the delightful occupation of decorating her rooms in the grim old Lombard Castello, which was more fortress than palace. Nothing was too costly, too rare and exquisite to satisfy her taste, and her own special chamber, overlooking the lake, with its inlaid woodwork and painted ceiling, its walls covered with priceless paintings, its treasures of rare books and musical instruments, silver and *niello* work, delicate glass from Murano . . . must have made this studio an ideal gem of the Renaissance. One little picture of Mantegna's which hung here is thus described:

"The dying of Our Lady, the Apostles standing about with white candles lighted in their hands; and in the landskip where the town of Mantua is painted is the water-lake, where a bridge is over the said water towards the town. In a little ebony wooden frame."

In the year 1494, when all the world was ringing with the discoveries of Columbus, Isabella paid a visit of state to Venice, where she was royally entertained; but soon after her return she had the great sorrow of losing her mother, the Duchess Leonora, to whom she was passionately attached. It was an eventful year, as on the last day of December was born her eldest child, a girl who was called Leonora Violante Maria. "In her the name and blessed memory of my mother shall live again," she wrote to her aunt, the Queen of Hungary.

At this time she had the comforting society of her dear friend, Elisabetta Gonzaga, the Duchess of Urbino, whom she was always so delighted to meet, "that they might tell each other all that had happened since they parted." Soon after this the young mother went on a pilgrimage of thanksgiving to Loreto, which a recent French writer * has thus poetically described:

"The sweet, tender Isabella d'Este set out thus to transport her soul across the plains of Umbria, towards the calm and glorious homes of peace and art, Loreto and Assisi. It was early spring, when the days were clear and sunny; every morning after mass the little caravan resumed its march with its picturesque escort, piously, tranquilly, ideally. During the Easter festival it made a halt with the Duke and Duchess of Urbino in the delightful palace of Gubbio, smiling down from amongst its gardens and fountains.

"The woman who has been able to live these hours of pure enthusiasm is conscious of accomplishing a large part of her dream. She is within sight of reconciling two opposite forces, the forces of Nature and the forces of the human heart. . . ."

Isabella had inherited from her father an absorbing love for travel and for art, and she had ample opportunity of gratifying both these tastes. She went to Ferrara, to Milan, where her brother-in-law Lodovico il Moro had recently become Duke, and everywhere was the centre of princely entertainments. Her little daughter was left meantime in the care of an accomplished governess, Violante de' Preti.

* R. de Maulde la Clavière.

In the year 1495 her husband was appointed captain of the armies of the League which had been formed against the French king, who had already conquered Naples. Francesco was covered with honour by his success at the battle of Fornova, and as a memorial of this event he was painted by Mantegna, kneeling in his armour before the Virgin, in the famous "Madonna della Vittoria," which was carried away from its forsaken shrine and now hangs in the Louvre. Peace had been made, but was not of long duration, and the next year we see the curious spectacle of the two sisters-in-law, Isabella, and Chiara Duchess of Montpensier, together amongst their books and music at Mantua; while their husbands fought in opposing camps, and good news to one would be disaster to the other. Such was the tangle of political interests and alliances in those days.

In this brief space, it is impossible to follow the varied course of that terrible war which ravaged Italy for so many years, and brought ruin and exile to so many friends of the house of Este. But through all the desperate perils and ever-present anxiety, Isabella so wisely ruled in Mantua, so delicately threaded her way through the bewildering maze of intrigues, and always hastened so judiciously to welcome and flatter the winner of the hour, that she kept her husband's dominion intact. Sorrow she could not keep away, and many losses befell her at this time.

Her sister Beatrice, the splendid young Duchess of Milan, died suddenly at the age of twenty-one, and her infant son was buried with her. She was taken from the evil to come, poor young princess, for not three years later, all the glories of her estate were at an end;

ISABELLA D'ESTE, MARCHESA OF MANTUA

Titian

the duchy was taken from her husband, whose fate was a French dungeon, and her young children were exiles. The same year Isabella had to mourn the loss of her young cousin, the gallant Ferrante of Naples, and she had the bitter disappointment of seeing her husband disgraced and dismissed from his post of Captain-General, on a suspicion of treason.

Through all her troubles she never lost her eager interest in art, and the collection of beautiful things. She had friends in every city who kept her informed of every event of interest, such as the bringing out of notable books or fine editions, the works issued from great studios, excavations, sales of collections. Her treasures overflowed from her "studiolo," and she arranged or rebuilt an exquisite suite of rooms, the world-renowned Studio of the Grotta. As de Maulde tells us: "She cherished in undisturbed harmony the Sleeping Cupid of Michelangelo and a choice collection of antique statues; she covered her walls with the works of Mantegna, Costa, and Correggio; Leonardo da Vinci and Titian were her portrait painters; she herself painted her soul in two words: 'Neither by hope nor by fear.' As an ideal for life and an emblem for her house, she commissioned of the great idealist master, Perugino, a Combat between Love and Chastity, and wished to arrange its composition to the minutest details. . . ."

Not until 1500, ten years after her marriage, was her first son born, to her great joy and pride, and henceforth the little Federico is the centre of all her hopes and affections. With her usual diplomacy she chose the all-powerful Cæsar Borgia as one of his sponsors, and she seems to have remained in high favour with him. Within two years after, she was selected to receive his sister, Lucrezia Borgia, when she came as a bride to Ferrara. It must be owned that this marriage of her brother Alfonso was extremely distasteful to her, but she made no sign, and acted her part to perfection. On this occasion her misgivings were not realised, for after her stormy past the Pope's daughter seems to have won respect and affection in her new position. She never forgot the gracious courtesy of her sister-in-law, and always looked up to her with admiration, as her letters bear witness.

Untouched by a breath of scandal herself, Isabella seems to have had large claims upon her tolerance. Amongst the refugees whom she received with hospitality after the fall of Milan, were the two mistresses of Duke Lodovico, Cecilia Gallerani and Lucrezia Crivelli. Her own husband was by no means faultless, and seems to have shocked even the lax feeling of that age, by appearing at a tournament at Brescia with a certain Teodora, in splendid attire, when his relations with her were a matter of notoriety. There were troubles, too, in after years, with some of her maids-of-honour, but she always behaved with wise and kindly discretion.

About this time we hear of a delightful visit to Venice, when Isabella and her friend the Duchess of Urbino travelled incognito, with only two ladies, in order to avoid the inevitable entertainments, and to enjoy themselves in their own way. With what longing they must have looked back upon that happy time, for only a few months later, the treacherous Cæsar Borgia seized Urbino, drove the duke and his wife into exile, and, with characteristic promptness, carried off the art treasures of that magnificent palace, to the value of close upon half a million.

The Marchesa of Mantua receives her friends, is deeply distressed at their misfortunes, but writes at once to secure an antique Venus and a Cupid, which she has long desired, from the spoils. One person's calamity is the opportunity of another.

The death of the Pope soon after, put an end to the Borgia power, and it is a satisfaction to know that Guidobaldo and his wife returned in triumph to Urbino—but Isabella kept the Venus.

In the year 1505 a second son was born to her, Ercole, the future Cardinal; and her daughter Leonora was betrothed to Francesco, the nephew and heir of the Duke of Urbino. Her letters of this period are all very full of the wondertul sayings and doings of her son Federico, but she scarcely mentions his sisters. As we are specially interested in the women of the Renaissance, it may be interesting to mention that on the birth of Leonora her mother received a splendid cradle, but she never used it for her girls, and only the baby boy was considered worthy of it.

When Federico was seven years old, she took him with her to Milan, there to meet as a matter of policy King Louis XII. of France, in the ducal palace where her sister had once reigned, and Lodovico, who was then a prisoner at Loches. A few years later a great misfortune awaited her. Her husband, who had taken an active part in the renewed wars, was made prisoner by the Venetians, with all the costly furnishing of his camp, his horses, and his fine suits of armour. It is curious to read how, in her despair, Isabella consulted priests, lawyers, and astrologers. The answer which she received with regard to the conjunction of the star of Jove and the dragon's head is extremely curious, as she is told to say her prayers at that exact moment.

But for thirteen long weary months poor Francesco was kept in the dreary prison at Venice, and when he was at length released, his precious son had to be sent as a hostage to Rome. Meantime his wife had governed Mantua with great ability, and used every effort by diplomacy and immense bribes to obtain the release of the Marquis. In order to gratify the Pope she hastened the marriage of her daughter, who was warmly welomed to Urbino, after the usual floods and narrow escapes on the journey ; for all these grand weddings seem to have taken place in the winter.

After this, we hear a great deal in the letters about the boy Federico's life in Rome, where he appears to have become a great favourite with the masterful old Pope Julius II., that indomitable fighter whose life was one long battle. During three years this precocious child was the spoilt darling of the brilliant society which filled the halls of the Vatican, and much as his mother wrote about his studies, they seem to have been quite secondary to his amusements. Nothing was too costly or too sumptuous for him, and Isabella pawned her jewels to supply the needed outlay. He would ride by the Pope's side on State occasions, in a magnificent suit of white satin, brocaded with gold embroidered letters, wearing a sword and cuirass, with a velvet cap and sweeping feathers fastened by a diamond clasp. We can fancy him bowing with courtly grace to acknowledge the cheers of the populace.

On the death of his patron, the boy returned home to Mantua, and did not see the splendid festivities of the Coronation of the new Medici Pope, Leo X. Many changes occurred after this. Alfonso of Ferrara made his peace with Rome, and the young son of Beatrice d'Este, Maximilian Sforza, ruled at Milan in the palace of his father, to the great content of Isabella. But his triumph was of short duration, for in 1515 he was compelled to abdicate finally in favour of Francis I.

She had much anxiety at this time about the health of her husband, who never recovered from his captivity at Venice, and who seems to have been querulous and irritable, always ready to find fault with those around him. A Venetian ambassador, who paid him a visit, gives a very curious account of finding the invalid sitting in a splendid chamber, with a great fire burning on the hearth, surrounded by his pets. A number of hawks and falcons in leash were about the room, immense greyhounds lying at his feet, with his favourite dwarf in gold brocade, while the walls were hung with portraits of his horses and dogs. Nothing gave him so much pleasure as the loan of a new jester, or contriving some rough practical joke. But when death came not long after, he made a devout end, and by his special wish he was buried in the habit of a Franciscan, and laid to rest in the church of San Francesco. Letters of condolence came from all parts of the world, one of the most interesting being from Lucrezia Borgia, who herself only survived the Marquis of Mantua two months.

His son Federico, who succeeded him, was just nineteen, and he must have made a handsome picture as, clothed in white, he rode out of the Castello to receive the sceptre at the gate of the cathedral.

The next year, Federico was appointed Captain-General of the Church, a great honour, which gladdened the heart of his mother, although the condition attached to it by Pope Leo X. was that the exiled family from Urbino should leave Mantua, for again the tide of war had turned against the Gonzaga family, and Elisabetta, with her son Duke Francesco Maria and his wife, Isabella's daughter, had taken refuge in her palace. But before the end of that year, 1521, the Pope himself died, and all was changed. The exiles returned with great joy to Urbino, where their people welcomed them with the old enthusiasm.

Meantime Isabella had her time fully occupied with affairs of State, where her counsel was needed more than ever, and in the ever-delightful task of arranging and decorating her *suite* of splendid new apartments in the Corte Vecchio, which was called her "Paradiso." She took the same keen interest in collecting more antiques, statues, and bas-reliefs, and in the minutest details of plenishing and adornment. But all this did not exhaust her marvellous energy, and her thoughts were much occupied with the future of her second son, Ercole, for whom she had chosen the Church as a profession, and who at fifteen was already a bishop. But her ambition went far beyond this; and the first step in his upward career would be an excellent education, so she decided to send him to Bologna, which had famous scholars, and where the university was in high repute. He had inherited his mother's love of learning and did well at Bologna, where he remained until the death of the great master, Messer

Pietro Pomponazzi, when he continued his studies at Mantua.

As years went on, Isabella does not seem to have lost any of her keen interest and delight in travel. In 1523 she paid another visit to Venice with her brother Alfonso, and her great friend and constant correspondent, Castiglione. As of old, she was never weary of visiting churches and picture galleries, meeting Titian and other artists and men of letters, not to mention making friends with the new Doge, whom she saw enthroned. Two years later she decided to go to Rome, that by her personal influence she might at length obtain the much-desired Cardinal's hat for her son Ercole. This was in February, and on the way she heard the news of that great victory of Pavia, where Francis I. was defeated and taken prisoner. At Rome she found Pope Clement VII. in terror of the Emperor, and only too glad to make close friends with the Court of Mantua. He even presented to Federico, Raphael's portrait of Leo X., and showed the greatest kindness to the Marchesa, who had established herself in the Colonna Palace on the Quirinal. As usual, she at once became the centre of a delightful literary coterie, she visited everything, and must have been perfectly happy in being at the very fountain-head of all discovery of antiques.

It was while Isabella was in Rome, that she heard of the death of her dearest friend, Elisabetta, Duchess of Urbino, whose loss was one of the greatest sorrows of her life.

Meanwhile, important events were happening in Italy, where, after the Treaty of Madrid, war broke out again with more violence than ever. But Isabella still remained in the splendid palace with its sunny gardens, following out all her wonted pursuits; and she had been more than two years in Rome when suddenly the blow fell. Duke Charles of Bourbon with the Imperialist troops, encamped under the very walls one Sunday in May 1527; an attack was made, the leader was killed, but his wild and savage army stormed the walls, and the hapless city was given up to pillage and destruction during three awful days. The Pope and most of the cardinals fled to the Castel St. Angelo, and escaped only with their lives, for all the priceless treasures of the Vatican were ruthlessly sacked and carted away. Isabella d'Este herself was safe, for she had kinsmen and friends in the invading army, and amongst them her son Ferrante. The crowd of distinguished people who found a refuge under her roof were compelled to pay a heavy ransom; Gregorovius gives the number as 1200 ladies and 1000 citizens. But she must have had a fearful time during that week in the Palazzo Colonna, before she was able to escape with a strong guard to the galleys, which took her safely to Ostia.

Leaving desolation and ruin behind her, the indomitable lady had yet one satisfaction, she bore away with her the Cardinal's hat for her son Ercole, which the Pope, in his desperate need for money, had sold to her for 40,000 ducats, when Bourbon was already under the walls of Rome.

The Marchesa found her beloved Mantua ravaged by famine and plague, which spread all over northern Italy. Again she pledged her jewels, and did all in her power to help the poor people, of whom we are told that nearly one-third fell victims to the pestilence.

But she still found means to add to her treasure, although one galley laden with spoils was taken by pirates.

"For all these little vexations, those were glorious days!" exclaims de Maulde. "What a lucky windfall the sack of Rome was to collectors!"

That was the true Renaissance spirit, and a while later we find Titian on a visit to Mantua, admiring the treasures of Isabella, and painting her famous portrait, in which she wears that wonderful turban-shaped cap which had been her favourite head-dress for twenty years. We next meet this indispensable lady at Ferrara, where once again it falls to her lot to receive and welcome a distinguished bride. It was a quarter of a century since the days of Lucrezia Borgia, and now the coming princess is Renée of France, daughter of Louis XII., and sister-in-law of King Francis I. Truly a great marriage for the son of the Duke of Ferrara.

As usual there were splendid festivities, but the time was unfortunate, for Ferrara, too, had been ravaged by the plague, and the unlucky city was once more on the point of war. But the next year, when the victorious Emperor arranged to meet the Pope and to be crowned at Bologna with the iron crown of Lombardy, Isabella d'Este had so many interests at stake that, aware of her own personal influence, she felt it her duty to be present at this great meeting, and went thither in great state and splendour. She was justified by the event, for she was entirely successful, both in mediation for her brother and her nephew of Milan, and also in obtaining for her son great favour with the Emperor, and the coveted title of Duke of Mantua.

Those three resplendent years which the young Federico spent at the Papal Court seem to have weakened his moral fibre, for he had entered into relations, unsanctioned by the Church, with one Isabella Boschetti, although he had been twice unwillingly betrothed. But now an opportunity presented itself for a splendid marriage with Margherita Paleologa, the heiress of Monferrato, and through his mother's successful diplomacy, all difficulties were overcome. With a stately escort of a thousand men, the Duke of Mantua rode to Casale, the ancient capital of Monferrato, and the wedding was celebrated with the usual pomp and magnificence. A few years later the bride came into her rich dowry, which was added to the duchy of Mantua, a princely inheritance for her little son born in 1533.

Was ever woman so favoured by fortune as Madonna Isabella? Every project of hers was crowned by success; she had but to form a wish and straightway it was gratified. To the last she kept up her enthusiasm for all beautiful things, for travel, for art, for poetry. She spent much time in her exquiste villa at Porto, and was never weary of adding to the choice flowers and shrubs of the terraced gardens. Surrounded by her friends, with frequent visits from her children and her grandchildren, she lived gaily and happily to the end. She died on February 13, 1539, and the world was the poorer by her loss.

We feel that for one who had laid up so much treasure here below, it must have been hard to lose it all—to die, and leave her earthly "Paradiso." But did some instinct tell her that she would bequeath an undying memory to the world of culture, that she would awaken the passionate envy of art-lovers yet unborn, and that she would go down to posterity as the most perfect flower of the Italian Renaissance?

RENÉE, DUCHESS OF FERRARA, AND OLYMPIA MORATA

WE cannot turn away from the Lombard cities of the plain, without a few pages on the subject of Renée of France, who for the greater part of her life was Duchess of Ferrara. She was daughter of Louis XII. and Anne de Bretagne, and was brought up at the French Court with her cousin Margaret, who became Queen of Navarre, and distinguished as a Platonist and a poetess. Both the young girls seem to have been drawn towards the new spirit of religious thought which was spreading over Europe, but their feelings were somewhat vague and speculative at that time, and they had no idea of rebellion against the powers of the Roman Church.

After the successful campaign of the French army in Italy, the Duke of Ferrara renewed his old friendship with King Francis I., and asked the hand of his sister-in-law, Renée, for his eldest son Ercole. This would appear to us rather a descent for a daughter of France, who seems, indeed, to have held this view herself; but, probably from reasons of policy, the marriage contract was signed, and on June 28, 1528, the wedding took place in Paris, at the Sainte Chapelle, with much magnificence.

We are not told the first impression which the princess made upon her bridegroom when she was presented to him, for she was very different in appearance from the beautiful women of his own family, being short and deformed, with a plain face and delicate health. Still it was a great match for him, and he could doubtless appreciate her intelligence and literary tastes. For the Court of his father at Ferrara, in which he had been brought up, was exceptionally gay and brilliant. Titian, Bellini, and other great painters were at his service to paint pictures for him or decorate his palace walls. Men of letters and poets were welcomed at his table, and the saying went that "Ferrara had as many poets as there were frogs in the country round." Most notable among them was Ariosto, whose "Orlando Furioso" told with splendid satire the passing away of the Mediæval Age, and the coming of the new vivid inquiring spirit of the Renaissance. It is possible that the thought of this polished circle of art and literature may have had its attraction for Renée.

When all the balls and hunting parties at St. Germain and Fontainebleau were over, the wedding party set out towards Italy in September. They proposed to travel by slow stages through Lyons, Turin, Parma, Reggio, and Modena, and did not expect to arrive at Ferrara before the middle of November. Great preparations were made to welcome the bridal pair, and the Duke of Ferrara, mindful of his sister's tact and kindness on the arrival of his own bride, Lucrezia Borgia, a quarter of a century before, begged Isabella of Mantua to help him in the reception. This was to take place at Modena, where the bride made her entry in great state, with much ringing of bells, and salvoes, and flare of trumpets, and enthusiasm. But the young princess must have appreciated most of all, the gracious presence and earnest friendliness of the Marchesa. After a fortnight spent in festivities, the bride and bridegroom spent a night at the beautiful palace of the Belvedere, which Duke Alfonso had built. It was situated on an island in the river, and has been made famous by Ariosto in the "Orlando." It was a dream of beauty, with its stately terraces and exquisite gardens, its orange groves and fountains, and its chapel painted by Dossi.

The next day they set sail in the great decorated bucentaur, and arrived at the river gate of Ferrara, where they were received by Ippolito, the Archbishop of Milan, Ercole's brother, the ambassadors, and all the clergy, and others who escorted them to the cathedral. The streets were hung with banners, and a large company of pages in black satin and pink, attended the cortege. Renée was carried in a crimson litter with a baldacchino of gold, and her ladies followed in chariots. The bride was presented with the keys of the city in a silver bowl, in the Piazza del Duomo, which was thronged with eager spectators, although the city had but recently been ravaged by the plague. On arriving at that huge fortress palace of Este, which stands four-square in the centre of Ferrara, Renée was led by the hand up the great marble staircase, in her gorgeous wedding dress of gold brocade and a priceless necklace of pearls, wearing a golden crown on her head. In the tapestried hall she received costly wedding presents from the ambassadors, while the chief merchants of Ferrara prayed her acceptance of oxen, goats, fowls, cheeses, and other articles of food, which waited below in the vast courtyard.

Poor princess! One wonders if in all her gorgeous array, she had misgivings as to the difference between herself and the Italian ladies, in their matchless charm and beauty. Did she remember hearing, as a child, that her wise mother, the Sovereign Lady of Brittany in her own right, had been dissuaded from paying a much-desired visit to Italy for this very reason? Her husband, King Louis XII., had frankly warned her that the very sight of such magnificent princesses as Isabella d'Este and Lucrezia Borgia would "crush her to the ground!"

It is rather touching to hear that Anne, Queen of France, she who "was so glorious of soul," meekly expressed her willingness to wear only "black or tan cloth and no fine robes," not to enter into rivalry with those ladies. In the end, however, the journey was given up, and she never saw Italy.

Renée does not seem to have made a very favourable impression at the court of Duke Alfonso. Probably she was shy and awkward in the middle of all these strangers whose language she could not understand, and she clung to the company of her French attendants, more especially to that Madame de Soubise who caused so much trouble in after years. The only Italian she took into her service was her secretary, Bernardo Tasso, the father of the famous poet.

More festivities followed, but in rather a half-hearted manner we gather, and the Marchesa of Mantua seems to have been very weary of them. There were quintain races, on which the court ladies and gentlemen looked down from the balconies, there was much dancing, and there were state representations of the comedies of Ariosto and some French plays in honour of the bride. Of one great entertainment given to welcome her, such full details have come down to posterity, that for once it will be worth while giving them, to bring before us a banquet of the Renaissance.

In the great hall painted by Titian, Bellini, and Dosso Dossi, a hundred illustrious guests sat round a splendid table, on which were rows of great figures, most ingeniously and artistically designed out of sugar and gilding, of the Olympian gods and goddesses. In the centre was a striking group of Hercules strangling the lion, in compliment to the name of the bridegroom. With the next course another composition was placed on the table, of Hercules grappling with the Hydra; and again another appeared, of the taming of the Minotaur by the same hero. Meantime the table groaned with the weight of great silver dishes, piled up with all the dainties of the age. Amongst these we may notice fish of many kinds richly stuffed, peacocks roast whole with the tail outpread, roast meats and galantine, boiled capons with spices, small chickens garnished with sugar and rosewater, quails and wild fowl, caramels made of pine seeds, and every variety of tarts and pasties and sweetmeats. Wines of the rarest vintage filled great silver jars and flasks, and were constantly handed round. Each course was brought in headed by a band of musicians, playing the lyre, viol, and harp, and singing rondeaux and madrigals, while the organ softly accompanied them from afar.

At the end of the banquet, the choicest and most costly perfumes were handed round, and a great golden pasty was placed on the table, full of exquisite jewels, for which the ladies drew lots. We do not wonder after all this, that wedding festivities often left a State impoverished for years !

It must have been unfortunate for Renée that, almost immediately after her marriage, the armies of France began to lose ground in Italy, and one defeat after another led up to the Treaty of Cambray, when it seemed that Ferrara would be sacrificed to the Pope's vengeance. But the Duke hastened to do homage to the victorious Emperor, who took a great fancy to his lively wit—escorted him with much ceremony through his dominions, induced his sister to act as mediator at Bologna with the Pope, and the peril was averted. Alfonso seems to have behaved kindly to his daughter-in-law even when the alliance with her family had lost all political value. He sympathised with her literary tastes, but we do not know how far he could enter into her love for philosophy, geometry, and astronomy. From various parts of Italy distinguished scholars gathered round her Court, where she seems to have presided over an academy, which met in her apartments. Amongst her friends were many of the new school of thought, and when the spirit of intolerance in France drove reformers from their native land some of them took refuge at Ferrara. Clement Marot, who has been called the first poet of modern France, was a guest of hers. He had written a nuptial hymn in honour of her, and he spoke of her as "Ce noble cœur de Renée de France." It was Marot who with the curious fantastic taste of the age, thus addressed the yet unborn child of the Duchess Renée : "You will find a century in which you can quickly learn all that a child can understand. Come then boldly, and when you grow older, you will find something better still: you will find a war already begun—the war against ignorance and its insensate troops." He also addressed these lines to Marguerite of Navarre, with regard to Renée, Duchess of Ferrara:

"Ha! Marguerite, escoute la souffrance
Du noble cœur de Renée de France;
Puis comme sœur plus fort que d'esperance
Console—la.
Tu sais comment hors son pays alla,
Et que parents et amis laissa la,
Mais tu ne sais quel traitement elle a
En terre estrange.

"Elle ne voit ceult a qui se veult plaindre,
Son œil rayant si loing ne peut attaindre;
Et puis les monts pour ce bien lui estaindre
Sont entre deux."

Calvin himself remained with Renée for a time before he settled in Geneva, and he continued a friendly correspondence with her until his death.

She seems to have spent much of her time in the country house of the Este princes, the Schifanoia or Sans Souci, which had been decorated by Cosimo Tura with celebrated pictures of pastoral and hunting scenes. She had a gay and brilliant life now that Ferrara was once more in peace and prosperity. We hear of many entertainments, and a description of the costumes of the ladies from the novelist Stabellino. On one occasion Renée wore a blue satin gown with a high French collar, with sleeves slashed to show a white chemisette, a little black velvet cap with a white feather on her head, and a gold fillet. Her ladies were dressed, some in black satin, others in crimson, with the same velvet caps. There appears to have been great interest shown as to whether Madame de Soubise would persuade her to wear the French mode instead of the Italian. This lady was a very bad adviser, and, after being the cause of much scandal, was ultimately sent back to France in disgrace.

The first child of the young Duchess was a daughter, whom she called Anna, after her own mother, Anne de Bretagne, and this child seems to have been a special favourite with Isabella d'Este, whom she greatly resembled in appearance and character. There was an early portrait of the Marchesa, which she lent her nephew to be copied, as it proved to be so strikingly like his little girl, who was destined in after years to marry Duke Francis of Guise, the most famous of his race. In November 1533 there were great rejoicings at the birth of a son, who was christened Alfonso, after his grandfather, and had the Pope Clement VII. for his sponsor. Both of these old enemies died the following year, when Ercole and his wife became the reigning Duke and Duchess.

Isabella d'Este seems to have kept up her connection with Ferrara, for we hear of her going there to spend the carnival two years later, to cheer the spirits of Renée, who was ill after the birth of her daughter Lucrezia. The Marchesa writes to tell her son about her visit: "To-day I arrived here half an hour after nightfall, and was received by the Duke and many nobles and ladies on the river bank. They escorted me with lighted torches to my lodgings. . . . Soon after I visited the Duchess, who has had a touch of fever, but not serious, and then went into the hall to see the dancing begin."

Later she writes that the Duke Ercole has given a great supper, "which was followed by a concert of excellent and varied music, and afterwards by dancing till bedtime." Another very curious letter of Isabella's is preserved, written to a court lady with regard to her famous dwarfs, whose suite of apartments may still be seen at Mantua:

"It was a promise of mine to give Madame Renée the first girl born to my dwarfs. The 'puttina' has now reached the age of two, and doubtless will continue to be a dwarf, though she hardly promises to be so small as my Delia. She can now walk alone without a guide, if the Duchess desires to have her."

Vittoria Colonna, Marchioness of Pescara, was drawn towards Renée through similarity of tastes, and paid her frequent visits at Ferrara. She was godmother to her youngest daughter, Leonora, made immortal by the love of Tasso. On this occasion Vittoria was anxious to enlist her friend's interest in that wonderful man, about whom opinions have differed so much, Fra Bernardino Ochino. He was a monk, and for three years general of the Capuchins, "fiery, proud, austere, with large bloodless face and long, shaggy white beard." His sermons had created quite an enthusiasm in Rome, where most of the Sacred College had flocked to hear him. But he was a man of rare mental independence, and his writings soon verged towards heresy, notably the "Dialogi."

We have another glimpse of the young Duchess in those days, or rather of her little six-year-old daughter on the occasion of more carnival fêtes. "Signora Anna played some pieces most excellently on the gravicembalo." Then the dwarfs, Morgentino and Delia, jumped and danced together, and Signora Anna joined them and danced several dances "alla gagliarda," which gave the Marchesa di Pescara and the Duke and every one the greatest pleasure. We were convinced that if the goddess Nature had danced before us she could not have danced in more perfect time or more exquisite taste."

In 1540, when Anna d'Este was only nine years old, Calcagnini thus wrote to her in Latin: "I have read the fables you have translated from the Tuscan into Latin, in an elegant and ornate style, as becomes a royal hand. On finishing the perusal I had only to regret that it was so soon ended. . . . I trust that these essays may be the seed of future compositions which will reflect honour on your name. I have already the pleasure of applauding these first steps on the path to fame."

Renée took the greatest interest in the education of her children, and when Anna was ten years old she selected as her companion and teacher, Olympia Morata, a most accomplished girl, only two years older than her pupil. She was the daughter of a professor in the university, Pelligrino Morata, and she had been taught all the learning of that day, was well versed in Greek and Latin literature, and was engaged in the study of rhetoric or public speaking. What progress Signora Anna made in this we do not know, but we hear that Olympia, at the age of fourteen, wrote Latin letters and dialogues in Greek and Latin in the style of Plato and Cicero, and that when she was scarcely sixteen she was asked to give lectures in the University of Ferrara on the philosophical problems of the "Paradoxes" of

Cicero. She was listened to with respect and critical admiration; but before long religious questions became of serious importance. Hitherto the spirit of Italian culture had been full of tolerance, but now the gulf between the old opinions and the new had grown wider, the Renaissance Popes were compelled to take strong measures, and the Inquisition set out in earnest to purge the land of heresy. France had become more Catholic under Henri II., who looked with suspicion on the freedom of thought encouraged by his aunt Renée. He joined with the Pope in requesting the Duke of Ferrara to put an end to heresy at his Court. Ercole had no wish to make political enemies, so he dismissed Olympia from the education of his children, drove away all Lutherans from the city, and insisted upon the outward orthodoxy of his wife.

It will be interesting to make a slight digression in order to see what became of this learned lady. Not yet twenty on her father's death, she was the only support of a delicate mother, three sisters, and a brother, all younger than herself. At this time she writes:

"I do not regret the fugitive pleasures which I have lost. God has kindled in me a desire to dwell in that heavenly home in which it is more pleasant to abide for one day, than a thousand years in the courts of princes." Two years later, Olympia married a young German doctor who was studying medicine at the university, and they found it necessary to leave Ferrara and make a home in Germany. She was devoted to her husband, but her short life was full of anxiety and trouble, and she died at Heidelburg at the age of twenty-nine. Her husband gives such a touching description of her end that it is worthy of record.

"When she was almost dying, waking a little out of sleep, I saw her look pleased and smile softly. I went nearer and asked her why she smiled so sweetly. 'I saw just now,' she said, 'a quiet place filled with the fairest and clearest light.' When she could speak no more through weakness. 'Courage,' I said, 'dear wife; in that fair light you will dwell.' Again she smiled and nodded her head. A little while afterwards she said, 'I am quite happy.' When next she spoke her eyes were already dim, 'I can scarcely see you any longer,' she said, 'but everything seems to me full of the most beautiful flowers.' They were her last words. Soon after, as if overcome by sweet sleep, she breathed forth her soul."

To return to Ferrara, Olympia must long have been a tender memory and a surviving influence with her pupils. We hear of them, when still under fifteen, as being sufficiently advanced to act a comedy of Terence before Pope Paul III., when he paid a visit to their father. The great Venetian scholar, Pietro Bembo, must often have spoken to them of his old friend, Olympia; he who said, "A little girl should learn Latin; it gives a finishing touch to her charm."

It is a very remarkable episode in the history of Ferrara that a reigning duchess should be an enthusiastic lover of the Reformation—that religious revolution which was to spread over the world, and deliver it from a Church of which the Borgia, the Rovere, and the Medici had been chief. Yet her courage was fatal to the happiness of the poor lady herself. Her husband placed her in a convent in the year 1554, but the noble princess remained absolutely faithful to her religious faith. When the Inquisition had succeeded in stifling the reforming spirit in Ferrara, and her son Alfonso was the reigning duke, she went back to France, where she lived at the Castle of Montarges, surrounded by her Huguenot friends, until her death in 1575.

DAUGHTERS OF VENICE.

CATERINA CORNARO, QUEEN OF CYPRUS.

BIANCA CAPELLO, GRAND DUCHESS OF TUSCANY.

HISTORICAL SUMMARY.

1454. Birth of Caterina Cornaro.

1468. Betrothal of Caterina Cornaro to Giacomo, King of Cyprus.

1472. Marriage of Caterina and Giacomo.

1473. Birth of a son to the Queen of Cyprus. He died the next year.

1477. Turks ravaged Friuli; defeated Venice.

1479. Venice made peace with the Ottomans, after fifteen years war.

1482. Sixtus IV. made a league with Venice to despoil House of Este. The Pope made peace with Este, and excommunicated Venice. Venice continued the war till the Treaty of Bagnolo secured her much Este property.

1489. Caterina resigns the crown of Cyprus to the Republic.

1509. League of Cambray. The Pope, Emperor, and Kings of France and Spain were against Venice, who was defeated at Aignadello. Venice made peace with the Pope and Spain, and defeated the Emperor Maximilian at Padua.

1510. Death of Caterina Cornaro, late Queen of Cyprus.

1548. Birth of Bianca Capello.

1563. Flight of Bianca Capello from Venice. Her marriage to Pietro Bonaventuri.

1565. Marriage of Francesco, son of Cosimo, Grand Duke of Tuscany, to Giovanna of Austria, sister of Maximilian II.

1574. Death of the Grand Duke Cosimo. Francesco succeeds him.

1576. Murder of Isabella dei Medici (Orsini).

1577. Birth of Filippo, son of Giovanna of Austria.

1578. Death of the Grand Duchess Giovanna.

1578. Marriage of the Grand Duke Francesco with Bianca Capello.

1582. Death of Filippo, son of the Grand Duke.

1587. Death of the Grand Duke Francesco and his wife, Bianca Capello, at Poggio a Cajano.

CATERINA CORNARO, QUEEN OF CYPRUS.

THE story of the Venetian maiden, suddenly called from her convent school to become the Queen of Cyprus, then returning to her peaceful home until such time as she sailed forth in stately pomp to her royal husband and her kingdom, is a picture so brightly vivid that it has all the charm of a fairy tale, and we follow, with breathless interest, the stirring adventures which befell her.

A few words on the history of Cyprus will be neces sary to explain its position in the middle of the fourteenth century. During three hundred years it had been in the peaceable possession of the descendants of Guy de Lusignan, the expelled King of Jerusalem, to whom our Richard I. had given it after the Third Crusade. He had become King of Jerusalem by marriage with Sibylle, the widowed daughter of Baldwin IV. Giovanni III. of Lusignan died in 1458, leaving the kingdom of Cyprus to Carlotta, his only legitimate child, who married her cousin Louis, Count of Geneva, second son of the Duke of Savoy and Anna of Cyprus. She was solemnly crowned at Lefkosia or Nicosia in 1460, but before many months her half-brother, Giacomo, natural son of the late king, had defeated and deposed her, with the aid of the Sultan of Egypt and his Mamelukes.

Having taken possession of the island, and caused himself to be crowned, Giacomo II. felt the importance of making a durable alliance with his powerful neighbours the Venetians, and he therefore sent a formal embassy to the Doge and Signoria, asking them to bestow upon him a Venetian maiden of good birth as his bride. We may imagine the flutter in the dovecotes of the city, and the careful consideration needed before the grave and reverend statesmen could make a suitable selection. At length the choice fell upon Caterina, the young daughter of the great Venetian merchant, Marco Cornaro, who, with two other patrician houses, happened to hold most of the island of Cyprus in mortgage.

The little girl, who had never been heard of before outside her own family, was born on Santa Caterina's day, 1454, and received the name of her patron saint. Her father must have been of noble birth, for in the archives of the city he is called Kavalier Marco Cornaro, and the name of his wife was Fiorenza Crispo. Their eldest daughter Violante married Marco Dandolo, and Caterina was sent at ten years old to be educated at the convent of San Benedetto at Padua. When the decision of the Signoria was made known, she suddenly became a person of much importance, and returned home at once to prepare for the great event. The chronicles of the day give a very full account of the espousals, which were celebrated with splendid pomp. Her father's home was at San Polo, in the centre of Venice, not far from the Frari, and here, on July 30, 1468, there came a stately company of forty patrician matrons, in the richest velvets and brocades, to fetch the destined bride, and accompany her in the Doge's own barge all down the gaily decorated Grand Canal, amid the eager curiosity of the pleasure-loving people, to the Ducal Palace. Here another group of noble Venetian ladies awaited her at the foot of the great staircase and conducted her into the Council Chamber. An eye-witness declares that "he had never seen so beautiful a child, and described her as being of middle height, though she looked tall in the magnificent robes covered with jewels, which set off her full round figure. She had soft black eyes, an open brow, a milky complexion, and the rich golden hair so much esteemed in Venice.

There was a distinguished assembly present to witness the marriage ceremony, and the Doge Christoforo Moro presented a consecrated ring to the Cyprian ambassador, who placed it on Caterina's finger, "in the name of Jacopo II. di Lusignano, re di Cipro, d'Armenia, e di Gerusalemme." Her dowry was fixed at the princely sum of 100,000 ducats, and it was decided by the Republic that a picture of the bride should be painted and sent to the King of Cyprus.

It must have been indeed an eventful day for this maiden of fourteen, to be taken from the quiet life at San Benedetto, to change her plain black dress for brocades and costly jewels, and to find herself the chief actress in a dramatic ceremony of such grandeur and importance. A simple little girl in the morning, she returns home at night a queen, at least in name. When she was back at home with her mother in that sunny Campo San Polo, while the husband she had never seen was far off fighting the Turks, Caterina must have been tempted to think at times that nothing had really changed, and that it was all a dream of the night.

The young bride had to wait four years before anything happened, and meantime Giacomo, under the influence of Ferdinand of Naples, was very much disposed to break off the alliance with Venice, and seek a wife elsewhere. However, after much negotiation, and no doubt strong language from the Republic, the King of Cyprus came to a better mind, and the day was fixed for the departure of Caterina.

Nothing was wanting in splendour for this festal voyage of thirteen hundred miles, and immense preparations had been made, for the bride took with her several members of her family, and a stately suite of ladies in waiting, attendants, and servants. Four magnificent Venetian galleys had been specially fitted up for her use, and on a sunny morning in late summer of the year 1472 she set forth on that triumphal expedition. We can trace her route to-day, on that changeless highway of the ocean, through many leagues of rippling waves, down the whole length of the Adriatic, past the ancient towered cities on the coast of Romagna and the Abruzzi, with many a rest and break on the way, through the Straits of Otranto, into the blue waters of the Mediterranean, skirting round the storied isles of Greece; onwards, ever onwards, driven hither and thither by the caprice of the wind, until at length, after two months' voyage, the great ships put in at Beyrout on the coast of Phœnicia. Beyond them rose those fabled peaks of Asia Minor, where Apollo and Pan made the flute discourse sweet music in the Phrygian highlands, while away to the north-west, beyond the snows of Lebanon, the wild swans of Ovid died in music, amid the reedy shallows of the Maeander. But at such a moment of eager expectation, dreams of the past would be swallowed up in the living present, for the young Queen of Cyprus was about to make her royal entry into her kingdom. Again she embarked, this time for the short voyage across to the port of Larnaca, and before her, like an island of enchantment, her future domain lay stretched on the horizon, a bank of misty blue, with gleams of light and stains of purple that told of headland and cliff, shining here and there like crags of amethyst. On the near shore, at the very edge of the water, minaret and campanile seemed to rise glimmering above the white dwellings, encircled to the east by an emerald grove of palm trees. Here beyond the open roadstead an escort awaited the travellers, with litters and mules for riding, and beasts of burden to carry all the magnificent trousseau and furnishing of the Venetian bride. It was still a journey of many hours, through a wild bare country, with undulating ridges and rocky boulders and broad marshy levels, bounded in the distance by purple mountains, until at length the capital, Nicosia, rose before them, that city of the crusaders, with its palaces, and mediæval churches, and minarets and temples of the old Greeks. Here with great solemnity Caterina made her entrance, splendidly dressed, with King Giacomo riding by her side, until the gay procession streamed into the palace of the Lusignan kings.

If there had been misgivings as to the warmth of her reception, they melted away at once, for her dazzling beauty triumphed over all. Her new life spread out before her as an endless vista of festal scenes and gay entertainments, in that delicious balmy climate, where even winter had no terrors.

It must have been like a vision of dreamland, that grand old castle with its sumptuous interior, of oriental colour and design, in the midst of its spice gardens and tropical flowers, and shady groves of palms and mulberry trees. All around were white Corinthian porticoes side by side with Greek basilicas and Gothic churches; while the streets were the scene of splendid pageants, and the markets full of all that wealth and luxury could desire. Caterina must have loved to hear the story and tradition of her classic isle; of its connection with ancient Egypt and of Greece; with Solomon and Haroun-al-Raschid; with Crusaders and Knights Templars; of the Byzantine Dukes of Cyprus who had built that very palace, and the love story of her husband's ancestor, Guy de Lusignan and the Princess Sibylle. Could she ever weary of hearing how the chivalry of the West inherited the romance of the East?

Then how full of charm and contrast to the convent-bred girl—whose out-door life was once limited to a demure walk in the shady gardens of the Monasterio at Padua—must it have been to set forth with a gallant cavalcade, hawking or hunting in the broad plains around. Or at times, with greater daring, she may have gone farther afield, when for her the "Queen's Lodging" was added to the Castle of St. Hilarion, on that rude mountain height where Richard Cœur-de-Lion once planted his standard. From thence she could hunt in the great forests beyond, still haunted by the legend of Adonis, and where still roamed the wild boars whose forerunner had slain the peerless youth. In verse and song, the fair young Queen of Cyprus had herself been likened to that Venus who rose from yonder sapphire waves, and chose for her ancient home the Mount Olympus of that sea-girt isle.

But those happy days were all too brief, and within a year her joy and triumph were changed to mourning. Her husband, Giacomo, had gone out on a hunting expedition, in the neighbourhood of Famagusta, and had been killed, and brought home to her dead. It must have been a fearful shock ; but Caterina kept up her courage, and took all needful steps to protect the throne, for the sake of her unborn child. A Council of Regency was appointed, for the island became at once in a state of unrest, and the news was sent to Venice, where steps were immediately taken for the protection of the queen, troops being sent to fortify and garrison the important fortresses of the island.

As for poor Caterina herself, all her thoughts and hopes were concentrated on the passionate desire that her child might be a son, to inherit his father's kingdom. She made pilgrimages and prayers to Saint Irene, and to St. Epiphanius, the good Bishop of Salamina, who had performed many miracles ; he was so pious and good ! She knew that there was a deadly conspiracy against her, that the partizans of Carlotta of Savoy were preparing a great effort ; but what did it matter ? If only an heir were born to her, God would protect the right.

As her biographer says, "stava apicato a un chavelo," her throne was on a volcano, and though many loved her, yet they were the gentle timid ones who could not protect her. One terrible day, the conspirators burst into the palace, forced their way to her presence, and her physician and one of her servants were murdered before her eyes. Her uncle, Andrea Cornaro, and a cousin who were hastening to her aid, were also put to death, and she herself had a narrow escape. But help was at hand, the expedition from Venice arrived, under the captain-general, Pietro Mocenigo; he put down the insurrection in the city, and hung the ring-leaders, who were ardent supporters of the Princess Carlotta of Savoy, and had hoped to place her on the throne.

On August 28, 1473, "al quatro hore de notte," the Queen of Cyprus gave birth to a son, born a king, and the happy mother forgot all her troubles in supreme content at the realisation of her fondest wishes. He was baptized on September 26, in the presence of General Mocenigo, the Venetian ambassador, and many other noble personages, and received the name of Giacomo III.

The Venetian Republic, with their usual astuteness, had sent with their army, two trusty Councillors and a Civil Commissioner to watch events, and obtain a firm grasp of the affairs of Cyprus. Caterina was too much absorbed in the care of her child to give her whole care to the government, and was glad of their help. But another sorrow was in store for her; her baby was scarcely a year old when he was taken from her by some sudden childish complaint, and she was left desolate indeed. The watchful Senators of Venice sent her father, Marco Cornaro, with his wife, Fiorenza, to comfort their bereaved daughter, and, at the same time they gave orders that the mother, sister and illegitimate son of Giacomo should be forthwith sent to

Venice. Marco Cornaro was also specially commissioned to keep the allegiance of the Cypriotes, and to take heed that there would be no change in the government. About this time a fresh conspiracy was entered into by the partisans of Carlotta of Savoy, and Ferdinand, King of Naples, sent a certain Rizzo di Mario to carry on the plot at Alexandria. But the Venetian government had received a warning, and they secured the person of Rizzo and carried him to Venice, where the Ten went through the form of a trial and condemned him to death. At this point, the Sultan, who had been friendly with the prisoner when he had gone to his Court as Ambassador, made a strong appeal in his favour, even going so far as to forbid the Republic to carry out the sentence. However, the unfortunate Rizzo di Mario was strangled in prison, and the Sultan was informed that he had taken poison in despair.

Meantime, Caterina continued to be the nominal mistress of Cyprus, and as her real power diminished, she seems to have gained ground in the sympathy of her people. As she was denied the joys and duties of a mother, her biographer tells us, she grew to care more and more for pomp and ceremony and the outward show of sovereignty. "She recalled to the Cypriotes those memories of independence which flattered their pride." And all the time, by means of the two Councillors and the Civil Commissioner, the Republic of Venice was slowly and surely gaining dominion of the whole island.

As time passed on, they gradually assumed absolute power, and the position became intolerable for the unfortunate queen. She wrote lamentable letters to the Doge of Venice, complaining of the insulting conduct and actual persecution of these envoys, both to her father and herself. And others in authority took their cue from them, for even the Archbishop, "without respect or reverence, would enter her chamber when he would," and she was constantly molested by brawls in her own palace. Years passed in this way, for with the achievement of their purpose certain in the end, the Senators of the Republic could afford to wait. At length, when the time was ripe for action, they won over to their side her brother Giorgio Cornaro, and sent him to persuade Caterina to abdicate in their favour. With him they also despatched General Diedo, with instructions that, "by wise and circumspect, cautious and secure means, they should get the queen on board a galley and bring her here to us at Venice."

This elaborate diplomacy was successful, and the unhappy lady yielded at length to persuasion and threats. Her brother had arrived on his mission in October 1488, but it was not until February 26, 1489, that the banner of St. Mark's floated over the castles of Cyprus.

An ambassador was at once sent to the Sultan of Egypt to announce that the event had taken place "with the full and free determination of our most serene and beloved daughter Caterina Cornaro," and also to ask for his friendly alliance. There is an Italian proverb, "A nemico che fugge, ponte d'oro," and so it was in this case. Magnificent fêtes and ceremonies were arranged in honour of the fallen queen, in which as much as 2000 ducats were freely spent. All the population of Nicosia found their way down to the shore to witness the departure of Caterina, which was of the most triumphal description. The Doge had sent his own state "Bucentaur," on which he was wont on Ascension Day to perform the solemn ceremony of wedding the sea. In this splendid wooden ship, with oars for many rowers, gorgeous with gilding and intaglio, and costly damask hangings, the poor deposed queen set forth on her homeward journey. With what other hopes had she passed that way more than sixteen years before, in her sumptuous youth and the gay prime of her beauty, now to return to the home of her childhood, widowed, and robbed of all save the glare of outward show; like the Dead Sea fruit, beautiful without, but dust and ashes within! The white moaning sea-birds which hovered around her in the salt sea breeze, must have been more in sympathy with her mood than the festive music on board the splendid "Bucentaur."

Once more she beheld that "golden city, paved with emerald," whose every pinnacle and turret gleamed above the face of the waters as the sun declined behind the great Campanile. The most magnificent reception awaited her; the "Bucentaur" was followed through the blue waters of the lagoon by an innumerable company of boats and gondolas in festive array, and decorated galleys and barques came to meet her with all the great nobles of the city, and their ladies in gorgeous attire. She was welcomed with the blowing of trumpets, the firing of guns, and thundering salvoes of artillery. All the palaces were richly adorned, and from each carved balcony, decked with flowers and hung with gay-coloured streamers, the fair Venetian ladies looked down with smiles and "vivas" as she passed onwards to the palace of the Duke of Ferrara, which had been made ready for her reception. The next scene in the drama is the solemn procession to the Piazza of San Marco, when Caterina, clothed in sumptuous black garments, is conducted in state within the great Byzantine temple, and there she "fece un libero dono alla Republica del regno de Cipro."

So far as the Republic of Venice was concerned, this was the end of the story, but the deposed queen had to be comforted with many gifts and much gold. A splendid yearly allowance was voted for her maintenance, and she was presented with "la terra e il Castello di Asolo, vago e piacevole castello posti negli estremi gioghi delle nostre Alpi, sovra il Trevigiano. . . ."

Caterina took possession of her new domain on Sunday, October 11, and this again was made an occasion of great pomp. The chronicler tells us that she advanced under a golden umbrella carried by four nobles, amid the acclamation of the people, who conducted her to the great church, where a solemn mass was celebrated, and the Te Deum sung in token of thanksgiving. Then the procession proceeded through the picturesque mediæval town to the castle on the hill, which had been sumptuously decorated for the queen's reception. Nothing was wanting; she was even consoled with a formal oration:

"O felice patria Asolani, o fortunata Grege, posciachè sarai retta e governata da così giusta e felice Paestorella; o avventurata nave, posciachè sarai guidata da si esperta nochiera. . . ."

It is interesting to notice how the Senators of Venice continue to exercise their grandmotherly care for this "most serene and beloved daughter," for they gravely put it on record that they chose Asolo for her abode; "afinche ella potesse godere del possesso, della bellezze e della salubrità di quel luogo." Beautiful "sparkling" Asolo; it was indeed a princely retreat. From the broad terrace of her stately castle the queen could see outspread before her the sunny plains of the Brenta and the Piave, girdled round by the encircling Alps and the blue Euganean hills. On a summer eve she could trace these classic rivers from the distant point where they rise amid the Alpine valleys, and wind their way like silver threads, with many a slow fantastic curve, across the vivid green of the wide pastoral plain, till they are lost to sight in the misty distance of the far off purple lagunes.

In this earthly paradise, Caterina was surrounded by a court of four thousand persons, and arranged her life in a routine of luxurious splendour. She had her rector from Venice, Nicolo Pruli, a capellano she had brought with her from Cyprus, a German doctor, at least one pet dwarf, her secretary, of whom we are told that he was an excellent poet and by no means a mediocre philosopher; and also many ladies in waiting and attendant pages. It is of one of these that Browning writes:

"Give her but a least excuse to love me!
When—where—
How—can this arm establish her above me,
If fortune fixed her as my lady there,
There already, to eternally reprove me?
('Hist!' said Kate the Queen;
But 'Oh!' cried the maiden, binding her tresses,)
''Tis only a page that carols unseen,
Crumbling your hounds their messes!'

Is she wronged?—To the rescue of her honour,
  My heart!
Is she poor?—What costs it to be called a donor?
Merely an earth to cleave, a sea to part.
But that fortune should have thrust all this upon her!
  ('Nay, list!'—bade Kate the Queen;
And still cried the maiden, binding her tresses,
  ''Tis only a page that carols unseen,
Fitting your hawks their jesses!')"

We cannot tell whether the exiled Queen of Cyprus was really satisfied with her mimic Court, her empty title; or whether, like a wise woman, she made the best of that which was within her reach, and ceased to sigh for the unattainable. But this we know, that under her genial rule, Asolo became a very citadel of pleasure, where one entertainment succeeded another, and life became one round of changing delights. There were gorgeous tournaments and tilting matches, and pastoral dances and moonlight festivals; there were gay hawking and hunting parties in which the Lady of Asolo was never weary. She had an unconquerable desire for joy and happiness, a very passion for magnificence, which she may perhaps have inherited from her grandmother, an imperial princess of the East. From all parts of Europe, visitors were attracted to this ideal spot, and were welcomed with royal magnificence.

We hear of the ambassador of Cyprus coming to present her an offering of rare sweetmeats, with many nobles in his train and thirty pages in white and gold. Theodoro of Aragon, Pandolfo Malatesta, Hieronimo Leone, with a retinue of two hundred persons, Isabella d'Este, the Duchess of Urbino, and Beatrice Duchess of Milan, were amongst her guests. She was the centre of an intellectual coterie, of which her kinsman, Pietro Bembo, the historian of Venice, afterwards made cardinal, was one of the most distinguished. His philosophical dialogues on the nature of love were named by him the "Asolani," in compliment to this society, and in them he describes Caterina's three Courts—of the Muses, of Love, and of magnificent and royal dignity.

Besides all this, the Lady of Asolo had a great love for gardening, and her summer resort on the plain was full of the rarest shrubs and flowers from Eastern lands, to which she was never weary of adding fresh treasures, as gifts came to her from her many friends. In the midst of her amusements she did not neglect more serious duties, and governed her limited domain wisely and well; dispensing even justice in her courts of law, founding a hospital and other charitable institutions, amongst them a kind of "mont de pieté" to help the poor in time of need. Like a true Lady Bountiful, in years of distress, she was most generous in distributing corn to all her subjects, and by her courtesy and kindness she won the affection of her people. Fra Bonaventura dei Minori, her confessor, speaks in high terms of her piety and good works. He tells us that she loved to read the life of Saint Caterina, the miracles of St. Giralomo, the legends of the Virgins and the lives of the Fathers. In the year 1506 she commissioned the artist Lorenzo Lotti to paint a great altar-piece for the church of Asolo.

For nearly twenty years the deposed Queen of Cyprus had spent her life in this sumptuous Arcadia, when rumours of approaching war induced her to take shelter in Venice. The warrior Pope Julius II. could no longer endure the encroachments of the Republic in Romagna, and at length induced the Emperor Maximilian and the Kings of France and Spain to join with him in a coalition against her, called the League of Cambray, and Venice was defeated at Aignadella, on the banks of the Adda. While the war still continued, Caterina was taken ill and died in the Palazza Cornaro della Regina on July 10, 1510.

She was universally mourned, for a strong feeling of respect and affection was felt by all her native city for the gracious and stately personality of Caterina Cornaro, Queen of Cyprus, Jerusalem and Armenia, and Signora of Asolo, as she signed herself to the end.

Yet her last wish was that she might be buried in the habit of St. Francis, with the cord, and cowl, and coarse brown cloak. A magnificent funeral was decreed by the Republic, who caused a bridge of boats to be made across the Grand Canal from the Cornaro Palace, not far from the Rialto, to the opposite side. An immense procession followed to do her honour, including the Patriarch, the Signoria, the Vice-Doge, the Archbishop of Spalato, and great crowds of citizens, all bearing torches in their hands. The crown of Cyprus was placed upon her coffin, an empty tribute to the dead, which had been denied to the living, by the fatherly Senate.

It was on the 11th, that Caterina was carried to the Cornaro chapel in the church of SS. Apostoli, where her father, Marco, and her brother Giorgio's tombs remain to this day. A terrible storm, long remembered in the city, took place at the time of her burial, with wind and heavy rain—the mourning of the elements. On the following day the funeral service was performed with extraordinary pomp, and the ambassador, Andrea Navagero, poet and scholar, pronounced her funeral oration, and her touching story moved the listeners to tears.

At a later period her body was taken to the church of S. Salvatore, and a tomb was raised to her memory in the right transept. The bas-relief represents Caterina giving up her crown to the Doge of Venice, Barbingo. She bequeathed her beautiful palace at Venice to the Papacy.

BIANCA CAPELLO, GRAND DUCHESS OF FLORENCE.

SHOULD we not humbly ask pardon from the noble ladies of the Renaissance when we dare to bring into their company a figure so notorious for evil as Bianca Capello? And yet, in this marvellous period of startling contrasts, good and evil were ever mingled, so that in princely hall and gorgeous festa the rich brocades of noble dame and base adventuress would sweep together side by side.

Bianca was the daughter of Bartolommeo Capello, of a noble Venetian family, and large fortune. She was born in 1548, when the earlier glory of the Renaissance in Italy was passing somewhat into decadence, with the increase of wealth and luxury. Unfortunately for the young girl, she lost her mother at an early age, and would not appear to have been carefully trained, for one chronicle tells us that "her habits of life were more free than is the custom with noble Venetian damsels." We are also told that her home life was made very unhappy by an unkind stepmother.

Fiction has been kinder to her story than is warranted by more recently discovered fact, for the old legend ran that when in her fifteenth year she had fallen in love with a young gallant, after chance meetings at mass maybe; she had granted him an imprudent interview at early dawn, the little side-door of the palace had been closed by accident, and nothing remained for the lovers but instant flight. But the chance discovery of an old volume of criminal trials belonging to the Archives of Venice has brought to light a curious marginal note written in Latin: "Effaced by order of the 'Ten.'" The historian Cicogna tells us how the passage, which was scratched out with a pen, was deciphered, and the secret revealed. This is a brief summary of the Latin entry which the "Ten" had thought to bury in oblivion:

"Whereas Pietro Bonaventuri of Florence, dwelling in this city with his uncle Giovanni Batista Bonaventuri, nigh unto the church of St. Apollinare, hath been accused before the criminal court of the Forty; that with hateful insolence and disrespect for the nobles of Venice, he, knowing that Bianca, the daughter of Bartolommeo Capello, was the heir to no mean fortune, and being minded to get possession of such property . . . dared to take her from the house of her father in the night following the 28th day of November in the year 1563, she being deceived by many lies and having scarce completed her sixteenth year; he did afterwards take her away from Venice, thus shaming the name and house of a noble Venetian, in contempt of law, and defiance of public morals; and whereas the said Pietro hath not yet been found, it is ordained that when he shall be arrested he shall be brought to Venice, and at the accustomed hour, on a lofty scaffold raised between the two columns on the Piazza, his head shall be stricken from his shoulders by the public executioner, so that he shall die." Then a reward is offered for this Pietro, alive or dead, and the judgment is given against a certain Maria Donati, a serving-maid in the house, who aided in the flight.

It is plain therefore that the elopement was planned, and there is reason to believe that the girl carried off all the jewels she could lay hands on. This Pietro Bonaventuri was a clerk at the Salviati Bank, but he persuaded Bianca that he was a member of the princely house, and, when their meetings could no longer be concealed, he induced her to fly with him to Florence one dark November night. The journey across the Apennines, so laborious and severe even for great ladies with a splendid escort, must have been rough and trying indeed for the fugitives, with the constant fear of pursuit at their heels, and the foolish girl must very soon have begun to repent of her wild step.

When at length she arrived safely in Florence it must have been a cruel awakening to find that Pietro had no noble connections whatever, and that his family lived in a poor house, a "tugurio," on the south side of the Piazza of San Marco. But it was now too late to protest, and the ill-matched couple were married in the house of Pietro's mother, and only too thankful to have a shelter over their heads, for the indignant Republic of Venice was offering large rewards for their arrest. They were very poor, for Pietro had no longer even his clerk's salary, and as for Bianca's fortune of six thousand crowns, which she inherited from her mother, that was declared to be confiscated. We are told that this high-born girl, accustomed to a home of wealth and luxury, was obliged to help in all the menial work of the house, and found her life most miserable. During this period she gave birth to a daughter, who received the name of Pellegrina.

Meantime the story of their flight had spread through Italy, for a price had been set upon the head of Bonaventuri, and it soon became known that they were in Florence. This, and the fame of Bianca's beauty, reached the ears of Francesco, the eldest son of the Grand Duke Cosimo, and he felt a strong desire to see the fair heroine. It is most difficult to form any idea of the attractions of bygone beauties, for taste changes from one age to another, while no description, and but rarely even a portrait, can recall the charm of a living woman. But such portraits and medals as remain to us of the Capello do not confirm the enthusiasm of her contemporaries, for we see a coarse, bold face, with a mass of red hair and an insolent smile of triumph ; but this, of course, was at a much later period of her history. When Montaigne saw her at the court of Florence, he describes her as "handsome according to the taste of the Italians, having a cheerful and plump face, with considerable stoutness of person. . . ."

At the time of Bianca's arrival in Florence, the court of the Grand Duke Cosimo I. was very different from the literary and intellectual society which had surrounded Lorenzo the Magnificent. It was a scene of dissipation and luxury of the lowest description, and never were there so many crimes and murders in the streets of Florence. The duke's three daughters met with tragic deaths later, and in 1562 two of his sons came to an untimely end. Giovanni, who was nineteen years of age and had been a cardinal for some time, was out hunting with his younger brother Garzia, near Leghorn, and the story goes that a dispute arose between them, when Garzia mortally wounded his brother with his rapier, and when he prayed for his father's forgiveness he was slain at once. Whether this be the true account or not, it is certain that the two princes died suddenly, and their mother, Eleanora di Toledo, died of grief within a few months.

The other sons of Cosimo were Ferdinando, who had recently been made a cardinal at the age of fourteen, and Pietro, a wild unmanageable boy of nine. His daughter Isabella, the wife of Paolo Giordini Orsini, lived a gay life in Florence apart from her Roman husband.

After the tragedy of his two sons' death, Cosimo resigned his power into the hands of Francesco ; and this young prince was not long in satisfying his curiosity with regard to the new beauty. The wife of his Spanish tutor, Marchesa Mondragone, made the acquaintance of Bianca and her mother-in-law, as it was suggested that her husband would try to obtain a pardon for Pietro. She arranged a meeting between Duke Francesco and Bianca at the Casino Mediceo, in the Piazzo of San Marco, not far from the house of the Bonaventuri. The girl was not troubled by any shyness, and at once appealed to him for protection against the Republic of Venice and her own family, who had offered a great reward to any one who should arrest or kill herself, or her husband Pietro Bonaventuri. Francesco was ready to promise anything, for he was captivated by the ripe charms of this Venetian girl of sixteen, with her ruddy golden hair.

But prince though he was, he had to use much diplomacy to conceal the progress of this love affair, for at that very time a marriage was being arranged for

BIANCA CAPELLO, GRAND DUCHESS OF TUSCANY

BRONZINO

him with Giovanna of Austria, the sister of the Emperor Maximilian II., and also, his father Cosimo, who, had he not formally abdicated the throne, might have been roused to assert himself. But this was in the early days, before Bianca had obtained such complete ascendency over the weak prince, that she ruled everything according to her will.

The marriage with the great Princess of Austria was celebrated with much pomp in December 1565; but the unfortunate Giovanna was not long in finding that her husband's affections were given elsewhere, and that she was even robbed of the influence and homage which her high position claimed. Meanwhile the Venetian favourite was loaded with wealth and favours; the palace in the Via Maggio, still known by her name, was given to her, and the famous Orti Oricelli, those Rucellai Gardens where the Platonic Academy, founded by the father of Lorenzo the Magnificent, held its meetings for a time at the invitation of the cultured Bernardo Rucellai. Here Machiavelli gave his celebrated discourse on Livy, and Giovanni Rucellai read the first Italian tragedy, Rosamunda, in the presence of the Pope Leo X. and a brilliant assembly. Henceforth this abode of culture and learning was to be profaned by the presence of Bianca, who gave the most sumptuous and dissipated entertainments in the beautiful gardens, to lighten the gloom of her royal lover.

Pietro Bonaventuri had a post at court, and a large salary found for him, and, freed from all clerkly duties, he threw himself recklessly into the wildest and most frivolous amusements of the young nobility. He engaged in several love intrigues, and more especially one which caused much scandal with a young and beautiful widow, Cassandra Bonciani, whose proud family, the Ricci, had already found means to compass the death of two of her lovers. But Pietro disregarded the warning; and one night when he was returning from a visit to her, and had reached the eastern side of Santo Spirito, near the foot of the bridge of Santa Trinita, across the Arno, suddenly he was attacked by a number of armed bravos; of his two serving-men one fled, and the other was stabbed, while Bonaventuri fought for his life, and actually succeeded in crossing the bridge, where he was near his palace in the Via Maggio. But after a desperate struggle, in which he killed one of his assailants, he was pierced with dagger thrusts, and left dead on the stones.

At that time, such night attacks were by no means of rare occurrence in the streets of Florence, for we are told that one hundred and eighty assassinations occurred within the city in less than two years. That very night, Cassandra's bedchamber was broken into by masked ruffians, who murdered her in her bed, and it was thus that the Ricci family redeemed their honour. But in the death of the hapless Pietro, the hand of Duke Francesco was distinctly traced, as every facility was given to the assassins for their escape, and all Florence was perfectly assured of the connivance of Bianca, who had absolute dominion over her lover. It appears that in the early days of their acquaintance she had obtained from Francesco a solemn promise, "made before a sacred image," that if a time should come when they were both free, he would marry her.

By the death of Pietro one obstacle was removed,

and the only bar in the way of Bianca's ambition was the unfortunate Austrian princess, Francesco's neglected wife. To marry a Duke of Milan had been a great descent to her imperial pride, but when to this was added her husband's neglect and indifference, and her contempt and horror of the loose morals of a court which treated her with open scorn, she was indeed to be pitied. Poor Giovanna had no charm of beauty to attract; her manners were reserved and haughty, and, unfortunately for her, she had not at that time given birth to an heir to the Duchy. Of her four elder daughters, Maria, born in 1573, became Queen of France, as wife of Henri IV., Romola and Isabella died in infancy, and Eleanora married the Duke Vincensio Gonzaga.

A number of letters of Bianca Capello have been collected from the muniment room of the Capello family at Venice, mostly written during this period, and addressed to "the very magnificent Signor Andrea Capello, my most respected cousin, and as it were my Brother, at Venice."

"1572, February 21 (Venetian style).

"... Seeing how greatly you desire my return, indeed I was resolved upon it after the event* which has taken place; but fortune ... made my father-in-law resolve on assuming the guardianship of my daughter, and depriving me of it, for so the laws and statutes of this city direct; that if the father of one defunct be yet living, to him rather than any other be conceded the care of his grandchildren. Now think what must be my state of mind ... yet I will not despair, and will trust in our Lord God and in your

* Probably her husband's murder.

illustrious excellency for the finding of some remedy, because the world for the most part is all out of order . . .

"Your magnificence's cousin and as it were sister,

"BIANCHA CAPELLO."

If the "event" alluded to in this letter is her husband's death, as it appears, that would fix the date, of which historians seem uncertain. A year later she writes in evident allusion to the constant appeals for money made by her grasping family at Venice:

"Your lordship writes me that it has been said I possess twenty thousand crowns in money, but in this I think there is some mistake . . . it is very true that I wrote to my most magnificent brother that in real and chattel, property and jewels, I have more than thirty thousand crowns . . . but you must consider that I ought to leave a part of this to my daughter . . .

"P.S. Most magnificent lord and brother, I beg of you to do me the favour to send me my Nativity, that is, the day and hour of my birth, and let no one beside yourself know of this thing . . ."

This must evidently have been required for the casting of a horoscope, as Bianca was perfectly devoted to necromancy and incantations of all kinds. In another letter to the same Andrea, she writes in April 1573:

". . . I was much grieved at heart by the discourse between my most noble father and your most magnificent lordship, from which I conclude that he is not at all well disposed towards me, and that his only wish to have me back in Venice is that he might bury me in a convent, which I will by no means do, for I know of a surety that so I should be lost, soul and body, and I do not choose, as I have often told your lordship, to change from a mistress to a slave; but excepting that match of which I spoke to your lordship, I will leave everything to return to my country and my kin.

"Your lordship's, &c.,

"BIANCHA CAPELLO."

Duke Francesco had kept his word, and done all he could to reconcile the Venetian Republic to her, as well as her own family, but from this letter it is plain that he had not succeeded.

Later on she alludes in various letters to "a matter which is of too great importance to be written," and she begs her cousin to come to Florence to discuss it. "Di troppa grande materia da mettere in carta."

Her biographer, Signor Odorici, believes this matter was her hope of marrying Francesco after the death of the duchess. Now as all this was written while the poor lady was still alive and well, it looks like rather a curious confirmation of the general belief in Florence, later on, that steps had been taken to hasten the death, so much desired, of Giovanna.

In the letters there are also frequent allusions to the great friendship shown to Bianca by Donna Isabella, and on one occasion she breaks off abruptly, saying that she is sent for by the Signora Isabella dei Medici to accompany her and Cardinal Ferdinando to a great hunting party at Pisa the fifth day of December, 1573.

This Ferdinando was Duke Francesco's next brother, about twenty-four years of age. He lived chiefly at Rome, where he was in good repute as a man of learning and ability; but he had friends in Florence who sent him news of the most secret events which took place there. Hc feared and hated Bianca, but he was politic enough to keep on good terms with her outwardly. The younger brother Pietro had grown up wild and profligate, a terror to peaceful citizens, and a constant source of anxiety to his cardinal brother. Before his father's death in 1574, he had married a Spanish lady, Eleonora di Garzia, of more than doubtful character, who paid for her frailty with her life, for only two years later Pietro put her to death with his own hand, in the Villa of Cafaggiuolo in the Apennines. This was the same old castle where, in bygone days, Clarice, the wife of Lorenzo dei Medici, and the tutor Poliziono had their difference of opinion on the subject of the children's lessons. Little did they dream of the awful tragedy which would be enacted in that lonely desolate spot by a degraded member of that Medici family, of which they were both so proud.

Nothing could more sharply accentuate the contrast between the quiet domestic life in the early days of the Renaissance, and the passion and crime of its decadence. But we have not yet had our fill of horrors until we touch upon the tragedy of the Lady Isabella dei Medici, mentioned above as the friendly patroness of Bianca. This princess, who was the sister of Duke Francesco, and the wife of Paolo Giordano Orsini, lived in open immorality, which gave great scandal to her brother, Cardinal Fernando. He strongly urged upon the duke the need of interference in the matter, and persuaded him at length to send for Orsini, who had taken up his residence in Rome. A secret consultation was held between the husband and brother of

Isabella, in which her fate appears to have been sealed, for the last words spoken by Francesco were overheard.

"When you have assured yourself of the shameful truth, bear ever in mind that you are a Christian and a 'gentiluomo.'" He also placed at the disposal of Orsini a villa which had been a favourite resort of Lorenzo the Magnificent, outside the Porta Romana, and now called Poggio Imperiale. Isabella must have been surprised to find her husband so attentive and affectionate, for he had brought her a present of a couple of greyhounds, and also invited her to a great supper at the villa; but she went thither without apparent misgiving, although it was afterwards remembered that she had seemed sad and restless that evening.

The next day it was announced in Florence that the great lady had died suddenly in the night of apoplexy, but the chroniclers of the day had little doubt that the unfortunate Isabella was strangled by her husband. It is a significant fact, that after this occurrence, Orsini was more friendly than ever with the Medici brothers, and Francesco, miser as he was, paid most of his brother-in-law's debts.

The death of this beautiful and accomplished woman took place on July 16, 1576, and after this time it was noticed that her brother the duke gave way more than ever to fits of gloom and violence. It was a cause of constant discontent to him that he had no son to succeed him, and to attain this end Bianca had consulted every necromancer and dealer in philtres and spells throughout Italy. But all her magic arts were in vain; and the story goes that at length she conceived the audacious plan of foisting a surreptitious child upon the Medici family. She seems to have arranged her plans, according to Galluzzi, with great skill; and on August 29, 1576, it was announced to the Court and city that a son had been born to the Grand Duke. He received the name of Antonio, as Bianca declared that his birth was due to the intercession of that saint, and Francesco bought for him a principality in the kingdom of Naples, at the price of 200,000 ducats. But in Florence no one believed in the child; and we are told that Cardinal Fernando, having obtained positive proofs from a poor woman, murdered by order of the duchess, who confessed on her deathbed—went with the whole story to his brother, who met it with absolute incredulity. Galluzzi sets him down as an accomplice to the fraud, after its successful issue.

It was a curious coincidence that a year later, in 1577, a son was actually born to the Grand Duchess Giovanna, to the immense satisfaction of all the Medici family, who cordially hated Bianca. Philip II. of Spain was godfather to the heir, who received the name of Filippo.

During the rejoicings which followed, Bianca found it wise to leave Florence for awhile; but the duke could not live without her; and when his first rejoicing at the birth of his heir had passed over, his Venetian favourite was recalled, and he loaded her and the child Antonio with gifts. Her brother Vittorio was invited from Venice, and his coming was made the occasion of an extraordinary entertainment in the Rucellai Gardens. The feast was under the management of a famous magician, and the contemporary writer, Celio Malespini, gives a very full account of it, from which this short sketch is taken.

In the beautiful wooded groves of that marvellous walled garden within the city walls, the wizard made all his elaborate preparation. He marked out a large circle in the centre of the greensward, under which a shallow pit had been already dug out, but it was carefully concealed from view by a kind of wooden platform covered with freshly-cut turf. On one side of this were two large braziers filled with live coals, and a vase full of drugs for fumigation, and a black and yellow rope was stretched all round the enclosure. When all was ready the necromancer, clothed in a black robe, with a mitre on his head covered with pentagons and strange figures, stepped out slowly to meet the guests, and invited them within the magic circle. Then he whistled loudly, to the east, north, south and west. He then seized a silver bell, and ringing it with a slow loud peal, he cried in a hollow voice: "Come hither, come hither, all spirits who owe me obedience, Barbicul! Solsibec! Tarmidor! Zampir! Borgamur!"

By this time it was long after sunset, and the growing darkness added to the weird effect, for the only light was from the lurid glare of the braziers. At this moment he gave orders for great handfuls of the noxious drugs to be cast on the flames, which sent forth a dense blue smoke and so abominable an odour that it was almost unbearable. Then he clapped his hands thrice; and instantly there came forth horrible cries and groans from below, with strange howling and clanking of chains. The guests being now thoroughly alarmed, suddenly the platform gave way, and they all fell into the pit, with the exception of the grand duke and a few others who were privately warned.

"Having thus fallen into the bowels of the earth," says Malespini, "the devils were upon them, making fearful noises, and hideous in the lurid glow of the flames; till the hapless creatures scarce knew if they were alive or dead." At that moment a bevy of beautiful girls came to the rescue, and "angelic voices sang hymns appropriate to the occasion." Those who were seriously injured amongst the victims were carried to beds prepared for them; and so the entertainment ended, to the great amusement of Bianca, who had watched the whole scene from a distance. Such were the orgies carried on in the historical gardens, where once Lorenzo and his learned friends had calmly discussed the philosophy of their beloved Plato.

It had been a fresh sorrow and disappointment for the unhappy Grand Duchess Giovanna to see Bianca resume her sway over Francesco; she was in bad health at the time, and too much overcome with sadness to have the energy to rally. On May 11, 1578, she passed away from a world which had given her so little joy. Although her cold, reserved manner had not won popularity, yet she was deeply mourned by all the city, and always spoken of with sympathy and respect. She had a magnificent funeral in San Lorenzo, the great mortuary church of the Medici.

W. Story tells us that when her coffin was opened in 1857 "she was as fresh in colour as if she had just died . . . in her red satin, trimmed with lace, her red silk stockings and high-heeled shoes, the earrings hanging from her ears, and her blonde hair as fresh as ever. And so, centuries after she had been laid there, the truth became evident of the rumour that ran through Florence at the time of her death, that she had died of poison. The arsenic which had taken her life had preserved her body." A strange confirmation of rumour, if indeed this be the true explanation.

After his wife's death Francesco wandered about his dominions, restless and troubled; but whether by remorse or by uncertainty as to his future conduct we know not. He consulted his court chaplain as to whether he should keep his promise of marrying Bianca, and was advised not to do so; but the lady, hearing of this, went to the duke's own Franciscan confessor, and pointed out to him that the bishopric of Chiusi was at that moment vacant. The friar took the hint and gave the required advice, with the result that the duke found his duty and his wishes coinciding. At the same time Bianca wrote him a touching letter, saying that she was resigned to his will, but that she could not survive his loss. This finally decided the duke, and the marriage was privately performed by the Franciscan friar, only twenty-four days after the death of Giovanna, in the little dark chapel of the Palazzo Vecchio. It was kept secret, even from Cardinal Ferdinando, for many months, then it was made known to King Philip of Spain; and next it occurred to Francesco that he would write a smooth letter to the senators of Venice, speaking of Bianca as a daughter of the Republic, and announcing his intention of making her his Grand Duchess.

The success of this message was beyond all his expectations. His envoy was received at the Capello Palace by the Patriarch of Aquileia, and attended by forty senators. Bartolommeo Capello and his son were made "illustrissimi cavalieri," with precedence over all others, and there were festal rejoicings in the city. On June 16, 1579, a vote of the Senate declared that "the Grand Duke of Tuscany having chosen for his wife Bianca Capello, of a most noble family in this city, a lady adorned with all those most singular and excellent qualities, and most worthy of any the highest fortune, it is decreed that she be created a true and particular daughter of the Republic." A splendid gold chain was bestowed on the Florentine ambassador, and a certain compromising entry in the public registers was erased by order of the "Ten."

It was now openly announced to all the courts of Europe that the duke's marriage with a daughter of the Republic would take place on October 12. A fortnight before the great event a magnificent embassy arrived from Venice "to place Bianca Capello in full possession of all prerogatives appertaining to a daughter of San Marco." The ambassadors were accompanied by a train of ninety Venetian nobles, and besides these, there were as many as eighty connections of the bride's family, and they were all entertained with such pomp and gorgeous festivities that the cost to Florence was reckoned at 300,000 ducats, an enormous sum, if we consider the much higher value of money in those days. The ceremony of Bianca's coronation and marriage began in the great hall of the Palazzo Vecchio, that ancient citadel of Italian freedom, and from thence Bianca was borne in state to the cathedral, with the crown on her head.

It was a time of dearth and famine in Florence, yet the subservient Venetians carried off many and costly gifts and the grand duchess was to receive an extra

100,000 ducats to be invested in the mint of Venice. She had attained the summit of her ambition, and could now afford to be gracious to her old enemies, for we find her writing to Cardinal Ferdinando : " I live more for you than for myself. Indeed I live but in you, for I cannot live without you. . . ."

The extraordinary and reckless extravagance of the wedding festivities must be looked upon as a test of Bianca's unbounded influence over the grand duke, for his strongest feeling was avarice. No means of adding to his wealth had been left untried ; he derived immense revenues from his trading speculations, which stretched over the whole of Europe, and there was no important city where he had not a large share in the banking interest. He carried on a prosperous trade with ships of his own, in wool, grain, silk, leather, pepper and other spices. Besides the gains of a great merchant and banker he had those of a sovereign, from heavy taxation, fines and confiscation. From his vast wealth, he advanced loans to foreign Powers which often turned the scale of war ; but through it all he had a miser's love for his gold. Another passion of his which gave him much trouble in negotiations about his time, was that of title. His father had obtained that of " Grand Duke of Tuscany " from Pope Pius V., and he was therefore a " Most Serene Highness " ; but the other States of Italy would not recognise his supremacy, and also called themselves " Serene," to the extreme indignation of Francesco.

He had a fresh trouble early in 1582, in the death of his little son, Filippo, the only boy of poor Giovanna ; and he felt the loss acutely. Indeed, after this time he fell into a terrible state of gloom and melancholy, and shut himself almost entirely in the lonely Villa of Pratolino, about eight miles from Florence on the way to Bologna. It stood on the slopes of the Apennines, of which Ruskin gives such a striking description in this immediate neighbourhood—"The country is on a sudden lonely . . . a scene not sublime, for its forms are subdued and low, only a grey extent of mountain ground, tufted irregularly with ilex and olive; not rich nor lovely, but sunburnt and sorrowful; becoming wilder every instant as the road winds into its recesses, ascending still until the higher woods, now partly oak and partly pine, dropping back from the central nest of the Apennines, leave a pastoral wilderness of scattered rock and arid grass, withered away here by frost, and there by lambent tongues of earth-fed fire."

Amid these grey surroundings Bianca lived a wretched life for more than five years, shut up with a husband whose melancholy was only varied by reckless excesses, and gusts of savage ferocity. Her highest ambition was gratified; a long coveted and splendid position was hers, and wealth beyond her wildest dreams, yet she was a miserable woman. The one thing she craved for—and for which she would have sold her soul, in the darkest magic and witchcraft—was denied her. No son was born to her, although constant rumours were spread as to her expectations.

Thus time passed on, and Cardinal Ferdinando was kept in a constant state of fear and suspense as to his own ultimate succession to the duchy. But, outwardly, he kept on the most friendly terms with Bianca, and in October 1587, he was invited to pay a visit to his brother at his country retreat of Poggio-a-Cajano, a low-lying villa on the banks of the river Ombrone, at the foot of Monte Albano, about half way between Florence and Pistoia. It had been a favourite resort of Lorenzo the Magnificent, who went there for his favourite amusement of hawking. An old proverb says:

> "Val piu una lustra di Poggio a Cajano
> Che tutte le bellezze d'Artemino."

Ferdinando was accompanied by the Archbishop of Florence, and they were most hospitably received by Bianca; ample sport being provided for them, as the neighbouring marshes abounded with game. All went well until October 19, when Duke Francesco was suddenly taken ill, and died at nine o'clock in the evening; the Duchess Bianca was also seized with the same complaint, and only survived until the next morning. These are the undoubted facts, but Florentine historians have held different views as to the cause of the tragedy. A very curious letter has been preserved, which was written shortly after the event.

"Quando, che alli giorni passati la Morte cavalcò sopra il suo destriero magro, e disfatto per investirsi del titolo di Grande. La Morte ottenne a Roma il titolo di Grande, e conseguita ch'ella ebbe cossifatta indecentissima intitolazione, se ne cavalcava frettolosa alla volta del Poggio a Caiano, e quivi con irresistibile forza e pari valore assaltò il Grande Etrusco di Firenze e Siena, e lo abbattè alli 19 di Ottobre, 1587, a 4 ore e mezzo di notte, e di 47 anni lo privò di vita dopo strani e disusati scontorcimenti, e ululati e muggiti diversi."

"When in these past days, Death rode on his thin

pale horse to invest himself with the title of Great. Death obtained in Rome the title of Great, and having received this most indecent title, he rode in haste towards Poggio a Cajano, and there with irresistible force and equal valour assaulted . . . &c." Giovanni Vettorio Soderini."

It has been suggested that Death rode from Rome in company with Cardinal Ferdinando, for the latest theory supports the popular opinion that he poisoned his brother and sister-in-law; although some suggest that Bianca had prepared the poison for the cardinal, while others assert that the duke and his wife died of malarious fever. When Pope Sixtus V. heard the news, he saw how strong the suspicion would be against Ferdinando, who had everything to gain by the event, and who at once succeeded to the duchy. A pompous funeral was accorded to Francesco under the dome of San Lorenzo; but with regard to Bianca, the new duke exclaimed: "We will have none of her among our dead!" Her body was wrapped in a sheet and thrown into the common grave for the poor, under the nave of the same church.

"There, at Cajano,
Where when the hawks were mewed and evening came,
Pulci would set the table in a roar
With his wild lay—there, where the sun descends,
And hill and dale are lost, veiled with his beams,
The fair Venetian died, she and her lord—
Died of a posset drugged by him who sate
And saw them suffer, flinging back the charge
The murderer on the murdered."—ROGERS' "Italy."

It is interesting to know that after the death of Francesca and his wife, their reputed son, Prince

Antonio, then a boy of eleven, was unmolested, and lived to enjoy many peaceful years in the "Casino Medici," where he devoted his time to the cultivation of art and science. Pellegrina, the daughter of Bianca, was happily married some years before, to Count Ulisse Bentivoglio.

GREAT LADIES OF ROME AND ROMAGNA.

CATARINA SFORZA, COUNTESS OF FORLI.

LUCREZIA BORGIA, DUCHESS OF FERRARA.

VITTORIA COLONNA, MARCHESA OF PESCARA.

HISTORICAL SUMMARY.

1460. Federigo, Duke of Urbino, marries Battista Sforza.

1462. Catarina Sforza born. Daughter of Galeazzo, Duke of Milan.

1471. Elisabetta Gonzaga born, daughter of Federico Gonzaga of Mantua.

1472. Guidobaldo born, son of Federigo, Duke of Urbino.

1473. Girolamo Riario betrothed to Catarina Sforza.

1476. Assassination of Galeazzo Maria Sforza, Duke of Milan.

1477. Catarino Sforza marries Count Girolamo Riario.

1480. Count Girolamo takes possession of Forli.

" Birth of Lucrezia Borgia at Rome.

1481. Sixtus IV. combines with Venice against Ferrara.

1482. Death of Federigo, Duke of Urbino. Guidobaldo I. succeeds him.

1483. Guidobaldo enters the service of Naples.

1484. Death of Sixtus IV. Treaty of Bagnuolo. Innocent VIII. succeeds.

1488. Assassination of Count Girolamo Riario at Forli.

" Duke Guidobaldo marries Elisabetta Gonzaga of Mantua.

1490. Birth of Vittoria Colonna, daughter of Fabrizio Colonna.

1492. Death of Lorenzo dei Medici. Alexander VI. becomes Pope.

1494. Lucrezia Borgia marries Giovanni Sforza, of Pesaro.

1495. Guidobaldo helps the Pope to restore Ferdinand II. to Naples.

1497. Guidobaldo defeated and taken prisoner by Bracciano.

" Divorce of Lucrezia Borgia, 1498. She marries Alfonso, Duke of Bisaglia.

" Catarina Sforza marries Giovanni dei Medici.

1498. Guidobaldo helps the Medici. His illness at Bibbiena.

1500. Cæsar Borgia takes Forli and Imola, and carries Catarina Sforza to Rome.

1501. Lucrezia Borgia marries Alfonso d'Este, Duke of Ferrara.

1502. Elisabetta, Duchess of Urbino, visits Venice.

" Cæsar Borgia takes Urbino by treachery. Duke's flight to Mantua.

1503. Death of Pope Alexander VI. Guidobaldo returns to Urbino.

1505. Guidobaldo visits Pope Julius II.

1507. The Pope visits Urbino. Baldassare Castiglione at Urbino. (Il Cortegiano.)

1508. Death of Guidobaldo, Duke of Urbino. Francesco Maria succeeds.

1509. Marriage of Vittoria Colonna to the Marquis of Pescaro.

" Death of Catarina Sforza at Florence.

" Marriage of Francesco, Duke of Urbino, to Leonora Gonzaga of Mantua.

1513. Leo X. dei Medici becomes Pope.

1515. Duke of Urbino deprived of his office as Gonfaloniere of the Church and of his duchy.

1519. Death of Lucrezia Borgia, Duchess of Ferrara.

1522. Death of Leo X. Duke of Urbino recovers his duchy after seven years of exile with the Dowager Duchess Elisabetta and his wife.

1523. Death of Elisabetta Gonzaga, Duchess (dowager) of Urbino.

1525. Death of Ferrante, Marquis of Pescaro, husband of Vittoria Colonna.

1527. Rome sacked by the Imperialists. Pope Clement VII. a prisoner.

1529. General peace in Italy.

1537. Vittoria Colonna visits Duchess Renée at Ferrara.

1547. Death of Vittoria Colonna, Marchesa of Pescara.

CATARINA SFORZA, "MADONNA OF FORLI"

CATARINA SFORZA is a splendid type of the "warrior woman," of which Italy has ever been so proud; the Virago, as she is called not in blame but honour. She was an illegitimate daughter of that notorious Galeazzo Maria Sforza, Duke of Milan, son of Francesco, whose passions he had inherited but not his ability. Born in 1462, the little girl was legitimatised at eight years old, and brought up by the Duchess Bona of Savoy, who treated her in all respects as her own child.

Her life may be said to have begun with tragedy, for she was still a child when her father was brutally murdered. It was a strange, and to us a meaningless crime, and yet Sixtus IV. was right when he exclaimed on receiving the news, "The peace of Italy is dead." This is the account we have of it. The Duke of Milan, unsuspicious of any danger, was quietly entering the Church of San Stefano at Christmastide 1470, when he was suddenly attacked and stabbed to death by three nobles of Milan and their bravos. He was accompanied at the time by two ambassadors, who caught him as he fell forward, but for the moment no one realised what had happened. It was a desperate adventurer, named Lampugnani, who struck the first blow ; pressing through the crowd, he fell on his knee before the duke to present a petition, and stabbed him with a dagger hidden up his sleeve. Then, as Galeazzo fell on the pavement, his assassins covered him with dagger thrusts.

Of the other two chief conspirators one, Visconti, avenged an insult to his sister, while the third, Olgiati, was a Republican who dreamed of freeing the State of a tyrant. The confusion was so great that these two escaped for the time, but Lampugnani tripped his foot in a woman's train and was put to death by the populace, who had no sympathy with the murderers. A chronicler of the time gives a striking account of the young prince setting forth in his gay suit of crimson brocade, from the Castello that morning, and smiling at the presentiment of his wife, Bona of Savoy, who had besought him not to enter the church that day.

The widowed duchess in her anguish at his loss, thus suddenly cut off unshriven, wrote an imploring letter to the Pope, praying him to give her dear husband plenary absolution for his many and grievous crimes. She promised to make all the atonement in her power, by redressing wrongs, and by building churches and hospitals, and other good works. This was rather a sudden change of mood for the great lady, who had been noted for her magnificence and worldly splendour, of which she and her husband gave a great display when they paid a visit to the Court of Lorenzo at Florence. He had been godfather to her infant son, and on that occasion had presented her with a magnificent diamond necklace ; and his friendship was a great help and support to her now in her regency.

Before the murder of Galeazzo he had arranged a

marriage for his daughter Catarina with Girolamo Riario, the nephew of the Pope, who expressed to the Duchess Bona his earnest wish that it should be carried out at once. So the young girl was married with great pomp in the month of April 1477, when she was scarcely in her sixteenth year.

As usual, the chroniclers give a very full and interesting account of the journey to Rome, and the young bride's triumphal entrance, as she rode in through the Porta del Popolo, the centre of a brilliant cavalcade, on a richly caparisoned dappled palfrey. On this occasion Catarina was very gorgeously dressed in a robe of the newest fashion, called a "Cyprian," which excited much interest, and was not entirely approved of, for it was cut square to the bust, in a manner which showed the whole neck. It was of crimson brocade lined with ermine, extremely full round the feet, and close fitting from the waist upwards, with very long and large sleeves, and a girdle of silver gilt worked with pearls.

Her hair was drawn back over a cushion and tied with strings of pearls, and over all she wore a veil of beautifully thin fine white lawn. She was greatly admired, and all Rome was soon at her feet, for she became an immense favourite with the Pope, her uncle (or father-in-law).

One contemporary historian describes her in flowery language: "When she issued from her litter, it was as if the sun had emerged, so gorgeously beautiful did she appear, laden with silver, and gold, and jewels, but still more striking from her natural charms. Her hair, wreathed in the manner of a coronet, was brighter than the gold with which it was twined. Her forehead was of burnished ivory ; her eyes sparkled behind the mantling crimson of her cheeks, as morning stars . . ."

Another biographer writes of her : "It would be difficult to find in history any woman who so far surpassed her sex, who was so much the wonder of her contemporaries and the marvel of posterity. Endowed with a lofty and masculine spirit, she was born to command . . ."

The splendid palace on the banks of the Tiber, now called the Corsini, with its stately halls, and delicious terraces, looking down on the Farnese palaces and gardens, was bestowed upon Riario and Catarina, and adorned with the most magnificent furnishings of every kind, and priceless works of art.

Sixtus IV., according to his promise, confirmed to his nephew the township of Imola, on the high road, south of Bologna, of which he was ecclesiastical lord, and gave him 40,000 ducats. Catarina appears to have had no lack of wedding presents, and we are told that two days after her marriage, Girolamo sent his bride a casket containing diamond necklaces, and robes of gold brocade and of velvet, embroidered with fine pearls ; one dress alone carried nearly 3000 pearls ; there was also a purse of gold, silver-embroidered girdles and many other precious things. The month following her marriage, her half-sister Anna, who was only three years old, was betrothed to Alfonso of Este, the son of Duke Ercole of Ferrara. There were solemn processions and thanksgivings on the occasion, and the infant bridegroom's wedding contract was signed.

Catarina was a beautiful girl, full of boundless spirit and energy. In those early years of her married life, when she was one of the most brilliant ornaments of the papal court, she had a constant round of gaiety and amusement. She was passionately fond of dancing, and a poet exclaims to her : " Catarina, if you make the dance go thus, Atlas will find the world a lighter burden." Another writer tells us " how well she knew, in the intervals of her frenzied existence, how to enjoy life, when she gave herself up to the beauty of her flowers, the charm of her gardens, the delight of seeing her splendid drove of cattle peacefully grazing in her parks. Dogs never had a more tender protectress. She evoked the people's enthusiasm and applause when, riding in a red skirt at the head of her huntsmen, like a legendary fairy, and reining up her horse with her delicate scented hand, she smiled upon them all, her beautiful white teeth flashing between her full ruby lips." *

We have a most interesting letter which she wrote in 1481 to the Duchess Leonora of Ferrara four years after her marriage.

" Illustrissima e Excellentissima Signora,—The credible accounts and perfect information brought in by innumerable persons about the extreme kindness and rare munificence of your excellency, inspire me with the boldness to address you in confidence. I know that the most illustrious lord your spouse and your most illustrious ladyship adore hunting and birds, and that you have always in abundance dogs of all kinds, excellent, perfect. I beseech your excellency very earnestly that you would deign to make me a very beautiful and very precious present, namely, a pair of

* De Maulde de la Clavière.

greyhounds, well-trained and fleet-footed, for the deer of the Campagna, which are very swift : a couple of good deer-hounds and a couple of handsome pointers, so good that I may hope to say regarding their exploits when they catch their quarry, 'these are the dogs the most illustrious Duchess of Ferrarra gave me.' I know that your excellency will not send me anything but what is really good."

Then she cordially recommends to the duchess the falconer she is sending to fetch the hounds, and probably to choose them.

The chase was extremely popular at Rome, and the hunts in the great Campagna were renowned of old for the deer were fleet, and the boars so fierce that they needed a special breed of hounds to cope with them.

But hunting alone did not absorb the thoughts of the brilliant princess, for so high in favour was she with the Pope, that we find great princes of Italy, courtiers, petitioners of every kind, making intercession to this young girl, in order to obtain their requests. No honours were beyond the reach of her husband. He was made a citizen of Rome with much ceremony, in the year of his marriage, and while Catarina was enjoying life to the full, he was steadily and craftily working his way, and increasing his dominions. Imola was already his, and he had set his heart on Faenza and Forli. But the Medici were suspicious, and on the watch for any overt act of aggression on the part of the Pope's nephew, who therefore secretly joined with the Pazzi family in that dark plot, which had for its aim the assassination of the Medici brothers, and met with fatal success in the murder of Giuliano, in 1478.

By the confession of agents employed in it, this disgraceful conspiracy was traced to the cruel and treacherous Girolamo, and Pope Sixtus himself was more than suspected of being an accomplice. On being accused of connivance, he at once excommunicated Lorenzo and all Florence, in punishment for the summary vengeance taken on the murderers.

Meantime endless festivities in Rome mingled with these crimes and ambitious designs. Distinguished strangers were constantly making pilgrimage to the Eternal City from all parts of Europe ; foreign ambassadors came to bring gifts, to plead some national cause, to obtain absolution, or seek help of some kind from the successor of Saint Peter.

It was the custom to receive visitors at the city gate. and conduct them in pomp through the streets to their abode with a great retinue, to the delight of the Roman populace, who knew that this was a prelude to outdoor festivities in which they could share. Thus when the Duke of Saxony arrived on March 22, 1480, to pay a vow, he was met at the Porta del Popolo by the Pope and all his Cardinals, and conducted in state with an immense following to St. Peter's and presented with the consecrated golden rose, which on this occasion was an oak-bough, the heraldic emblem of the Della Rovere family.

The chronicler, Jacopo di Volterra, tells us that on this occasion Girolamo and his countess gave a great hunting party in honour of Duke Ernest on April 10, in the immediate neighbourhood of Rome, towards the Fonte Malliane, to the great joy of the citizens, as they could all join in the sport. It must have been a splendid sight to see the princes riding out on their fine horses, with the hounds in leash; themselves "shining with gold and jewels," accompanied by Catarina and her ladies in crimson and scarlet costumes, and followed by a gay retinue. Then as they reached the woods on the hillside, the horns sounded with the eager cry of the hunters and woke the echoes far and wide. A great number of stags and deer were taken, and after the chase a great banquet was prepared under the ilex woods for all to join in, high-born prince and citizen alike, to "their no small content."

During her four years of residence in Rome at the magnificent Palazzo Corsini, the Countess Riario had four children born to her. The eldest, a daughter who received the name of Bianca, was born in March 1478, and was her only girl. Ottaviano was born in September 1479, and Cesare in August 1480, just a month before his father received from the Pope the longed-for investiture of the city and domain of Forli. The infant heir of the Ordelaffi, who had so long held dominion there, had most opportunely died, whereupon Sixtus declared that the fief was forfeited, and had devolved to the Holy See.

Forli is about sixteen miles south-east of Imola, in the same fertile district, lying between the Apennines and the Adriatic, and is one of the most important towns of Romagna, forming a most useful link, with its strong fortress, between the Papal States and Imola. A few days after this investiture, Girolamo was appointed generalissimo of the army, and this being September 8, the birthday of the Virgin, there was a solemn mass, and Riario in complete armour knelt before the Pope, received the staff and standard, and took the oaths, in the presence of all the cardinals.

It was at daybreak on June 30, 1481, that the Count and Countess of Forli set forth on the eventful journey to their new home; the day and hour having been carefully selected by the court astrologer. During the whole of the previous week, long trains of laden mules and carts might have been seen passing out of the city, guarded by men-at-arms, and making their slow way by Orte and Spoleto to Perugia, on over the rough bridle paths of the Apennines, through the broad alluvial plains, by the Via Emilia to distant Forli. The old chronicles speak with awe and amazement of the immense treasure in richest stuffs, tapestries, clothing, furnishing, jewels and gold and silver plate, which was carried away from Rome in this slow laborious manner, each load being covered with an emblazoned cloth, bearing the united arms of Rovere and Sforza. The children had also been sent on in advance, and expectation in the provincial town was at its very highest, when at length Girolamo and Catarina reached the city gate on July 15. They were met by a company of youths and maidens clothed in white, and bearing olive-branches, with all the priests and bearers of office.

The people of Forli had never seen anything so magnificent as Catarina in her sumptuous robe, glittering with pearls and diamonds, and they were much impressed by the great Roman nobles who rode with their new count. Then followed the usual festivities, tournaments, balls, banquets and orations, in return for which loyal welcome Girolamo remitted the duty on corn. Building was at once commenced; to complete the strong fortress, enlarge the palace, and found schools and other public works. After a while, they went on a visit to Imola, and were received in much the same manner.

The chronicler of Forli says that, "charming it was to see the lady countess and all her damsels come forth in different magnificent dresses for a whole week, and the great buffets, ten feet high, in the banqueting hall of the palace, loaded every day with a fresh service of silver and gold." Every room in the grim palace of Forli was adorned with splendid hangings of tapestry, and magnificently furnished with the priceless spoils brought from Rome.

Elated by his previous success, the count's ambition extended to new conquests, and he now turned his eyes towards Ferrara. The moment seemed propitious, for Ercole Duke of Ferrara had quarrelled with Venice, and had been excommunicated by the Pope for having taken the post of general, on the side of Florence. Girolamo therefore found a pretext for a visit with his wife to Venice. Now the wily Venetians always looked on with approval at the ruin of hereditary rulers by papal nephews, who could have no permanent rule; for they knew that in the end the spoils would fall to them.

Girolamo and Catarina travelled to Venice by Comacchio and the marshes, to avoid Ferrara; the count giving as a pretext for his visit the urgent need of a league against the Turks, who had taken Otranto. A bucentaur with the Doge and Senators came to meet him at St. Clement in the Lagoon, two miles from Venice. He and his wife were received with princely honours in the Doge's palace, where "the noble virgins of Venice to the number of one hundred and thirty-two, loaded with gems, gold, and pearls," were assembled to welcome them. The Doge, Giovanni Mocenigo, took his place on a high dais, with the count on one side and the countess on the other, and all the nobles of Venice and their ladies sat around the hall. The afternoon and evening were given up to dancing and feasting; candles of white wax being lighted in such profusion that "the night was turned into day." The dresses of the ladies on this occasion were said to be worth 300,000 gold pieces. The next day, the Senators proceeded to business with their guest, privately discussed the division of the Este property, and found an excuse to declare war against Ferrara, in May 1482.

After this, the object of the journey being apparently attained, the count and countess returned to Imola; but they had not been there long before they received news of a conspiracy at Forli to restore the deposed family of the Ordelaffi. This, however, was promptly suppressed by the zeal of Francesco Tolentino, the governor, and Girolamo was able to set out for Rome with his wife, on October 14. The negotiations with Venice had not been kept so secret but that rumours had reached the King of Naples, who prepared a force to help the Duke of Ferrara. This was the signal for general hostilities, and offered a splendid opportunity for the condottieri to make their fortune. The Pope and Venice were on one side, while Florence, Naples, and Milan were on the other, with all the smaller States joining in, according to their private feuds. Roberto Malatesta commanded the armies of Venice, and the opposing league chose the distinguished Duke Federigo of Urbino.

In this brief sketch we cannot follow the varying fortunes of the struggle which followed, but it curiously illustrates the nature of this internecine war —that the two rival generals, both losing their lives, though not on the field of battle—had previously bequeathed to each other the care of their children and property. Roberto died in Rome, probably of fever, but rumour hinted that Girolamo had poisoned him out of jealousy. He was buried in St. Peter's with great honour; endless torches, banners and standards, one of which bore his arms with the motto: Veni, vidi, vici; victoriam Sixto dedi; Mors invidit gloriæ."

Infessura cynically tells an anecdote, in recording this pompous funeral: "A great captain had once saved Siena, and the people were at a loss how to reward him fitly. Then a citizen rose and said: 'Let us put him to death, and then worship him as a saint, so making him our perpetual protector,' which was done. Now it is said—not that I altogether believe it," adds Infessura honestly—"that the Pope followed the example of these Sienese, in the matter of Malatesta's death, and his funeral honours."

We can believe anything of Pope Sixtus IV., the promoter of the Inquisition, after reading his cruel treatment of the Colonna family in his feud with them at this time, and his judicial murder of the Protonotary. Meantime, a Congress was held, and the Pope found it to his interest to withdraw from the Venetian alliance, while Girolamo, who had not distinguished himself in the war, was ready enough to grasp the spoils of the victor, in the shape of Ravenna and Cervia. Italy was weary of war, and peace was made, without consulting the fiery Sixtus, who was furious at the

CATERINA SFORZA, COUNTESS OF FORLI

MARCO PALMEZZANI

thought that Ferrara would never belong to his nephew, and his rage is said to have killed him.

At this critical moment, when the triumphant career of Riario was brought to an abrupt end, he was away from Rome, engaged in harassing the Colonna family in their fastnesses; but Catarina, who was then on a visit, rose to the occasion. She at once took possession of the Castello St. Angelo, in the name of her husband, who was commander of the forces, and thus secured a safe refuge for herself and her children, in the fearful tumult and disorder, which followed upon the Pope's death. The city was given up to anarchy, many houses were pillaged and destroyed, especially all that belonged to the family of the late pontiff, even those of the Genoese merchants, because they were his countrymen. In the palace of Girolamo, they found little of value, as all the treasures had been safely carried to Forli, but they tore down the marble doorways, the carvings, &c., all they could not remove they destroyed. Catarina had a farm in the neighbourhood of Rome, and here they carried off hundreds of cows, goats, pigs, asses, geese and poultry, besides enormous stores of salt meat, round Parma cheeses, and casks of Greek wine.

Catarina, being in possession of the citadel, Girolamo was able to make terms with the cardinals, and insist upon his arrears of pay, some 4000 ducats, and a safe conduct for himself and family to Forli. Before they had arrived there, on August 29, 1484, Cardinal Cibo was made Pope, under the name of Innocent VIII. His election had been assisted by the Riario family, and the Count of Forli was confirmed in all his possessions. But he had no longer the boundless wealth of the Holy See at his command, and with his habit of reckless extravagance, especially in the way of building, he was soon in difficulties. Great sums were spent on the fine vaulting of the cathedral, as well as on the fortress of Ravaldino, which was strengthened and enlarged until it could hold 2000 men-at-arms, with stores for them. As time passed on there was growing discontent amongst the citizens and the cultivators of the rich alluvial fields around Forli at the heavy taxes which they had to pay for the maintenance of an extravagant court.

In May 1487 Girolamo was seriously ill at Imola, and his wife was nursing him, when one night a messenger arrived from Forli with news that Codronchi the seneschal of the palace, had murdered the castellan and seized the fortress. Catarina lost not a moment; she was in the saddle at once, and, riding hard, reached Fort Ravaldino at midnight, and called on her seneschal to account for his conduct. He answered her with respect, but begged her to wait till the morning for his answer. She had no choice but to yield, and at daybreak she was admitted through the gate with one servant. What followed within the citadel was never known, but the undaunted lady came forth safely, appointed a trusty friend, Tommaso Feo, as castellan, and rode off to Imola with Codronchi. "And the next morning, two hours after sunrise, Catarina gave birth to a son," says the chronicler.

So ended this surprising adventure, and soon afterwards, Girolamo having quite recovered from his illness, he returned to Forli with his wife. As the dissatisfaction still continued, in a despairing effort to win the favour of his subjects, Girolamo lightened their burdens of taxation, and the natural consequence was that he could not satisfy the ever-increasing demands of his courtiers, or pay his soldiers. A conspiracy was formed against him by two captains of his mercenaries and two of his most pampered favourites at court, Lorenzo and Cecco Orsi, who decided on his murder, and watched their opportunity. One afternoon, it was April 14, 1488, they went to his chamber after dinner, and found him leaning against the cushion of the open window, which looked out on the Piazza. He was in excellent spirits, and, instead of showing annoyance at their intrusion, he turned to greet them with a jest. Under the usual pretext of a petition Lorenzo stabbed him as he raised his hand to receive it. Girolamo made a desperate struggle for his life, but he was pierced with dagger thrusts again and again, and then his body, half naked, was hurled through the window to the public square below, and dragged about the streets by the populace.

The little town was already in the hands of the murderers; but the fortress, which stands on high ground at the apex of the fan-shaped city, was in the faithful guard of Tommaso Feo, and commanded the streets, which it could sweep with its guns. On receiving the terrible news Catarina, with marvellous presence of mind, at once despatched the messenger to her castellan Feo, bidding him send off courtiers to Lodovico il Moro at Milan, and to her husband's friend, Bentivoglio, Lord of Bologna. She was only just in time, for the murderers burst into her rooms and carried her off with her children to the Orsi palace.

This done, a hasty council decided to secure the

help of the Pope by offering Forli to him; and the conspirators lost no time in sending this message to the Cardinal Savelli, who was governor for the Church at Cesana, about twelve miles south of Forli. The cardinal was much troubled in mind, but, "not willing to have it said that by his default the Pope should suffer loss," he accepted the offer, rode off to the rebellious city, and even had an interview with Catarina. He wisely suggested that she and her family would do well to seek a safe refuge in a strong chamber above St. Peter's gateway, under the guard of trustworthy citizens chosen by him. She agreed, and that night we are told that "twelve persons of her family and suite were led through the city by torchlight to their new prison."

Next day, Tommaso Feo the castellan, was summoned to give up the citadel; he refused, and Catarina was brought to the barred gate and compelled to repeat the order. But he knew her too well to be deceived, and persisted in his refusal to surrender. Full of rage the conspirators tried again the next day, and at length in despair assented to the suggestion that the Lady of Forli should have a private interview with her obstinate castellan. She was admitted alone into the fortress on the understanding that she was only to remain there three hours. We may imagine the anxious suspense and excitement in the crowded streets below when the great bell on the Piazza rang to announce that the time was up. Summoned by a trumpet blast Feo appeared on the ramparts and made some futile remarks about his mistress and her need of repose; she was asleep, and he dared not wake her. Furious at the ruse, which they now began to suspect, the rebels fetched the Riario children from the gate-house and vowed they should instantly be put to death if the fortress were not surrendered. Historians differ as to the exact words of the haughty refusal, but Catarina undoubtedly dared them to do their worst, with a hint that children might be more easily replaced than a realm, and a threat that any harm to them would bring a fate worse than Sodom and Gomorrah on the city itself. Possibly the cardinal's influence prevailed, for the five boys and their sister were taken back to the prison unhurt.

The murder of Girolamo had taken place on April 14, 1488, and on the 18th a herald arrived from the Lord of Bologna, to demand the safety of the Riario family, and that Ottaviano, the eldest son of the murdered prince, should be proclaimed Count of Forli. To this Savelli made reply that the children were safe, and that the fief had been offered to the Pope. But when, two days later, there came to him a messenger from Milan using still stronger language, he became alarmed, and took a dangerous step. As no troops had yet come from Rome, not even a letter from the Pope, he resolved to forge the Bull of which he stood in such urgent need. This did him no service, and proved to be a terrible mistake on his part, for the peaceable Innocent VIII. was not tempted by the offer of this turbulent little State, and absolutely disowned all that had been done by his agent, who had a very narrow escape with his life from the later vengeance of Catarina. Meantime the troops of Bologna, and those of Milan, under young Galeazzo di Sanseverino, were drawing near the city walls, and on the 29th the situation was hopeless for the conspirators, who after an unsuccessful attempt on the lives of Girolamo's children, fled by night from the scene of their crimes.

The magistrates went in procession to the fortress to offer their lady the key of the city, and the next day she made a triumphant entry on horseback, in company with the generals sent to her help: Ottaviano is proclaimed count, and his mother appointed Regent, while the hapless Girolamo is buried with much pomp at Imola.

The murderers had sent an envoy at once to Lorenzo dei Medici, describing their crime as due vengeance for the murder of his brother Giuliano, and begging for his support, but they received no answer. The ruler of Florence was not vindictive, and he was quite willing to help and protect the widowed countess and her son, for it was his policy to encourage weak States. As soon as her power was established, Catarina took a cruel vengeance on all who had taken part against her, and nothing can excuse her brutality to the aged head of the Orsi family.

As regent for her son, now nine years old, she ruled her State with vigour and ability, making a great name for herself, so that in France they called one of their most formidable pieces of artillery, "Madame de Forli." There is a curious little notice of Catarina in one of the diplomatic despatches of Cardinal Bibbiena; he writes:

"To-day there took place an interview between the Duke of Calabria and the divine lady of Forli. Needless to say, his excellency was admirably groomed and attired in the height of Neapolitan fashion. His arrival at Bagnara was welcomed with a salute of musketry, and he stayed to dinner. He spent two hours with the countess here, but it is patent to every one that Feo has the lady well under his thumb. His excellency took his leave very well contented, but he was only moderately taken with the countess; he told me that they joined hands very gingerly . . ."

In her exuberant energy she had also taken up the study of magic and medicine, and it was her strange taste to collect uncanny exotic recipes of every kind. We are told that "she spent hours in a private laboratory, receiving a Jewess who had brought her a universal salve, or verifying formulæ for a celestial water, a cerebrine made of the marrow of an ass, a magnet intended to compose family squabbles, and a thousand other prescriptions of like virtue." An ambassador sends her a drug compounded chiefly of eggs and saffron, of which he writes: "I wish to be present when you test it . . . and I would not change places with the King of France, so happy am I in contemplating so admirable a thing; and besides your excellency would not find another man like me, for courage is required not to be afraid of spirits; faith to believe, and secresy to betray nothing."

This princess is described to us as a magnificent woman, endowed with nature's most prodigal gifts; tall, strong, of a good presence, and with a clear superb complexion; in speech eager, impulsive, her voice ringing out for the most part like a trumpet call, but capable of alluring softness. The Giacomo Feo of Savona, mentioned in the last letter, was the brother of her faithful castellan, and became her husband or lover. He was a man of great power and violence, "threatening constantly to sell his soul to the devil, and (a more serious matter) the State to the Turks, and

Catarina was subjugated by him." "Feo became an odious tyrant; denunciations, persecutions, tortures are his wedding gifts." As was to be expected, Feo fell by the hand of the assassin. He was stabbed to the heart one day, under the very eyes of his sovereign, as they were returning together from the chase. Directly she saw that he was past all hope, she lost not an instant, but mounting her horse at once, she rode at the head of her guards to the quarter inhabited by the murderers, and there she caused to be massacred without distinction every living creature, even the women and children. Such was the savage vengeance of Catarina Sforza.

Yet in times of tranquillity she showed many qualities of a wise ruler. She built various useful public institutions, amongst others an Academy of Fine Arts, and was a liberal patroness of learning. She was generous and open-hearted, and not willingly unjust unless her passions were aroused, but she was a true despot in her government. Always in need of money, it occurred to her that as Imola and Forli were on the great Via Emiliana, it would be a lucrative thing to set up toll-bars at each end of her dominions. This brilliant scheme was not, however, a success. It naturally brought her into constant feuds with her neighbours, while the passing merchants and travellers found some way of evading her tolls, either by making a circuit round, or by crossing the rough open country at night. Finding it hardly paid the needful expense, the Madonna of Forli reluctantly gave up her toll-bars.

At the time of her first husband's death in 1488 she had been left a young widow of twenty-six, with six children, of whom five were boys; Giorgio Livio,

Galeazzo named after her father, and Francesco Sforza, being the three younger ones.

She had many tastes and interests in common with her uncle Lodovico Sforza, the Duke of Milan, and she kept up a constant correspondence with him during the troubled years of her rule at Forli. He had been the earliest to send help to Catarina after the murder of her husband Riario, and continued a most useful ally to this warlike niece of his, in her constant feuds with her neighbours and her own restless subjects.

"Were it not for the trust I place in your excellency, I should drown myself!" she exclaims on one occasion.

At this time she had aroused the anger of the Venetians by her alliance with Florence, for in the end she had taken to herself in 1497 another husband. He was the ambassador from Florence, a member of the younger branch of the Medici family, Giovanni, a man of delicate idealistic temperament, who must have attracted her by the very force of contrast. She gave to the son of this marriage the name of Lodovico, but this was later on changed to "Giovanni," on the death of her young husband, six months after the birth of her child. He was only thirty years of age, but he appears to have been for some time in delicate health, and he died at a little village amongst the Apennines, San Piero in Bagno, where he had gone to take the baths.

In consequence of this connection with the Medici, all her children were made citizens of Florence later on, when troubles had driven her to take refuge in that city.

Catarina lost her husband in 1497, and seems to have

mourned him deeply ; indeed, her heart was so much touched that she turned her thoughts seriously to religion. A very curious correspondence took place between her and Savonarola. She wrote to him in the full fervour of her new piety to request his prayers, and he replied in a gentle and dignified letter of mingled serenity and strength, in which he takes high ground in rebuking her life. This letter is dated June 18, 1497, the very day on which all the churches of Florence were thundering with the denunciation of the Pope against him. It shows a marvellous aloofness of soul from his own cares, that at such a time, he could devote thought and charity to a distant penitent in distress.

As for Catarina, she was a creature of impulse ; in the days of her prosperity she would dance all night, and go on a pilgrimage the next day. In time of famine or plague, she would go fearlessly amongst her people like a genuine sister of mercy. Her wonderful force of mind would assert itself under the most trying circumstances, as when she wrote to her sons, later on, from the depth of her dungeon in the Castle of Sant' Angelo, bidding them not to be concerned for her.

"I am habituated to grief ; I have no fear of it."

After war had been declared against her, and a Venetian army had already invaded her dominions, the Duke of Milan sent a gallant soldier, Gaspare Sanseverino, better known as the Captain Fracassa, to help her with troops, and later on his eldest brother, the Count of Caiazzo. But even those who went to her assistance did not find her easy to deal with, and she was always appealing to the Duke. A great condottiere, a captain of mercenaries, who bargained with Kings and Emperors, could not be expected to take rough words meekly even from a lady, and she would quarrel violently with Fracassa one day, to make it up again the next. Then, too, with regard to the marriages of her children, she gave Lodovico a great deal of trouble. He had suggested a bride from the house of Gonzaga for her eldest son; but this she rejected, and suddenly bethought herself that she would accept the proposal of Count Caiazzo for her daughter Bianca. Then she changed her mind and said he was too old, and wrote to her uncle to ask him what he thought of Galeazzo di Sanseverino as a husband for the young girl. This was another brother of Fracassa, one of twelve sons of Roberto Sanseverino, all famous, but Galeazzo was the most distinguished both with his sword and his pen. But the countess was promptly told that the knight had no intention of marrying again.

Catarina Sforza was a very capable woman, and a most able diplomatist; indeed, on one occasion, she more than held her own against Macchiavelli himself. He had been deputed by the Signoria of Florence to enter into negotiations with the Lady of Forli. He was to buy guns and ammunition from her if possible, but the chief point was that he was to renew the engagement of Ottaviano, her eldest son, now about twenty years of age, as a general in the army of the Republic. This appointment the young man had held for a year past, and the salary agreed upon was to have been twelve thousand ducats, but as yet he had received nothing. Now Macchiavelli was instructed to offer a stipend for the coming year of ten thousand ducats, instead of the twelve thousand already agreed upon, and it is a noticeable fact that Ottaviano himself keeps out of the way, and leaves his mother to do the bargaining for him.

Macchiavelli soon discovers with whom he has to deal, for he writes to Florence: "That words and reasoning will not avail much to satisfy her, unless some partial performance be added to them."

In the end the ambassador is beaten all round, and has to pay the astute lady the full amount agreed upon.

The days of trouble for Lodovico himself were fast approaching. After the death of his young wife Beatrice, nothing seemed to succeed with him. Now the King of France and Cæsar Borgia and the Venetians all combined against him, and Catarina, who sent a troop of horse from Forli, was almost his only ally in Italy. His fate was sealed, and before many months the most magnificent prince of the whole land was an exile and a prisoner. But Catarina was too much engrossed in her great and final struggle, to have much thought or pity for others. The year of the Papal Jubilee, when thousands of pilgrims crowded to Rome, to seek indulgences from the hand of Alexander VI., was a fatal one for the Madonna of Forli.

In the course of his career of conquest in Romagna, Cæsar Borgia reached Forli early in January, and, after a desperate and heroic defence on the part of Catarina Sforza, the citadel fell into his hands on January 12. Only after forcing his way into the innermost retrenchments, did he at length succeed in capturing her. There is a legend that the Duke of Romagna was so proud of his victory, that he caused his captive to be bound in chains of gold, like another queen of Palmyra, to conduct her to Rome, where he made his triumphal entry on February 20. We are told that she wore a black satin dress, and rode between Cæsar Borgia and a French general. Pope Alexander assigned the Belvedere to Catarina as her place of captivity. The city was full of pilgrims at that time, and amongst others who came that spring was Elisabetta Gonzaga, Duchess of Urbino, who must have been deeply touched by the sad fate of the Countess of Forli, the sister of her brother Alfonso's first wife, Anna Sforza. The kind-hearted duchess must have felt it all the more, that her own husband and her brother Francesco, being both in the service of France, must have had their share in the fall of this unhappy lady.

Elisabetta had scarcely left Rome before Catarina received the bad news that both her uncles, Lodovico and Cardinal Ascanio, had fallen into the power of the King of France. They had retaken Milan in February that year, by the aid of Swiss mercenaries, but they were shamefully betrayed by them on April 10 before Novaro. Lodovico was taken to France, where he died after ten miserable years of captivity in the dungeon of Loches; and Ascanio himself, formerly so powerful a Prince of the Church, was also taken a captive to France. It must have been a sad reflection for the proud woman, in her prison, that all her family were involved in these tragic fatalities.

The gaolers of Catarina, the Borgia Pope and his son, were more to be dreaded than any other men of their time, and the thought of being at their mercy may well have been a terrible one. She must have lived in dread of dagger or poison, and have felt that only by a miracle had she escaped death. After a disastrous attempt to escape, the Pope confined her in the grim castle of Saint Angelo. But some French knights in the service of her conqueror, and especially Yvon d'Allegre, had the honour of saving her by a chivalrous protestation to the Pope. After eighteen months of captivity, she was permitted to take refuge in Florence. The following is the somewhat surprising letter of recommendation which he wrote to the Signoria on the occasion.

"ROMA, *Juglio* 13. 1501.

"DILECTI filii Salutem et ap. ben. Our dear daughter in J. C., the noble lady Catarina Sforza, to whom we have given our pardon, after having, as you know, kept her prisoner for valid reasons, is on her way to you. Having not only acted with clemency, as is our habit and our pastoral duty, towards the aforesaid Catarina, but wishing to provide for her wants with paternal goodness as much as we can with the help of God, we have thought well to write to you to recommend warmly to your kind offices the said Catarina; so that, as she has the greatest confidence in our benevolence, and turns to you as to her own country, she may not be disappointed in the hopes which she has founded upon our commendations. It will, therefore, be very agreeable to us to learn that, as a recompense for the respect shown by her towards your city and from consideration for us, she has been well received and well treated by you.

"Given at Rome, at Saint Peter's, under the seal of the fisherman, on the 13th of July, the ninth year of our pontificate.

"HADRIANUS."

Thus it was that Catarina, the great Madonna of Forli, after her stormy and eventful life, took refuge in Florence. But even here she did not think herself safe, and more especially felt much anxiety as to the protection of her youngest son, the little Giovanni dei Medici. A curious idea occurred to her; she dressed him in girl's clothes, and took him by night to the Annalena Convent in the Via Santa Maria, where she prayed the nuns to keep him under their care until the evil days should have passed away, and the exiled Medici should once again hold their own. The good sisters were delighted to receive the little boy, and promised to keep the secret.

It was a remarkable episode in the early history of this distinguished warrior, the last and greatest of the condottieri of Italy, who was to be so famous in the military history of his time. When quite young, he began to serve as a soldier under Leo X., and was subsequently appointed Captain of the Republic when he gained the name of "Invitto" (the Invincible). It was under his training that the infantry first began to acquire fame. While in Lombardy fighting against the Spaniards, he was mortally wounded near Mantua, and carried through the falling snow to the house of Lodovico Gonzaga. We have a very touching account of his death, at the age of twenty-nine. "Love me when I am dead," he said to the Duke Federigo, who replied in broken accents, "I will indeed."

"En vérité, c'était un grand homme de guerre," wrote the French ambassador. The soldiers who fought under Giovanni were so devoted to him, that they never laid aside the mourning which they put on at his death; and from their black garments, the name of their leader remained famous in history as "Giovanni delle Bande Nere." He was the founder of a noble line, for his son Cosimo was the first Grand Duke of Florence.

Catarina never lived to see the fortunes of her house revive. She found a shelter in the Convent of Santa Maria delle Muriate, where she spent the few remaining years of her life, and died in the year 1509. But it is in the ancient town of Forli that her memory is most truly enshrined. In the secluded church of San Biagio, half forgotten in its moss-grown corner, the frescoes of Palmazzano still show us Catarina painted as the Madonna, and adored by all the Riario family. There, too, as we turn from the broad piazza, with its lovely campanile of San Mercuriale, and pass up the long arcaded street, we see before us, rising grim and threatening, the fortress of Ravaldino, and call to mind that stirring chronicler, how the Madonna of Forli won her fame.

LUCREZIA BORGIA, DUCHESS OF FERRARA

THE very name is a term of reproach, nay even of opprobrium, to many who read it; only suited to point a moral, in hateful contrast to the famous Lucrezia of old. But the researches of modern historians have done more than cast doubt upon the evil legend which has haunted this unfortunate lady through the ages. Countless letters and documents of the period have been hunted out from the dusty recesses of old libraries; family archives have been diligently searched, and the result has been to avenge the memory of this much maligned princess. Those who would seriously study the proofs advanced will find them in the pages of Roscoe, and more fully in the exhaustive "justification" of the historian, Gregorovius, made more impressive by sixty-five original documents of the time.

The Borgias were so justly hated in their own day, that their enemies were not satisfied with holding up to public execration Pope Alexander VI. and his son Cæsar, as monsters in human form, but they included in the same condemnation every member of the abhorred race. This at least we know, that when Lucrezia escaped from the poisonous atmosphere of the papal court, and became Duchess of Ferrara, she i ved a dignified and blameless life for more than twenty years, winning the esteem and respect of all. On her marriage with Alfonso d'Este, Ariosto pays her the tribute of "rivalling in the decorum of her manners as in the beauty of her person, all that former times could boast."

After this brief introduction, we will turn to the known facts of her eventful life. She was born April 18, 1480. Her father, Cardinal Borgia, was to become Pope Alexander VI. twelve years later, and her mother was a Roman woman of great beauty, Vanozza Catanei, who had already two sons of his, Giovanni and Cæsar. For some years these children were together in their mother's house, and the company of these two elder Borgia brothers cannot have been good for the character of little Lucrezia. She was probably their meek slave, for in after days she never seems to have greatly asserted herself, or to have had much voice in the mapping out of her life. The little girl seems to have been carefully brought up with the classical training of the day, and special attention was paid to her religious knowledge, whatever moral value that may have had. At this point, it is interesting to note that in the Catalogue of seventeen books which she took to Ferrara, at least eight were breviaries and religious works, besides a Dante, a Petrarch, and some books on Philosophy.

At twelve years old we are told, "she speaks Spanish, Greek, Italian, French, and a little Latin also, very purely; she writes and composes poetry in all these languages." Several hundreds of her letters have been preserved, some in Spanish, but mostly in Italian, written in a very natural and easy style, full of liveliness and feeling, but without much depth. She was quite young when she left her mother's house, and was placed under the care of Madonna Adriana Orsini, a connection of Cardinal Borgia, and a great lady of position and influence, and with her Lucrezia must have learnt to take her place in society. She is described as being a beautiful girl, with golden hair, well-formed features, laughing blue eyes and a very fair complexion.

Before her father became Pope, he had arranged for her betrothal with a Spanish grandee of an ancient and noble house, Don Cherubin Juan de Centelles. But the project was never realised, for, on his promotion to the Chair of St. Peter a year later, he set his heart upon a more brilliant alliance; nothing short of a prince would content him, and Giovanni Sforza, Lord of Pesaro, was selected as his son-in-law. He had married Maddelena, the younger sister of Elisabetta, Duchess of Urbino, but she had died the following year, and he gladly accepted the hand of Lucrezia. There was some trouble with the young Spaniard, but the masterful Alexander had his way. The marriage was celebrated with great magnificence, and the bride had a dowry of 31,000 ducats, and presents of immense value. She already had a palace in Rome, where she spent much time with her husband, and Madonna Adriana lived with her as dame of honour; also the daughter-in-law of this lady, Julia Farnese, whose intrigue with the Pope was of common notoriety. In a letter of that date we have a curious account of a visit to this palace of "Santa Maria in Forticu," where the three ladies were found sitting round the fire in the greatest intimacy. They were dressed in velvet and fur, but Julia had recently washed her magnificent hair, which fell round her to the ground, and Pucci adds: "shone like the sun." Can we conceive any more evil society for an impressionable girl of fourteen?

Meantime her husband was in great difficulties, for there was every appearance of war between the Pope and the Duchy of Milan, and he was in the pay of both. There was a clause in his marriage contract, authorising him to take his wife with him to Pesaro, and he availed himself of this, taking with him Madonna Adriana, Julia Farnese, and also Vanozza, as the Pope was afraid of the plague for them. A few months later, a curious adventure befell two of these ladies. In travelling from their Castle of Capodimonte to Viterbo with a suite of twenty-five horsemen, they were taken prisoners by a French troop, under Monseigneur d'Allègre. The Pope had to pay a ransom of 3000 ducats to redeem them, and all Europe smiled at the story. Pesaro is situated in a broad valley open to the sea, and protected by an amphitheatre of hills, an ideal situation on the shore of the Adriatic, the very garden of Italy. But it was in a torrent of rain which blotted out the landscape, that Lucrezia arrived to take possession of the ancient Sforza palace, which was to be her home for so short a time. It must have seemed to her like escaping from a prison, to live in this lovely spot, with the Apennines to separate her from her father and brother. For the summer she had several country resorts, but the most beautiful was the palace on Mount Accio, with splendid views over land and sea, and grounds like the gardens of Armida. If the young wife had been happy in her marriage, she would have been like some queen of Arcadia, but she had been simply a docile victim in the hands of her relations, tossed as a prize to the highest bidder.

In this brief space it is impossible to trace out the complicated politics and wars of Italy, and we can only follow the fortunes of Lucrezia, who found herself the next year recalled to Rome, and established in the midst of the brilliant and licentious court of the Borgia Pope. The Sforza alliance was no longer of any use to him, and, with his usual unscrupulous ambition, he decided to find his daughter another husband. It is said that Giovanni would have fallen a victim to the dagger or poison, had not his wife sent him an urgent warning, on which he made his escape, riding in all haste to Pesaro, where his horse fell dead under him. She does not seem to have cared much for him, but she opposed the divorce which followed, without success, for her father and brother had absolute power in their hands. But she so far asserted herself as to leave her sumptuous palace and take refuge, for a time, in the convent of nuns of San Sisto, on the Appian Way. It was while she was in this cloistral retreat that she received the terrible news of her brother, the Duke of Gandia, having been murdered in the streets of Rome, and public report accused Cæsar Borgia of the foul crime.

Close upon this followed the scandalous lawsuit in which the Borgias declared the marriage with Giovanni Sforza annulled, on June 10, 1493; and the shameful reports with regard to poor Lucrezia appear to have had their origin about this time. The Pope had already found another husband for her, Alfonso, Duke of Bisaglia, nephew of the King of Naples, whose daughter was greatly desired as a wife for Cæsar Borgia.

The unfortunate Alfonso, who was only seventeen, must have felt himself a sacrifice to the family ambition; he came to Rome sadly and unwillingly, and the marriage was celebrated at the Vatican, with the old custom of a knight holding a naked sword over the head of bride and bridegroom—a meet emblem of the troubles in store for them both. The Pope had bestowed on his daughter a dowry of 40,000 ducats, the duchy of Spoleto and the territory of Sermoneta. But he was much disappointed at the refusal of the hand of the Princess Carlotta of Naples for his son, and joined with Louis XII., who had designs on the throne of Naples. Some time after this, Alfonso, warned by a friend, thought it wise to escape from the fatal shadow of the Vatican, to the great indignation of Alexander, and the sorrow of his wife, who had become much attached to the amiable and handsome young man, and persuaded him to return to Rome. Her son was born three months later, and was baptized with great pomp in the Sistine Chapel, borne in state by the captain of the papal guards, and accompanied by all the ambassadors and cardinals.

Once more Lucrezia had a short time of peace and happiness, and her palace became a centre of artistic and intellectual society. Young Michelangelo had recently come to Rome, and attracted much interest; he was at that time working at his wonderful Pietà, which Lucrezia must often have seen. We have very full details of all that happened at Rome during this period, in the private Journal of Burchard, the papal master of the ceremonies, who, like our Pepys, never allowed his contemporaries to see his writings. Indeed, had he done so, it would certainly have cost him his head ; as it was, he continued to write every day, his short dry account of all he saw, under the rule of five Popes.

Alexander VI. had a narrow escape of his life in the month of June 1500, when a chimney fell in the Vatican, but he was rescued from the ruins only slightly hurt. He would suffer no one to nurse him but his daughter, and ascribing his escape to the special protection of the Virgin, he went in a procession to Santa Maria del Popolo, with rich offerings. As Gregorovius remarks, the Saints of Paradise may have interposed to save a great sinner, but they suffered an innocent man to be murdered only eighteen days afterwards. One evening, Alfonso was mounting the steps to meet his wife, when he was set upon by a band of men in masks and stabbed. He had just strength to rush into the Pope's apartment, where at the sight of her husband covered with blood, Lucrezia fell fainting to the ground. Alfonso was carried into a chamber in the Vatican, and a cardinal gave him absolution. But he was tenderly cared for by his wife and did not die, indeed he was on the way to recovery when Cæsar Borgia burst into the sick-room, with a bravo who finished the bloody deed.

Never was a crime sooner forgotten. The whole affair was hushed up, no steps were taken to punish the murderer, and only poor Lucrezia had to bear her burden of grief, in that most terrible moment of her life. The sight of her tears was distasteful to her father and brother, and they readily assented to her leaving Rome for a time. At the end of August, with an escort of six hundred horsemen, she set out for the old Etruscan town of Nepi, of which she was sovereign. The grim medieval castle stands on a height in the Campania, in the midst of a sombre and melancholy landscape, like all that volcanic country. A vast panorama spreads out before the eyes, the wooded hills of Viterbo, Mount Soracte, like an island in the middle of the sea, and to the north, the broad valley of the Tiber, bounded through a misty haze by the blue mountains of the Sabine.

The young widow of Alfonso took a portion of the court with her, and her little son Roderigo ; but it was a time of strict mourning, and there was nothing to distract her mind from her grief. There are a few letters preserved which she wrote at this time, signed, "La principessa infelicissima de Salerno." They chiefly treat of domestic affairs and the mourning clothes which she needs for herself and for little Roderigo, and for black hangings to her bed. But more than once she writes to her faithful servant in Rome, bidding him have prayers said in all the monasteries. "Fa far nove orationi per tutti li mònasterii per queste nove mie tribulationi."

She writes again on October 30 :

"Vicenzo. Having decided to cause a commemorative service to be celebrated for the soul of the lord duke, my husband,—santa gloria habia,—you will see to it.

"From the castle of Nepi. La infelissima."

"Sia data in mano de Vicenzo Giordano."

There can be no doubt that she sincerely grieved for the loss of her young husband, but before the end of the year we find her longing to return to Rome, and, twelve months later, the disconsolate widow was to all appearance gay and lighthearted as ever. It was true that her father left her no time for regrets, as he had already another marriage in view. He had set his heart on another Alfonso, the eldest son of the Duke of Ferrara, as by such an alliance he hoped not only to win over Ferrara to the cause of Cæsar Borgia, but also the allied houses of Mantua and Urbino. His first proposal was absolutely rejected by Ercole d'Este, and received with horror by his daughter Isabella d'Este, and the Duchess of Urbino, her sister-in-law.

Nothing daunted, the wily Pope continued to press the matter, feeling certain of ultimate success. After a time, more pressure was brought to bear upon Ercole by the King of France, and these humiliating negotiations for Lucrezia proceeded slowly. In June 1501, the Pope joined the army at Sermoneto, and actually installed his daughter in his own place at the Vatican, and Burchard writes in his Diary: "His Holiness before leaving the city, confided all the palace and the care of current affairs to Donna Lucrezia Borgia, his daughter, and his Holiness has given her full power to open all the letters which arrive. . . ."

What a scene at the Vatican! This young woman, the Pope's own daughter, presiding at the consistory, composed of cardinals! This one fact speaks for itself more than a thousand satires. It seems that Alexander had at last received the longed-for consent of Duke Ercole, and he may have thought to give her a more assured standing by raising her to this high position as a political personage.

There had been great difficulty in overcoming the repugnance of Alfonso himself to the proposed marriage, although his first wife, Anna Sforza, had died four years before, and had left him no son and heir. That Lucrezia was illegitimate does not seem to have been of most serious account; the sumptuous Renaissance was a golden age for children who had no legal right to be born. The young d'Este had but to look in his own family—at his grandfather, King Ferrante of Naples, of the proud house of Arragon, at his two uncles, Leonello and Borso d'Este, the late reigning Dukes of Ferrara—who were all of the "bar sinister." There must have been a dark shadow of sacrilege resting on this daughter of the Pope, but through it glimmered dim suggestions of unique advancement, for who of all the princes of Europe could offer so splendid a dowry ?

As to the lady herself, it was singularly unfortunate that at the age of twenty-one she should already have been twice betrothed, twice married, and twice deprived of a husband under criminal circumstances, of which she had been the too passive spectator. She had lived in the licentious atmosphere of the papal court, she was sister of the infamous Cæsar Borgia, the "Prince" of Macchiavelli, scandalous reports had spread with regard to her, but nothing had been proved—it was all *si dice*. Most anxious inquiries were made about her character, and a special envoy wrote to Duke Ercole that "there was nothing sinister about her." He also spoke of Madonna Lucrezia as "sensible, discreet, of good and loving nature . . .

her manners full of modesty and decorum; a good Christian filled with the fear of God . . . in truth, such are her good qualities that I rest assured there is nothing to fear from her, nay, rather everything to hope from her."

The Duke of Ferrara was quite won over by the immense advantages offered to his State; and as his son still hesitated, he used the final argument that he would marry Lucrezia himself if Alfonso remained obstinate. When at last the consent of the bridegroom was obtained, Duke Ercole took a purely business view of the matter, and determined to sell the honour of his house at the highest possible price. It is curious to note at this point, that in the long negotiations which followed, his future daughter-in-law was his best ally. Always at the elbow of the Pope when he received one exorbitant demand after another, she persuaded him in the end to agree to everything, although he was much enraged with all this haggling, and exclaimed: "Che il procedere del duca era un procedere da mercatante." Ercole wrote her several most friendly letters to thank her for her valuable help, but in truth she was herself intensely eager for the marriage.

Surely it speaks well for Lucrezia that she should so ardently desire to escape from the polluted air of Rome, from her fatal past; and to have a fresh start, with the chance of an honourable and peaceful life. She seems to have been strangely unconscious of any personal humiliation in being thus pressed upon an unwilling husband; no troubles could quench her gay, light-hearted, childish nature, and when the marriage was at last publicly proclaimed in Rome, she showed her joy by dancing all night with such exuberant spirits that she was ill the next day.

The dowry was indeed magnificent—100,000 ducats to be paid down in gold at Ferrara, and 100,000 more in plate, jewels, fine linen, clothes, costly hangings, and trappings for horses and mules. The yearly tribute of 400,000 ducats paid by the duchy as a fief of the Church was to be remitted, and the towns of Cento, Pieve, and Porto Cesenatico, and many valuable benefices, including the bishopric of Ferrara, were to be given to the duke. Every detail has been preserved of this amazing marriage, and we gaze bewildered on such lavish and wasteful prodigality.

A splendid retinue was sent from Ferrara to fetch the bride, composed of relations and friends and vassals of the house of Este; the great lords leading the way, splendidly dressed, with massive gold chains round the neck, and preceded by thirteen trumpeters and eight hautboys. This nuptial cavalcade consisted of about five hundred persons, under the command of the light-hearted young Cardinal Ippolyto d'Este, who thus gaily crossed the plains of Italy, living at the expense of the cities through which they passed. The journey took thirteen days; it was during the depth of winter, and when they reached Monterosi, fifteen miles from Rome, they were sadly weather-beaten, wet through, and covered with mud. The cardinal sent forward a trumpeter to take the orders of the Pope, with the result that the grand entry into the city, by the Porte del Popolo, was fixed for the next day. After a state reception by the people, the cardinals, and the Pope; the princes of Ferrara were introduced to Lucrezia, who came to meet them as far as the staircase of her palace. She wore a dress of white cloth brocaded with gold, with closely-fitting sleeves of gold brocade, a necklace of pearls, and a mantle of brown velvet trimmed with marten. "A charming and gracious lady," was the general verdict; and Cardinal Ippolyto wrote a long letter that evening to his sister Isabella at Mantua, giving a very pleasing account of his new sister-in-law.

He had brought a costly present of jewels, which he presented himself; and although the marriage had already been concluded by procuration at Ferrara, this formality was repeated at the Vatican, and his brother Ferrante placed the ring, in the name of Alfonso, on the bride's finger. On this occasion she wore a gown of gold brocade and crimson velvet, trimmed with ermine, the sleeves reaching to the ground, and her long train borne by her ladies of honour. Her fair hair was tied with a black ribbon, she wore a coif of some golden material, and priceless jewels.

There were great festivities every day—a bull-fight in the Piazza San Pietro, endless theatrical representations and state balls, in which Lucrezia's dancing was much admired. At length, on the 6th of January, she set forth on her journey to cross Italy like a queen, with so magnificent a procession as the world has rarely seen. A number of chariots and 150 mules laden with her trousseau had been sent on beforehand, and she took with her "everything she desired, and there was to be no inventory kept." The immense retinue with which she travelled made up almost a thousand persons, and amongst these were 180 of her own special Court, including Madonna Adriana and her other ladies, and Cæsar Borgia had equipped an escort of honour of 200 noble cavaliers, with a choir of musicians and jesters to entertain his sister on the way.

The Pope had carefully mapped out the whole route, and sent special orders that everywhere his daughter was to be received with triumphal arches, illuminations, and solemn preparations. She was to go by Castelnovo, Civita Castellana, Narni, Terni, Spolete, Foligno. Here the Duchess of Urbino was to meet Lucrezia, and had promised to accompany her as far as Ferrara. They would cross the States of Cæsar through Pesaro, Nimini, Cesena, Forli, Faenza, and Imola, to arrive at Bologna, from thence by the river Po to Ferrara, a long and tedious journey at that period, when the roads made it necessary to travel chiefly on horseback, and when we remember what even an Italian winter can be.

Even this light-hearted young woman, in the hour of her triumph, must have had some sad leave-taking. She was parting with her little boy, Roderigo, whom she was never to see again, for the young Duke of Bisaglio died at Bari a few years later. She may have said a last good-bye to Vanozza, but her name is never mentioned at this period. When her father had taken leave of her at the Vatican, he moved from one window to another to have a last view of her, until the cavalcade had quite passed out of sight. All the cardinals, the ambassadors, and the magistrates of Rome accompanied the bride to the Porto del Popolo. She rode a splendid white horse with a golden bridle and her travelling garb was of red silk trimmed with ermine, and a plumed hat. Thus she turned away from her stormy past to enter upon a new life.

The journey was tedious rather than eventful, although the new duchess was received everywhere with great honour, as though she were a royal personage. On the seventh day she arrived at Foligno, where, amongst other pleasing masques, was a triumphal car, from which Paris declared that he had made a mistake in giving Venus the golden apple, and that he now presented it to the lady who excelled all the three goddesses, with beauty, wisdom, and power combined.

On the outskirts of Gubbio, a remote little town on the western slope of the Apennines, Lucrezia was met by the Duchess Elisabetta, who conducted her in state up the steep road to her splendid palace on the grey hillside. It must have been a supreme effort on the part of this great lady to receive with any show of friendship the woman who had first married the widower of her young sister, Maddelena, and had then divorced him with public scandal. Yet nothing was lacking to the princely courtesy of her welcome at Gubbio and again at Urbino two days later, when Duke Guidobaldo and all his court came down the hill to meet her and escorted her to the palace, while he and the duchess lodged elsewhere. The Montefeltro may have hoped that the influence of Lucrezia would secure the safety of Urbino, and could never foresee that only a few months later the vile perfidy of her brother, Cæsar Borgia, would drive them from their dominions.

After a day's rest, the two duchesses continued their journey over the mountain pass, and arrived late at night at Pesaro, which now belonged to

Cæsar, and Lucrezia was accompanied by a train of children with olive branches to the very home of her first married life. We cannot imagine anything more painful for her than the thought of those days, and of Giovanni Sforza still burning for revenge; but our deepest pity would be for the tender-hearted Elisabetta, for whom these walls would be haunted by sad memories of her young sister's wedding, so soon to be followed by her death. It must have been a relief to both ladies to continue their journey. Passing through Forli and Faenza on Friday they reached Imola, where Lucrezia declared that she must rest a day to wash her head. Probably that golden hair required a great deal of attention. On reaching Bologna, she was very glad to take the easier route by water, and on the last day of January she arrived at Castel Bentivoglio, where she was agreeably surprised by an impromptu visit in disguise from Alfonso, her husband. She received him with "much deference and grace," and he made a gallant response during the short interview. The Pope was delighted to hear of this little episode from his daughter, who wrote to him every day. He had felt great anxiety as to her reception by the Este family, and this news set his fears at rest.

The next day, at Malalbergo, Lucrezia met Isabella Marchesa of Mantua, who had required much persuasion from her father to induce her to do the honours of the state reception. But she acted her part graciously, and greeted her new sister-in-law with a kiss. At Torre della Fossa the Duke Ercole, with his son Alfonso and all the Court, awaited their coming, and received them on a gorgeous bucentaur, where the ambassadors and others were presented to the bride. At Ferrara itself the preparations for her arrival were on a scale of royal prodigality, and the solemn entry was one of the most brilliant spectacles of the age. It was the great moment of her life.

We have a very full account of the magnificent procession—the archers, the trumpeters, the bishops, the cavaliers, the ambassadors, those of Rome in long cloth-of-gold mantles lined with crimson satin. The scene must have been one dazzling mass of colour. Alfonso wore red velvet and a black velvet cap with a beaten-gold ornament. His brown horse was covered with trappings of crimson velvet and gold. As for the bride, we are told she was sparkling with beauty and joy. She wore a "camorra" of black velvet with wide sleeves and delicate fringes of gold, and a "sbernia" of gold brocade trimmed with ermine. Her head was covered with a net shining with gold and diamonds, and round her neck was a chain of great pearls and rubies, which Isabella remembered with a sigh, having seen them worn by her mother. Her beautiful hair fell freely over her shoulders. A purple baldachino was carried over her head by the doctors of law, of medicine, and of mathematics, in turn. Behind her rode the duke, her father-in-law, in rich black velvet.

When Lucrezia reached the palace, she was greeted at the foot of the great staircase by Isabella d'Este; it was already late, and the great halls were lighted with torches and candelabra. The bride and bridegroom were conducted with music to the reception room, where they took their places on a throne. The court was presented to them, and then the pompous wedding oration was recited. Amongst the poets who paid homage to the newly-wedded pair was a rising genius of whom great things were expected. Ariosto had composed a Latin epithalamium in the bride's honour, of which these lines will give an idea :

Est levis haec jactura tamen, ruat hoc quoque quicquid
Est reliquum, juvet et nudis habitare sub antris,
Vivere dum licet tecum pulcherrima virgo.

These words must have been received with a smile by those who understood them.

Lucrezia appears to have made a most favourable impression, not so much from her beauty as by a certain undefinable charm of person and manner, which won over even those who had been most hostile to her coming. Her constant brightness and sunny good humour must have been very attractive. There is a hint of jealousy in some of the letters of Isabella d'Este ; possibly this "prima donna del mondo" could not brook a rival so near the throne, and also she may have looked with wistful eyes at the slight graceful figure of the bride, for she herself was always afraid of growing stout. There is no very satisfactory portrait extant of Lucrezia, but this is the description of her appearance by a contemporary : "Di mediocre statura, gracile in aspetto, si faccia alquanto lunga, il naso profilato bello, li capelli aurei, gliocchi bianchi, la bocca alquanto grande con li denti candidissimà, la gola schietta e bianca oenata con decente valore, ed in essere, continuamente allegria e ridente."

Alfonso d'Este's secretary, Bonaventura Pistofilo writes of her : "Tu essa Lucrezia di venusto e mansueto aspetto, prudente, di gratissime maniere negli atti, e nel parlare di molto grazia e allegrezza."

The wedding festivities lasted for six days, and we

have the most minute description of every masque and comedy, of every opera and dance, of priceless gifts and dazzling costumes. One day Lucrezia wore a robe of woven gold and a chain of the most precious gems; then she next appeared in one of black satin and gold foliage, with flowing sleeves, with a hem similar to a flame of gold; and of another dress we are told it had cost fifteen thousand ducats. As to the wonderful performances she witnessed, we can only imagine, as her biographer remarks, that we are transported into Shakespeare's "Midsummer Night's Dream," and that Theseus Duke of Athens is before us in the person of Ercole Duke of Ferrara. He certainly had a marvellous gift in the way of entertainments, even for those sumptuous days of the Renaissance.

After all these gay doings there followed a period of retirement and economy, which must have been rather trying to the bride, but she quietly felt her way and won golden opinions from all around her. She had strong proof of this before the end of the year, when she was very ill after the birth of a daughter, and received the greatest kindness and devotion. But a terrible blow awaited her the following autumn, nothing less than the sudden death of Pope Alexander and the consequent ruin of Cæsar Borgia's ambitious projects. Poor Lucrezia must have been overwhelmed with grief and despair, for she cannot have closed her ears to the chorus of malediction which rose up from all Italy, and must have known on what a slender thread hung her position and hope of happiness. But in point of fact, she was securely established at Ferrara, and does not seem to have lost respect and consideration after the death of her father. She was even able to give some help to Cæsar, whose failing fortunes she watched with anxious interest.

Early in 1505, after the death of her father-in-law, she became really Duchess of Ferrara, and availed herself to the full of her new advantages. She became the very centre of the intellectual life of Ferrara, and her court was frequented by all the poets and learned men of the day. Endless sonnets and epigrams were written in her honour, comparing her to every goddess of antiquity, and praising her beauty and virtue in no measured terms. Ariosto, in the "Orlando Furioso," places her in the temple of famous women, above the Lucrezia of old, in beauty and chastity. In some instances the language of adulation took a more tender form, as in the letters of Bembo, the distinguished Venetian; but of these we must form a judgment by the standard of that day. The young duchess had not Isabella's great love for painting and sculpture, or the same eager desire for collecting works of art, but she was a liberal patron to the artists who painted the Este palace walls.

Her husband Alfonso had but little taste for literature or for courtly show. He was a wise ruler and a good soldier, and served Ferrara well during the stormy times which followed his father's death. As often as he had a little leisure from his fortifications and diplomacy, he spent it in painting china vases. When he had to take the field against the fighting Pope Julius, or against Venice, he always left his wife as regent of Ferrara, and she showed herself thoroughly worthy of his confidence. On one occasion when the Jews had been persecuted in the city she proclaimed an edict to protect them, and caused those who were guilty of the outrages to be severely punished. She was greatly beloved by the people, towards whom she behaved with much generosity; for more than once, in time of famine, or misery caused by war, she pawned her jewels to help them. But we really hear very little about the latter half of her life, for the chroniclers of the period only mention her to record the birth of her children. The heir to the duchy was not born until 1508, and he received the name of Ercole, from his grandfather. There were two other sons, Ippolytus, afterwards the Cardinal d'Este, remembered by his villa at Tivoli, and Francesco, Marquis of Massalombarda. Her daughter Leonora became a nun at the convent of Corpus Domini, where she herself spent so much of her later life.

In her peaceful and dignified career at Ferrara she had yet her fair share of trouble. The captivity and death of her brother Cæsar Borgia, killed while fighting for his brother-in-law of Navarre, at the age of thirty-one, was a great blow to her; then the fatal love affair with her beautiful maid-of-honour Angela, which brought ruin on the two brothers of her husband; the death in 1508 of her eldest son Roderigo, whose varied fortunes she had followed from afar with loving eyes, and, ten years later, the loss of her mother Vanozza, her last link with the past.

As time went on, she devoted herself more and more to religious duties, and works of charity. As Paolo Giovio tells us, she renounced the pomps and vanities of the world, to which she had been accustomed from her childhood; she founded convents and hospitals, and was a mother to the sick, the poor, and the destitute. We have another interesting record of Lucrezia from the biographer of the famous Bayard, the "chevalier sans peur et sans reproche," who was received by her at Ferrara.

"La bonne duchesse, qui était une perle de ce monde, fit aux Français un merveilleux accueil et tous leur jours leur faisait festins et bancquets à la mode D'ytalie tant beaux que merveilles. Bien ose dire que de son temps, ne devant ne s'est trouvé de plus triomphante princesse, car elle était belle, bonne, deuce et courtoise à toutes gens, et rien n'est plus sûr que, quoique son mari fut un prince sage et vaillant, ladite dame lui a rendu de bons et grands services par sa gracieuseté."

Other homage was not wanting, on every side. Caviceo even sought to flatter the splendid Isabella d'Este, by offering her, as his highest praise, that "she closely approached the perfection of Lucrezia." The relations between these two great ladies had been very friendly, and on the death of Francesco of Mantua, the Duchess of Ferrara wrote to his widow to express her sorrow.

"Illustrious Signora, my sister-in-law and much honoured sister,—The cruel loss of your most illustrious husband of happy memory has caused me so much grief and sorrow that I have too much need of consolation myself to offer any to your excellency, for whom this great loss must be so bitter an affliction. I share the regrets with which this misfortune overwhelms your excellency, and I cannot succeed in expressing how much it touches and afflicts me." . . . She adds a few words about submission to the will of God, and signs herself, "Your sister-in-law, LUCREZIA, Duchess of Ferrara. The last day of March 1519."

She herself only lived a few months longer. On June 14 she had a child, born dead. In expectation of her approaching end she dictated a letter to Pope Leo X., which, written in sight of death, reveals to us the deepest feelings of her soul.

"Sanctissimo Patre et Beatissimo Signor mio Colendissimo,—With all possible reverence of soul, I kiss the feet of your Holiness, and humbly recommend myself to 'La sua Santa gratia.' . . . So great is the favour granted to me by my merciful Creator, that I know the end of my life approaches, and in a few hours I shall have gone hence, having first received all the Holy Sacraments of the Church. And at this point, I am reminded as a Christian, though a sinner, to supplicate your Holiness to bestow from your spiritual treasures, some comfort to my soul with your holy benediction, and this I devoutly pray. And to your holy grace, I recommend il Signor Consorte, and my children, all servants of your Holiness.

"De Vostra Beatitudine,

"Humil Serva,

"LUCREZIA DA ESTE.

"FERRARA, the 12th June 1519, at the 24th hour."

Two days later she passed away, to the deep and lasting grief of her husband, who had never left her side. She was buried in the Convent of the Sisters of Corpus Christi, in the same tomb as the mother of Alfonso, the Duchess Leonora of blessed memory. The whole city mourned for her, and instances of her goodness and piety were on every tongue.

But the poor duchess was unfortunate in that her

good deeds were soon forgotten, while the evil traditions of her youth survived, and were carried down alone to posterity. The study of celebrated characters of former days must always be a most difficult problem. If we are often mistaken about our own contemporaries, how much more likely are we to form a wrong judgment with regard to those who are only shadows from the past?

If her latest great biographer, Gregorovius, has succeeded in dethroning Lucrezia Borgia from the pedestal of wickedness where legend had placed her by the side of Phædra, Medea and Clytemnestra, this unhappy lady still remains an essentially tragic figure. Everything was against her; her birth, her early training, her surroundings, the evil character of her nearest relations, who merely used her as a tool for their ambition. And, even when she had weathered the storm and left Rome for ever to live for more than twenty years, not merely blameless, but honoured and beloved in her new home,—it was the very irony of fate that she should still be held up through the centuries, as the type of infamy for novelist, historian, and dramatist.

But the last word has not yet been spoken. The character of Lucrezia Borgia still awaits the final verdict of a broader knowledge.

VITTORIA COLONNA, MARCHESA DI PESCARA

Vittoria è 'l nome; eben conviensi a nata
Fra le vittorie, ed a chi, o vada, o stansi,
Die trofei sempre, e di trionfi ornata,
La Vittoria abbia seco, o dietro, o innanzi.
Questa è un'altra Artemisia, che lodata
Fu dl pietà verso il suo Mausolo; anzi
Tanto maggior, quanto è più assai bell' opra
Che por sotterra un uom, trarlo di sopra.

Orl. xxxvii. 18. ARIOSTO.

THE very name is music in our ears, and calls up the image of a gracious presence, which is perhaps better known than that of any other lady of the Renaissance. Princess and poetess, she combined the learning of her day with the religious mysticism of a later age, and her renown has come down to posterity as much from her friendship with Michelangelo as from her own merits.

Vittoria was the daughter of Fabrizio' Colonna, Grand Constable of Naples, and of Agnesina di Montefeltro, of the great house of Urbino; sister of one duke and daughter of another. She was born in the year 1490, in the ancient walled city of Marino, which nestles amongst the Alban hills between Castel Gondolfo and Grotta Ferrata, not far from the Lake of Albano. Under Pope Innocent VIII. there was at that moment a brief interval of peace before the death of Lorenzo dei Medici and the invasion of Italy by the French under Charles VIII.

For a child of such illustrious lineage, her marriage would certainly be a matter of political arrangement, and in this case it was the King of Naples who, to secure the somewhat doubtful fealty of her father, the Grand Constable, caused Vittoria's betrothal to Ferrante Francesco d'Avalos, the only son of the Marquis of Pescaro, a subject of his own. The boy and girl were about the same age, four years old, when this "marriage for the future" took place, according to the very frequent custom of that age. We have an interesting glimpse of the little Vittoria in the year of Jubilee 1500, when the Duchess of Urbino, Elisabetta, came on a pilgrimage to Rome, and paid a visit to her sister-in-law Agnesina at the castle of Marino. The young girl seems to have given early promise of beauty and intelligence, and was carefully educated, first under her mother's care, and then for some years in the guardianship of Ferrante's elder sister in the island of Ischia.

Costanza d'Avalos, the widowed Duchess of Francavilla, was a woman of strong character, who had greatly distinguished herself some years before, by her gallant defence of the citadel when attacked by the forces of Louis XII. In acknowledgment of her heroism, the government of the island was settled upon her family. It was here that King Federico of Naples took refuge with his wife and children, and his two widowed sisters, after the French had taken and sacked Capua, and were advancing on Naples, in the year 1501.

VITTORIA COLONNA

The wedding of the young Marchese of Pescaro and Vittoria Colonna took place in their nineteenth year, at Ischia, on December 27, 1509. There were splendid festivities, of which the chroniclers give us the most minute particulars, but all these pompous entertainments greatly resemble each other. A list of the wonderful presents is preserved in the Colonna archives, and amongst them we notice the furniture of a bed in crimson satin and blue taffeta, fringed with gold, and pillows of crimson satin edged and garnished with gold ; also the housing for a mule of wrought gold brocade, given by the bride ; while the bridegroom offers priceless jewels, diamond crosses, gold chains, &c., and costly robes of satin, velvet, and brocade, chiefly scarlet and crimson in colour, with the richest of gold embroideries.

Ferrante had inherited his title and property at an early age by the death of his father, and he is described to us as a singularly handsome man, of knightly bearing, very proud of his noble Spanish blood. He had cultivated tastes, and could sympathise with his young wife in her love of poetry and literature. They seem to have been devotedly attached to each other, and their marriage gave every promise of a happy life. Their home was in that beautiful island of Ischia, where mountains and valleys, sea and sky, the luxuriant vegetation of the tropics, the charm of old story—all combine to make this spot the ideal dream of a poet. Two years of delightful leisure were spent here in the cultivated society of the Duchess Costanza and her friends, and then the long honeymoon came to an abrupt end.

Ferrante was called away by his military duties, for

there was war between France on one side, and Naples and the Papal States on the other. With his father-in-law, Fabrizio Colonna, he joined the army of Italy, which was entirely defeated under the walls of Ravenna, on April 9, 1512. Pescaro and Colonna were both made prisoners, and carried to Milan, where the young Marchese nearly died of his wounds, but he was well cared for by Gian Trivulsio, Marshal of France, who had married his aunt, Beatrice d'Avalos. On his recovery he was ransomed by the payment of six thousand ducats by his wife, who had sought to relieve her distress and anxiety during his captivity, by writing a poetical letter to him of one hundred and twelve lines in *terza rima*. Ferrante on his part had composed a "Dialogo d'Amore" in his prison, which he dedicated to Vittoria. Neither of these compositions have much literary merit, but they are very characteristic of the age. For a short time the young soldier remained in his beautiful home, enjoying this interval of peace with his wife, but her happiness was of brief duration. Pescara was soon recalled to the field of war in Lombardy, and after this time Vittoria seldom saw him. Indeed, after the month of October 1522 they never met again. In his brilliant military career, as general of the Imperial forces, he was always engaged at a distance from home.

We have an interesting account of Vittoria's appearance on a great occasion at the Court of Naples, for the marriage of Sigismond, King of Poland, with Bona Sforza, the daughter of the unfortunate Isabella of Arragon. In the midst of the most magnificent festivities and revels, we are told: "The illustrious lady, Madonna Vittoria, Marchesa of Pescara, was mounted on a black-and-white jennet, with housings of crimson velvet fringed with gold. She was attended by six of her ladies-in-waiting, clad all alike in azure damask, and followed by six grooms on foot with cloaks and jerkins of blue and yellow satin. She herself wore a robe of brocaded crimson velvet, adorned with large branches of beaten gold, a crimson satin cap, with a head-dress of wrought gold above it, and a girdle of beaten gold round her waist." She was a very beautiful woman at that time, with delicately-moulded classical features, large bright eyes, the smooth, high forehead so much admired then, and golden hair.

The Marchesa had no children of her own, and she decided to adopt and educate a young cousin of her husband's, Alfonso d'Avalos, as an occupation during the long absences of Pescaro. The boy was very intelligent, but he had Spanish blood in his veins, and was most unruly and difficult to manage. However, she acquired great influence over him, and became very much attached to him. Vittoria also found many intellectual interests; for, besides the men of letters and poets who came to her court, she had much literary correspondence. Castiglione, then ambassador in Spain, writes to her thus: "I have felt so much joy in the victories of the Marchese that at first I would not write a letter—a letter is so common a thing! One writes letters about events of no importance. I had thought of fireworks, fêtes, concerts, songs, and other vigorous demonstrations, but reflection has shown me that these are inferior to the concert of my own affections; and so I am come back to the idea of a letter, convinced that my marchesa will be able to see what I have in my soul, even though my words fail to express it. . . And as to my duty towards your highness, seek, I pray you, the testimony of your own heart, and give it credence, for I am sure your heart will not lie to you on what not only yourself, but the whole world, sees shining through my soul, as through the purest crystal. And thus I remain, kissing your hands, and humbly commending myself to your good favour. Madrid, March 21."

On one occasion Vittoria Colonna wrote a charming letter to Paolo Giovio, in which she spoke with great enthusiasm of her "divine Bembo." Paolo Giovio lost no time in passing this letter on to him. "I send you," he writes, "a letter from your lady-love, the most illustrious marchesa. It is very pretty, and speaks of you, and I send it to you at once without any of that resentment which rivals are so apt to feel, for I am fully assured that her excellency's love for your lordship is in all points like to my own love for her, that is, celestial, holy, altogether Platonic. Her excellency is come to Naples from Ischia, with the other noble dames. I mean the serene Amalfia and the superb Vasta, with the Francavila (the Duchess Costanza, her sister-in-law), a mirror of virtue, and verily a matchless beauty." *

This must have been at the time of the King of Poland's wedding.

Meantime, great events were happening in Italy. The French were defeated at Novaro, then for awhile there was peace between the Pope and the French king; then again the French take Milan and hold it

* De Maulde.

until the Pope and the Emperor Charles join against them and drive them from Milan in 1521. Then at length comes the final rout, when, under the leadership of Pescara, the battle of Pavia is won in 1525, on February 24; and Francis I., taken prisoner, sends home to his mother the one brief message: "Tout est perdu fors l'honneur."

Pescara was wounded, but not dangerously, in the battle, and he claimed the custody of the royal prisoner, who was, however, taken away from his charge into Spain. He was at this time general-in-chief in all Lombardy, and high in the confidence of Charles V., and he felt himself sorely aggrieved at losing his captive. Until this time, whatever his private character might have been, he had not only been successful, but crowned with honour and glory. But now, in his rage and discontent, he appears to have listened to plans of secret treachery. It was suggested to him that if he would turn against the emperor, he should be offered the crown of Naples. We do not know exactly how far he wavered in his allegiance, but some rumour must have reached his wife, for she wrote to him a most touching and earnest letter, begging him:

"That you consider well what you are doing, mindful of your pristine fame and estimation; and in truth, for my part, I care not to be the wife of a king, but rather to be joined to a faithful and loyal man; for it is not riches, titles, and kingdoms which can give true glory, infinite praise, and perpetual renown to noble spirits desirous of eternal fame; but faith, sincerity, and other virtues of the soul; and with these man may rise higher than the highest kings, not only in war, but in peace."

From all we know of the Marchese di Pescaro's character, it is very doubtful if this letter had any effect. Historians believe that having reason to doubt the success of the plot, he resolved to betray his friend Morone, and revealed the whole scheme to Charles V., vowing that he had never wavered in his allegiance, and had but drawn on the conspirators to their own betrayal. In return for this double treachery he received the title of Generalissimo of the imperial troops, but he did not live to enjoy this splendid position for many months. He fell ill of a mysterious complaint, which some biographers attribute to anxiety and remorse, and grew so rapidly worse that before the end of the year there was no hope of recovery.

An urgent messenger was sent by him from Milan, to tell the news to his wife, who set off at once in anxious haste, but when she arrived at Viterbo she heard of his death. This was in November 1525, and he was first buried at Milan, but his body was afterwards removed with stately ceremony to Naples. In the church of S. Domenico Maggiore, amongst the huge chests covered with velvet which bear the names of the "Princes and Princesses of the House of Aragon," is one which contains the bones of "Ferrante Francesco d'Avalos," and over his tomb hang his portrait and his banner.

In her loyalty and her love, Vittoria forgot all her husband's faults, and for a time was absolutely brokenhearted. Her first impulse was to flee from the world, and she sought a refuge in Rome in the convent of San

Silvestro in Capite. This was of the order of Santa Chiara, and was founded especially for noble sisters of the house of Colonna, who might wish to dedicate themselves to God. The first desire of the widowed lady, still only in her thirty-fifth year, was to take the veil, in her affliction. But it is a curious proof of the importance which she had in the eyes of her friends, that Pope Clement VII. was persuaded to send a brief to the abbess and nuns of San Silvestro permitting them to receive into their convent the Marchesa di Pescara, and to offer her all spiritual and temporal consolations, but forbidding them, under pain of the greater excommunication, to permit her to take the veil in her distress. "Impetu potius sui doloris, quam maturo consilio circa mutationem vestium vidualium in monasticas. December 7, 1525."

If she could not enter the sisterhood, at least she could consecrate her whole life to the memory of her beloved husband, and to religion. She remained at San Silvestro until the following autumn, when she was at Marino, during the great feud between the Colonna family, who took part with the Emperor, and the Orsini who were on the side of the Pope. Upon this Clement VII. declared the estates of the Colonna family confiscated, and Vittoria returned to her safe haven at Ischia. She must have been indeed thankful for so peaceful a retreat, when the very next year saw that terrible sack and plunder of Rome, to the horror and dismay of all the civilised world.

In her quiet island home, the young widow slowly recovered from the first overwhelming grief for her husband's loss, and reached the stage when she could find relief in writing tender sonnets to his memory ; a kind of "In Memoriam." Of these about one hundred and thirty-four have been preserved, and she always calls her Ferrante, "mio bel solo." Her fame as a poetess, even during her lifetime, procured her the title of "La Divina." The following translation will give some idea of one of the sonnets:

Hither did my fair sun to me return
From the fierce fight, all laden with his spoils.
Alas, to me what grief bring these fair scenes,
Where once his dazzling beams shone bright and clear!
A thousand honours did his valour win
Of faith and glory and of knightly zeal,
Proclaimed with joy by many-tongued renown
While on his brow the victor's laurels rest.
At my fond prayer he showed me his dear wounds,
And to my ravished ears revealed the place,
The hour, of all his mighty victories.
As erst my joy, so great my sorrow now,
While my sad memories the past recall
With sweet regrets and many bitter tears.

This certainly deserves the contemporary praise of being written "in very choice Italian;" and a high authority has described her poetry, as "penetrated with genuine feeling, it has that dignity and sweetness which belong to the spontaneous utterances of a noble heart."

Thou knowest, Love, I never sought to flee
  From thy sweet prison, nor impatient threw
  Thy dear yoke from my neck; never withdrew
What, that first day, my soul bestowed on thee.

Time hath not changed love's ancient surety;
  The knot is still as firm; and though there grew
  Moment by moment fruit bitter as rue,
Yet the fair tree remains as dear to me.

And thou hast seen how that keen shaft of thine,
'Gainst which the might of Death himself is vain,
Smote on one ardent, faithful breast full sore.

Now loose the cords that fast my soul entwine,
For though of freedom ne'er I recked before,
Yet now I yearn my freedom to regain.*

After three peaceful years in Ischia, Vittoria was driven away by the plague, so frequent a follower of war and devastation. She turned her steps to Rome, which was now beginning to revive after the horrors of that terrible pillage and ruin of 1527. Many distinguished exiles had already returned thither; amongst them her adopted son the Marchese del Vasto, and she found herself warmly welcomed, and soon became the centre of a delightful literary and artistic circle. That same year we find that Titian paints a Magdalen, which the Duke Federico of Mantua had promised her for a present. He writes thus:

"I sent to Venice at once, and wrote to Titian, who is perhaps the best master now living, begging him earnestly to make a picture of this saint, as beautiful and tearful as possible, and to let me have it directly."

On receiving this princely gift, Vittoria expresses the warmest gratitude, and sends the duke an exquisitely wrought casket filled with rare perfumes and cosmetic of roses. She continued her friendly relations with him, and on his marriage with Margherita Paleologa, the heiress of Monferrato, she sends him her warmest wishes; "she could not wish her own Marchese del Vasto greater joy or good fortune." She also encloses

* De Maulde's Trans.

two of her latest sonnets as a wedding offering. On another occasion she asked one of her friends who was going to Mantua, to offer Federico "a friendly and sympathetic greeting," with some small token of her regard. The friend presented the duke with a basket of roses, and he wrote at once to thank the lady with his deepest respect. Whereupon Vittoria wrote him a formal apology that her envoy had "honoured him so little" as to give so small an offering.

It was only natural that a lady of such wealth and beauty should be sought in marriage, but she refused every offer, and would make reply: "My husband Ferrante, who to you seems dead, is not dead to me." At the time of her loss, amongst the many letters of condolence she received, Castiglione had written: "Calamity has fallen upon you like a deluge. I durst not write to your highness at first, for I deemed that you had died with the Marchese; to-day in all verity and admiration I hold that the Marchese still liveth in you." This indeed was the universal feeling of sympathy towards her; her love for her husband was known to have been "passionate as youth and enduring as age, mutual, whole and faithful."

In the year 1528, "Il Cortigiano," of Baldassare Castiglione, was first printed in Venice, and it is interesting to remember that, before giving it to the world, the author submitted the manuscript to Vittoria for her approval. She kept it a long time, and praised everything most warmly; the freshness of the subject, the refinement, elegance, and animation of the style. She is quite jealous of the persons that are quoted in such a book, even if they are dead. When at last she returns it, she omits to add that she has lent it rather indiscreetly.

At Rome she was for a time the guest of her sister-in-law, Madonna Giovanna d'Aragon, the wife of Ascanio Colonna, whose family had made peace with Pope Clement, and recovered the princely estates. She survived her husband for two-and-twenty years, of which she spent a portion in her lovely home at Ischia, and sometimes in convents at Orvieto and Viterbo, while she found interest and variety in many journeys. Amongst her many correspondents was the famous Marguerite of France; but these two ladies, who had so much in common, never had the opportunity of meeting. In one of her earliest letters Vittoria writes that while awaiting the infinite happiness of a meeting, she ventures to reply to the "high and religious" words of the princess.

"In our day the long and difficult journey of life compels us to have a guide. It seems to me that every one in his own sex can find the most appropriate models. . . . I turned towards the illustrious ladies of Italy to find examples for imitation, and though I saw many virtuous among them . . . yet one woman alone, and she not in Italy, seemed to me to unite the perfections of the will with those of the intellect; but she was so high placed and so far away that my heart was filled with the gloom and fear of the Hebrews when they perceived the fire and glory of God on the mountain top, and durst not draw near because of their imperfection."

After these personal compliments she speaks of her

group of friends ; of Monsignor Pole, "who is always in the heavens, and only descends to earth to do service to others" ; of Bembo, one of the labourers of the eleventh hour, but by reason of his ardour worthy of the wages of the first, and she adds that "all this company unites in contemplating from afar the queen of gems so rich in radiance that she enriches others."

In another letter the Marchesa enters more deeply into the burning question of the day. She is full of respect for reason, but with her "religion is first, the supreme perfection of our soul, the perfect beauty." More fully to explain her meaning she encloses a copy of her sonnets. These verses had a curious adventure. Although addressed to the great Lady Marguerite, sister of the King of France, they were intercepted in the post by order of the Constable de Montmorency. We do not know if he read the sonnets, but he strongly disapproved of the correspondence, and only gave up the book "after a stormy scene at the king's table." With regard to the handwriting of Vittoria, in which some people see a "mirror of the soul," we are told that it was clear and plain, "somewhat masculine in character, but both nervous and irregular, with a multitude of abbreviations and splotches."

The remark in her letter to Marguerite of France that with her "religion was first," touches the key-note of all her later life. Her most intimate friends were chosen from those earnest thinkers who were deeply interested in Church reform and the new influences of the Reformation, without ceasing to be, for the most part, loyal sons of the Church. In April 1557 the Marchesa went to Ferrara on a visit to the Duchess Renée, who, like herself, was much interested in religious questions, and she stood sponsor in June to her new-born daughter, the Leonora of Tasso's love. Her arrival there is thus described:

"Madonna Vittoria Colonna, famed for her elegance in the poetic art, not less than for Christian virtues, arrived at Ferrara in humble guise, accompanied by six of her ladies, on her way, as was said, to Venice, whence she purposed to make a pilgrimage to the Holy Land. She, who was a great patroness of Bernardino Ochino of Siena, as long as he remained in the right path, by the influence of the duke obtained the gift of an oratory, together with a small piece of ground in the Borgo della Misericordia, on the Po, and there having built a modest retreat, she placed Ochino and a few Capuchins of his brethren. Fra Bernardino, during the time he dwelt there, preached in the cathedral in the Advent of that year, and subsequently was elected general of his order."

Vittoria seems to have been greatly interested in this friar, whose sermons had a remarkable success. Agostino Gonzago writes from Rome in Lent 1537 about him: "He is a man of most holy life himself, and his sermons are devoted to the exposition of the Gospels. His whole object is to teach men how to walk in the steps of Christ, and he has the most admirable fervour, as well as a most perfect voice. He is not afraid of saying what is good for his hearers, and aims his rebukes chiefly at those in high station, so that all Rome flocks to hear him. . . . The Marchesa di Pescara is always present at these sermons, and is living in seclusion with the sisters of San Silvestro, receiving no visits, and wearing the humblest of habits, and is so devoted to religious exercises that it is expected she will soon take the veil."

Later on Cardinal Bembo writes from Venice : "I am prayed by divers gentle souls in this city to intercede with your grace, that you would be pleased to persuade your Padre Fra Bernardino da Siena to come hither next Lent and preach in the church of the Holy Apostles, to the reverence and honour of our Lord God ; which thing they greatly desire to obtain from his reverence. Nor they alone, but all the citizens are in infinite expectation of hearing him." After his request had been granted, the cardinal expresses his admiration of the friar's eloquence and piety ; "he had never heard such preaching."

When Vittoria left Ferrara, she had won all hearts. "This morning the Signora Marchesa di Pescara started for Bologna," writes the Cardinal of Ravenna, "to the incredible grief of his excellency the duke, of myself, and of the whole city. We have indeed been divinely entertained by her presence, and can only comfort ourselves with the promises she has made to return before long. Last night we enjoyed a rare treat. The duke and I as well as the Marchesa, supped with the duchess, and after supper the Marchesa read us five sonnets of her composition, which were so beautiful that I do not think an angel from heaven could have written anything more perfect."

It was about this period that occurred the great event of Vittoria's later life, her friendship with Michelangelo, who was then in his sixty-third year, while she was nearly forty-eight. A strong sympathy grew up between these two, who were alike in the melancholy of their natures, in their deep religious feelings, and in their cultivated artistic and intellectual tastes. This is one of the first letters which Michelangelo wrote to the marchesa, in 1538:

"I am going in search of truth with uncertain step. My heart, floating unceasingly between vice and virtue, suffers and finds itself failing, like a weary traveller wandering on in the dark. . . . Ah! do thou become my counsellor. Thy advice shall be sacred. Clear away my doubts. Teach me in my wavering how my unenlightened soul may resist the tyranny of passion unto the end. Do thou thyself, who hast directed my steps towards heaven by ways of pleasantness, prescribe a course for me."

It was the custom of this great master to show friendship by the gift of a drawing, and for Vittoria he designed sketches from the Passion of our Lord. Ascanio Condivi says:

"At the request of this lady he made a naked Christ, at the moment when, taken from the cross, our Lord would have fallen like an abandoned corpse at the feet of His most holy Mother, if two angels did not support Him in their arms. She sits below the cross with a face full of tears and sorrow, lifting both her wide-spread arms to heaven, while on the stem of a tree above is written this legend: 'Non vi si pensa quante sangue costa.' The cross is of the same kind as that which was carried in procession by the White Friars at the time of the plague of 1348, and afterwards deposited in the church of S. Croce at Florence."

This is a portion of the letter in which she writes acknowledging it:

"I had the greatest faith in God that He would bestow on you supernatural grace for the making of this Christ. The design is in all parts perfect and consummate, and I could not desire more. I tell you that I am greatly pleased to see the angel on the right hand is by far the fairer; since he, Michael, will place you, Michel Angelo, upon the right hand of God in that day. Meanwhile, I cannot serve you better than by praying to this sweet Christ, whom you have drawn so well and perfectly, and begging you to hold me ever at your service."

The superscription on one of her letters was: "Al mio piu che magnifico e piu che carissimo M. Michel Angelo Buonarotti." And in another letter she says: Our friendship is stable and our affection very sure, it is tied with a Christian knot."

There is something very touching and beautiful in the relation between the man of genius, to whom this cultured lady was a revelation, with her sensitive feeling and delicate insight—and the widowed princess who found a solace and a keen interest in the creative mind of the master painter. She had many friends, brilliant men of the world, cardinals and courtiers, who laid their wit and talent, their learning and their piety at her feet, but she had never met a friend like this before.

Messer Francesco d'Ollanda, architect, illuminator, and miniature artist, who had been sent into Italy by the Portuguese government to study art, has left us an exquisite little miniature in words, which, although well known, will bear repeating once more. It is an account of a meeting with the Marchesa di Pescara and Michelangelo, and he thus tells it:

"Among the days that I passed in this capital, when I went to see, as was my wont, Messer Lactantius Tolomei, who had become friendly with Michel Angelo, they told me at his house that he had left word for me that he would be at Monte Cavallo, in the convent of San Silvestro, with Madonna, the Marchesa of Pescara, to hear a reading from the Epistles of St. Paul. Away I went, then, to Monte Cavallo, and was graciously received by the noble lady. She made me sit down, and, when the reading was over, she turned and requested some one to go to Michel Angelo and say to him: 'Messer Lactantius and I are in this chapel, which is cool and fresh, and the church is closed and pleasant. Ask him if he will be good enough to come and lose a part of the day with us, that we may have the benefit of gaining it with him, but do not tell him that Francesco d'Ollando the Spaniard is here.' After some moments of silence we heard a knock at the door . . . it was he. The Marchesa rose to receive him, and remained standing for some time, until she placed him between Messer Lactantius and herself. I sat a little apart. She spoke of one thing and another with much intelligence and grace, without ever touching upon the subject of painting, so as to make sure of the great painter. . . . At last she said: 'It is a well-known fact that a man will always be beaten if he tries to attack Michel Angelo on his own ground. . . . As for you,' she said to him, 'I do not think you less praiseworthy for the way in which you isolate yourself, and avoid our trivial talk and refuse to paint for every prince who asks you . . . .'"

A most interesting dialogue followed on painting, in which Vittoria makes these characteristic remarks:

"Painting," she said, "better than any other means, enables us to see the humility of the saints, the constancy of the martyrs, the purity of the virgins, the beauty of the angels, the love and charity with which the seraphim burns; it raises and transports mind and soul beyond the stars, and leads us to contemplate the eternal sovereignty of God. . . . If we desire to see a man renowned for his deeds, painting shows us him to the life. It brings before our eyes the image of a beauty far removed from our experience, and Pliny held this to be a service of priceless value. The widow in her affliction finds solace in gazing every day upon her husband's picture; young orphans owe to painting the happiness of recognising, when they have come to man's estate, the features of a beloved father."

The Marchesa di Pescara must have had most excellent judgment in the matter of artistic work, as we gather from the following letter, which she wrote on receiving a drawing for a crucifix from the great master, who suggested that if she liked it, he would entrust the execution of it to one of his workmen, probably Urbino:

"Unique Master Michel Angelo and my most singular friend, I have received your letter and examined the crucifix, which truly hath crucified in my memory every other picture I ever saw. Nowhere could one find another figure of our Lord so well executed, so living, and so exquisitely finished. Truly I cannot express in words how subtly and marvellously it is designed. Wherefore I am resolved to take the work as coming from no other hand but yours, and accordingly I beg you to assure me whether this is really yours or another's. Excuse the question. If it is yours, I must possess it under any conditions. In case it is not yours, and you want to have it carried out by your assistant, we will talk the matter over first. I know how extremely difficult it would be to copy it, and therefore I would rather let him finish something else than this; but if it be in fact yours, rest assured, and make the best of it, that it will never come again into your keeping. I have examined it minutely in full light and by the lens and mirror, and never saw anything more perfect.—Yours to command,

"LA MARCHESA DI PESCARA."

The lady shows her insight in discovering that the sketch is by the hand of Michelangelo himself, and is evidently resolved to keep it. She more than hints that she would like the crucifix to be executed by the same hand as the drawing. She always writes in the manner of a great princess, with a delicate touch of patronage in her admiration.

Only a few of Michelangelo's letters to Vittoria Colonna are preserved, and the following is one of the most interesting, evidently written after receiving some sonnets from her. For some years past there had been a strong religious tendency in her poetry:

"I desired, lady, before I accepted the things which your ladyship has often expressed the will to give me —I desired to produce for you something with my own hand in order to be as little as possible unworthy of this kindness. I have now come to recognise that the grace of God is not to be bought, and that to keep it waiting is a grievous sin. Therefore, I acknowledge my error, and willingly accept your favours. When I possess them, not indeed because I shall have them in my house, but for that I myself shall dwell in them, the place will seem to encircle me with Paradise, for which felicity I shall remain ever more obliged to your ladyship than I am already—if that is possible.

"The bearer of this letter will be Urbino, who lives in my service. Your ladyship may inform me when you would like me to come and see the head you promised to show me."

This letter is the more worthy of insertion, in that it is written below the autograph of a sonnet sent at the same time :

Seeking at least to be not all unfit
  For thy sublime and boundless courtesy.
  My lowly thoughts at first were fain to try
What they could yield for grace so infinite.
But now I know my unassisted wit
  Is all too weak to make me soar so high,
  For pardon, lady, for this fault I cry,
And wiser still I grow, remembering it,
Yea, well I see what folly 'twere to think
  That largess dropped from thee like dews from heaven
  Could ere be paid by work so frail as mine!
To nothingness my art and talent sink;
  He fails who from his mortal stores hath given
  A thousand fold to match one gift divine.

Translated by J. A. Symonds.

VITTORIA COLONNA

Everything from the hand of Michelangelo in connection with this famous friendship is of great interest, and it will be an appropriate place to quote another sonnet, which must have been written about the time, and in the same spirit of tender gratitude :

Blest spirit, who with loving tenderness
  Quickenest my heart, so old and near to die,
  Who 'mid thy joys on me dost bend an eye,
  Though many nobler men around thee press
As thou wert erewhile wont my sight to bless,
  So to console my mind thou now dost fly;
  Hope therefore stills the pangs of memory,
  Which, coupled with desire, my soul distress.
So finding in thee grace to plead for me—
  Thy thoughts for me sunk in so sad a case—
  He who now writes returns thee thanks for these.
Lo! It were foul and monstrous usury
  To send thee ugliest paintings in the place
  Of thy fair spirit's living phantasies.*

In this slight sketch of Vittoria's life there is no space for her many religious poems, but it may be interesting to give the following :

HYMN ON GOOD FRIDAY

Gli angeli eletti al gran bene infinito
  Braman oggi soffrir penosa morte,
  Accio nella celeste empirea corte
  Non sia piu il servo, che il signor, gradito.
Piange l'antica madre il gusto ardito
Ch'a figli suoi del ciel chiuse le porte;
  E che due man piagate or sieno scorte
Da ridurne al cammin per lei smarrito.
Asconde il sol la sua fulgente chioma;
  Spezzansi i sassi vivi: apronsi i monti

* J. A. Symonds' Trans.

Trema la terra e'l ciel; turbansi l'acque;
Piangon gli spirti, al nostro mal si pronti,
Delle catene lor l'aggiunta soma
L'uomo non piange, e pur piangendo nacque.

Which may be rendered thus:

The angels to eternal bliss elect
Desire this day to suffer painful death
Lest in the courts celestial it befall
The servant be more favoured than his Lord.
Man's ancient mother weeps the fatal deed
That closed the gates of heaven against her sons,
The two pierced hands she weeps, whose work of grace
Found for His own the path which she had lost,
The sun in dread doth veil his shining mane,
The living rocks are torn, the mountains burst,
Earth and sky tremble and the waters quake,
The evil spirits weep, who wish us ill,
The added burden of their captive chains.
Man only weeps not, yet was weeping born.

It is noticeable both in the writings of Michelangelo and his friend the Marchesa, that they do not give us Catholic legend, but ever the Gospel simplicity of the Christian religion. We find the doctrine of "justification by faith," of Christ the Mediator—doubtless much dwelt upon in the evangelical teaching of Luther and Calvin—and yet as old as Saint Augustine. Both the illustrious friends were ardent students of Dante, and yet were one in heart with Savonarola. In her later years, Vittoria incurred the suspicion of the Holy Office.

But the life of the widowed Marchesa was not one undisturbed scene of devotion to religion and literature. There had been a temporary truce between Pope Paul III. and the Colonna family, but it was again disturbed by so small a matter as an increased tax on salt. Ascanio Colonna refused to pay it, pleading some ancient privilege; and some of his vassals also refusing to pay it, they were thrown into prison by the papal tax-collectors. Thereupon Ascanio made a raid into the Campania, and carried off some herds of cattle, with the result that the indignant Pope declared war on the house of Colonna, took their chief fortresses, and levelled them with the ground.

During this disastrous warfare, Vittoria left Rome and took refuge at Orvieto, in that beautiful hill-city, rising above the fertile plain, where the river Paglia winds like some creeping snake, in ever-changing light and shade. There she must have seen that exquisite Duomo, in all the fresh glory of Signorelli's frescoes, painted recently in her lifetime; and the perfect rose window amid the marvellous mosaics of the great façade, which can be seen from far below, like a glittering shield in the sunlight.

During her voluntary exile at Orvieto, the Marchesa received visits from many of her distinguished friends at the court of Rome, and it is a high tribute to the respect and admiration felt for her personal character, that her friendship and influence with the Pope were unbroken. She was persuaded to return, after less than two years, to the Eternal City, where her absence had been a serious loss; and from this time until her death she remained there, except for occasional visits to Viterbo, where she took great interest in the new convent, which had been founded recently, of Saint Catherine of Alexandria, for Dominican nuns of the second order. Viterbo, which is only thirty miles north of Rome, was looked upon as a healthy change from the closer air of the city, and must have been exceedingly picturesque in those days, with its multitude of high battlemented towers, so common a feature of the fortified hill towns of the Middle Ages.

Towards the close of the year 1544, Vittoria Colonna retired to the Convent of the Benedictines of Saint Anna, in Rome, for a time. She was in ill health, and caused great anxiety to her friends, who wrote to a famous physician and poet, Fracostoro of Verona, for his counsel and advice. He does not seem to have thoroughly understood her illness, but was disposed to attribute it to prolonged depression of spirits. She had indeed much to sadden her closing years, for the fortunes of her family were in evil case, and the disputes between the Pope and her brother must have been a serious trouble to her. But her greatest sorrow was the loss of her adopted son, the Marchese del Vasto, to whom she was tenderly attached. As her end drew near, she was carried to the palace of her kinswoman Giulia Colonna, the wife of Giuliano Cesarini, and there she passed away in the month of February 1547, dying, as she had lived, in calm serenity and simple, lowly faith.

Condivi gives a pathetic account of Michelangelo's last sight of her beloved face. "In particular, he greatly loved the Marchesa di Pescara, of whose divine spirit he was enamoured, being in return dearly beloved by her. He still preserves many of her letters, breathing honourable and most tender affection, and such as were wont to issue from a heart like hers. He also wrote to her a great number of sonnets, full of wit and sweet affection. . . . He, for his part, loved her so that I remember to have heard him say that he regretted nothing except that when he went to visit her upon the moment of her passage from this life, he did not kiss her forehead or her face, as he did kiss her hand. Her death was the cause that oftentimes he dwelt astonied thinking of it, even as a man bereft of sense."

Under the sharp pang of bereavement, he composed two sonnets which fitly enshrine her memory.

SE'L MIO ROZZO MARTELLO

When my rude hammer to the stubborn stone
  Gives human shape, now that, now this, at will,
  Follows his hand who wields and guides it still,
It moves upon another's feet alone.
But He who dwells in heaven all things doth fill
  With beauty by pure motions of His own;
  And since tools fashion tools which else were none,
Its life makes all that lives with living skill.
Now for that every stroke excels the more
  The higher at the forge it doth ascend,
  Her soul that fashioned mine hath sought the skies;
Wherefore unfinished I must meet my end,
  If God, the great Artificer, denies
That aid which was unique on earth before.

When she who was the source of all my sighs
  Fled from the world, herself, my straining sight,
  Nature, who gave us that unique delight,
Was sunk in shame, and we had weeping eyes.
Yet shall not vauntful Death enjoy the prize,
  This sun of suns which then he veiled in night;
  For Love hath triumphed, lifting up her light
On earth and 'mid the saints in Paradise.
What though remorseless and impiteous doom
  Deemed that the music of her deeds would die,
And that her splendour would be sunk in gloom?

> The poet's page exalts her to the sky
> With life more living in the lifeless tomb,
> And Death translates her soul to reign on high.*

It will not be out of place to quote here a letter written seven years later by the aged Michelangelo to his nephew Lionardo :

"I have been asked if I possess any writings of the Marchesa. I have a little book bound in parchment, which she gave me some ten years ago. It has one hundred and three sonnets, not counting another forty which she afterwards sent on paper from Viterbo. I had these bound into the same book, and at that time I used to lend them about to many persons, so that they are all of them now in print. In addition to these poems I have many letters which she wrote from Orvieto and Viterbo. These then are the writings I possess of the Marchesa."

We have no marble monument to record the memory of this most noble and perfect lady of the Italian Renaissance. She desired to be buried in all respects like a Benedictine Sister, and her wish was obeyed, for not a stone or tablet marks the place where her body rests. But she has left us a touching prayer, a petition for peace and happiness in this world and the next, which is too typical of her character to omit.

"Grant, I beseech Thee, Lord, that by the humility that becomes the creature and by the pride Thy greatness demands, I may adore Thee always, and that in the fear Thy justice imposes, as in the hope Thy

* J. A. Symonds' Trans.

clemency justifies, I may live eternally and submit to Thee as the Almighty, follow Thee as the All-wise, and turn towards Thee as towards Perfection and Goodness. I beseech Thee, most tender Father, that Thy living fire may purify me, Thy radiant light illumine me ; that this sincere love for Thee may profit me in such wise that, never finding let or hindrance in things of this world, I may return to Thee in happiness and safety."*

* Translated from the Latin original.

ELISABETTA GONZAGA, DUCHESS OF URBINO

(WIFE OF DUKE GUIDOBALDO I.)

ALSO AN ACCOUNT OF "IL CORTIGIANO," BY
COUNT BALDASSARE CASTIGLIONE,
BEING CONVERSATIONS AT THE COURT OF URBINO

Come to the court, and Balthazer affords
Fountains of holy and rose-water words.

GUILPIN, in his "Skialethia.'

ELISABETTA GONZAGA, DUCHESS OF URBINO

AND CASTIGLIONE'S DESCRIPTION OF THE COURT OF URBINO

AMONGST the women of the Italian Renaissance, Elisabetta Gonzaga stands out as one of the central figures, not only on account of her unique position as queen of that court of Urbino, which has become the very ideal of intellectual culture, but also from her own most interesting personality. Brought up in an atmosphere of art and scholarship, she inherited a taste for letters from a line of distinguished ancestors, and her sweetness of nature lent a new charm to her learning and accomplishments.

She was born at Mantua in 1471, the daughter of Federico, eldest son of the reigning duke, Lodovico, most illustrious of his race. Her mother was Margaretta of Bavaria, daughter of Duke Sigismond, and the old chroniclers give us a very quaint account of her arrival in Italy. Her followers were rough and uncouth in their speech and manners, they wore coarse garments of a red colour and grotesque shape, and altogether appear to have shocked the more civilised Mantuans. We learn that Federico was most unwilling to accept this foreign bride, who is described as unattractive; but the Emperor Frederick had arranged the marriage, and it had to be carried out. Poor Margaretta seems to have been of a placid, gentle disposition, a good wife and mother, but we do not hear much about her. She died a year after her father-in-law, Lodovico, in 1479, leaving a young family of six children.

Of these, Elisabetta, and her sister Maddelena, who was seven at her mother's death, were the two youngest girls. Their eldest sister Chiara was married a couple of years later to the Duc de Montpensier, cousin of the King of France, to the great satisfaction of her grandmother, the famous Barbara of Brandenburg, who died shortly afterwards. Duke Federico was very much devoted to his two little daughters, and took great pains about their education. An accomplished lady, Violante de' Preti, was their teacher and constant companion. They learnt Latin from the learned Colombino of Verona, a noted writer on Dante, and they had masters for dancing, the lute, and singing. Amongst other interesting letters about their early education is one written by Violante to their father.

"Illustrissimo principi et excellentissimo domino,—You will hear with pleasure that your illustrious daughters are well in health, happy and obedient; thus it is pleasure to see them at their books and embroidery. They are very docile, and they delight in riding their new pony, one having the saddle and the other on pillion. Thus they ride in the park, closely followed by men on horseback, and we attend them behind in the chariot. This pony gives them much enjoyment, and no present from your excellency could have been more acceptable. By the grace of God I will endeavour to send you each day good tidings, that your highness may rest content, and I commend myself to your favour.—Your servant to command, Violante de' Preti.—14 August, 1481.—Porto."

They had been spending the summer in the country at the villa of Porto, which was probably needful for the health of Elisabetta, who was always delicate. The Marquis Federico was much away from home at that time, as he took the field in alliance with Ferrara and other States, against the Venetians and the Pope's nephew. But he kept up his keen interest in works of art, and we find him constantly giving directions to Andrea Mantegna with regard to the decorations of his Mantuan palaces. Had not the constant expenses of war been so heavy a drain on his treasury, he would have added to the Castello until it rivalled the wonderful palace of Urbino.

Another letter from Violante de' Preti gives an account of a visit paid to Mantua during the absence of the marquis, by Lorenzo dei Medici. He was on a journey to Cremona, where a congress was to be held, and Francesco, the eldest son of Federico, received him in the place of his father. His little sisters were introduced to the Magnifico, who sat down and talked with them, and seems to have been delighted with their courtesy and intelligence.

The death of their father in 1484 must have been a great loss to all his children. He was succeeded by Francesco, who was barely eighteen, but who had been already betrothed for some years to Isabella d'Este, the daughter of the Duke of Ferrara. Sigismondo, the second son, was studying at the University of Pavia, as he was destined for the Church, and ultimately became a cardinal. Giovanni, the youngest, was a bright, merry boy of ten years old. The young Marchese seems to have taken his position as head of the family very seriously, for two years later we find him arranging suitable marriages for his two young sisters.

There had always been a close friendship between the princes of Mantua and those of Urbino, dating from the time when Federico di Montefeltro and Ludovico of Mantua were together under the teaching of that most delightful of pedagogues, Vittorino. Now the two houses were to become allied by the marriage of Guidobaldo, the son and successor of Federico, with Elisabetta, and at the same time her sister Maddelena was betrothed to Giovanni Sforza, lord of Pesaro, who was destined to have so sad a history. Their sister Chiara, who had now been married five years, came to congratulate them, and spend Christmas in her old home.

Elisabetta's wedding was settled to take place early in 1488. She had already seen the young Duke of Urbino, who was almost her own age, a handsome boy, of cultivated tastes, but afflicted with hereditary gout. They appeared to have been mutually attracted to each other, and there seemed to be every prospect of happiness. But it was a great trial for the tender-hearted young girl to leave her home and be parted rom her sister and the brothers she was so fond of. She set out in February with her escort on the way to

Urbino, where the wedding was to be celebrated, in stormy wintry weather, and broke the journey at Ferrara. There she was received with motherly kindness by the Duchess Leonora, and renewed with the young Isabella, her future sister-in-law, the warm friendship which lasted all their lives. They had already met at Ferrara several years before, when the duchess and her daughter came on a visit to meet Francesco.

When the bride-elect resumed her travels, passing through Ravenna and by the spurs of the Apennines, the weather was still worse, the rain came down in torrents, and the rivers were so swollen as to be almost impassable. But after this trying and dangerous journey, at length Elisabetta saw the hill-city of Urbino, rising up against the sky on the highest and furthest ridge, as though it must command the whole width of Italy. Here a magnificent reception awaited her. "Ranged upon the hill-slope were the ladies of the city, exquisitely dressed, and the children bearing olive-branches in their hands. As soon as the bridal party came in sight, a screen of mounted choristers rose up before them, accompanied by nymphs in antique garb; dogs started off in pursuit of hares let loose for them; the hills resounded with the strains of a cantata specially composed; the Goddess of Mirth in person descended the slope and offered the young duchess her congratulations and good wishes."*

Guidobaldo led her by the hand into the splendid palace which seemed to climb the last height above the city, and whose walls were draped with tapestry and cloth of gold, while on every side were bronzes and antiques and costly pictures, and books the best

* De Maulde.

and rarest. She must have looked with dazzled eyes; but when the time came for parting with her favourite brother Giovanni and the escort from Mantua, she felt so desolate and forsaken that she burst into tears.

Still she was not forgotten by her family; her brother, the young Marchese, found time to pay her a visit in the summer, and we hear of a constant interchange of letters and presents between them. She was also greatly interested in the preparations for the marriage of her sister Maddelena, which took place in October the next year at Pesaro. This lovely spot on the sunny shores of the Adriatic is at no great distance from Urbino, and it must have been a joy to the sisters to feel that they were within reach of each other. The Duke and Duchess of Urbino were present at the wedding, which was celebrated with much festivity; but the strain of all the fatigue which she had gone through, was too much for the delicate health of Elisabetta, which broke down altogether before the winter. She was also full of anxiety with regard to her brother Francesco, who had been appointed captain-general of the armies of Venice and her allies, a position of danger as well as honour, which he filled for nine years. But he did not cease to take the most affectionate interest in his favourite sister, and when he heard of her illness he sent his own physician to attend her, accompanied by his secretary, who wrote such an unsatisfactory account that it was decided she must have a change of air as soon as she was strong enough to travel. The bracing winds of the hill-city were too keen for her that severe winter, and she longed for her native climate of Mantua.

Thus it happened that she was present in February

at the wedding entertainments of her brother and Isabella d'Este, and was able to receive the bride on her arrival, at the foot of the great staircase of the Castello di Corte. She had brought with her from Urbino much gold and silver plate, and also the splendid tapestries of the Trojan War to hang round the great hall, for on such a sumptuous occasion as this, princes had no scruples in borrowing from each other. The festivities lasted for days; there were public banquets in the Piazza, torchlight processions, dances, theatrical entertainments and tournaments in rapid succession. We cannot wonder that after all this the invalid required some rest, and we find that she remained at Mantua with Isabella until the following June. The two princesses were devoted to each other, and their friendship was one of the most earnest and lasting which we read of in history.

In those troublous days, when political changes were so sudden, when every State in Italy had to struggle for bare existence, and when a household and family was so constantly divided against itself, their unbroken affection was almost unique. They had many tastes in common; they both keenly enjoyed travel, they were both highly cultured, and had the same passion for art and literature and music. Elisabetta had not the splendid vitality of her friend, nor her undoubted beauty, but she was more gentle and winning, more unselfish and affectionate. We read of her in after years that she had "the love and reverence of all," "that peerless lady who excelled all others in excellence."

A charming picture of the happy time spent together by these two friends is given by the chronicler of

Isabella, whose words I venture to quote: "Together they sang French songs and read the latest romances, or played *scartino*—their favourite game of cards—in the pleasant rooms which Francesco had prepared for his bride on the first floor of the Castello. . . . Together they rode and walked in the park, and boated on the waters of the lake, or took excursions to the neighbouring villas of Porto and Marmirola." By the middle of March the Duchess's health was sufficiently improved to venture on a longer trip, and on the 15th Isabella writes: "To-day, after dinner, with your highness's kind permission, the Duchess of Urbino and I are going to supper at Goito, and to-morrow at Cavriana, where the wife of Signor Fracassa will meet us, and on Tuesday we are going to the lake of Garda, and I have let the Rector of Verona know, so that we may find a barge at Sermione." *

A few days later she wrote from Cavriana: "The Duchess of Urbino and I, together with Signor Fracassa's wife, went on Thursday to dine at Desenzano, and to supper at Tuscullano, where we spent the night, and greatly enjoyed the sight of this Riviera. On Friday we returned by boat to Sermione, and rode here on horseback. Wherever we went we were warmly welcomed and treated with the greatest attention, most of all by the captain of the lake, who gave us fish and other things, and by the people of Salo, who sent us a fine present. To-morrow we go to Goito, and on Tuesday back to Mantua."

"These Madonnas have been indefatigable in making excursions by boat and horseback, and have seen all the gardens on the lake with the greatest delight. The

* Mrs. Ady.

inhabitants have vied with each other in doing them honour, and one Fermo, of Caravazo, caused his garden to be stripped for the marchesana and her party, and loaded them with lemons and pomegranates." So wrote one of the gentlemen in waiting.

It was well that Elisabetta should have recovered her health before the terrible blow which awaited her a few months later—the sudden death of her sister Maddelena. The young wife had been looking forward with joy to the birth of her child, when the fatal event occurred, and mother and babe were laid in the grave, scarcely a year after the festal welcome to Pesaro. It was long before her loving sister recovered from the shock of this unlooked-for grief, and she little dreamed that the day was not far distant, when she would visit Pesaro again under other auspices. The Duchess of Urbino was in delicate health for some time, and we hear of her visiting the baths of Viterbo, where her brother sends his chamberlain, Silvestro Calandro, to enliven her loneliness, and Isabella writes her the following letter:

"DEAREST SISTER,—In my love to you I would have you resolve, when you take your first bath, to live only on such things suitable to give health and strength. And I would have you compel yourself to take daily exercise of walking and riding, and to take part in cheerful talk, and thus drive away sadness and melancholy, whether from causes of mind or body . . . think of your health and comfort, for in this fickle world we can do no otherwise, and they who spend not their time aright suffer their lives to slip away with much sorrow and little praise. . . ."

The next year, after a visit to the baths of Porretta, Elisabetta again went to Mantua, and in the bucentaur which met her she found a poet with his lyre, sent to cheer the journey with music and singing. Perhaps it was on this occasion that Isabella felt a desire to play this instrument, and wrote to Milan to borrow a marvellous silver lyre to practise on. The next loan she asked for was that the Duchess of Urbino would send her the "foreign master," Giovanni Santi, the father of Raphael, that he might paint some portraits for her. Of course the artist at once set out for Mantua, but unfortunately he fell ill with fever there, and had to return to Urbino before the work was finished. He never thoroughly recovered, and died the following autumn. Elisabetta thus mentions his loss: "Our painter, Giovanni dei Sancti, passed out of this life, being in full possession of his senses, and in the most excellent disposition of mind. May God pardon his soul!"

When Isabella went to visit her friend at Urbino that same year she was very much impressed with the princely magnificence of the palace. In the chronicles of the time it is described as "furnished in the most sumptuous manner, with vases of silver, rich draperies of gold and silk, and other rare and splendid articles. To this was added a great collection of statues and busts in bronze and marble, and of the most excellent pictures; but the pride of the palace and the envy of other princes was the superb and copious collection of books in the Greek, Latin and other languages, with which the library was adorned, enriched with ornaments of silver and gold." The Duke Guidobaldo could richly appreciate these precious works, for he was a cultivated scholar. With the Latin language, we are told, "he was as conversant as others are with their native tongue, and so intimate was his knowledge of Greek that he was acquainted with its minutest peculiarities, and its most refined elegance."

But, unfortunately, from early life he was crippled with gout, and quite an invalid. Isabella d'Este remarked of him : "He holds a fine court here, and lives in royal splendour, and governs the State with great wisdom and humanity, to the satisfaction of all his subjects." She paid a long visit on this occasion, and when she left, Elisabetta wrote her this characteristic little note : "When you departed hence, I felt not alone the loss of a dear sister, but of life itself. I can but seek to assuage my sorrow by writing to you, and telling you on paper that which my lips desire to say. I think you would come back out of pity to me, if I could clearly express my grief. If I feared not to be a burden to you, I would gladly follow you myself. Neither is possible. I can but beg your highness to think of me as often as I bear you in my heart."

The next event of special interest in the life of Elisabetta was her visit to Rome, in the year of Jubilee 1500. It was a critical time for public affairs, as the ambition of Cæsar Borgia filled all Italy with alarm and suspicion. The Marquis of Mantua, feeling anxious about his sister's safety, wrote at the last moment to discourage the pilgrimage. "If you are in need of change, come to Mantua, and give us the joy of your society. The year is long, and we will go to Rome together and visit the holy places at a more convenient season."

But the duchess had already started, and the letter

only reached her at Assisi. She wrote at once in answer, much disturbed at going contrary to his wishes.

"Illme. Princeps et Exme. Dne. frater."

"Having left Urbino these few days, and being already on my way to Rome to keep the Jubilee, I reached Assisi this morning, and your letter arrived which would persuade me to desist from going. This has given me the greatest distress and immense annoyance, as I would wish in all things to yield and be obedient to your will, looking up to you as in the place of a father. On the other hand, as I have said, I am already on the journey, and beyond the State, and Signor Fabrizio Colonna and Madonna Agnesina, my honoured sister-in-law, have taken a house in Rome for me and made all needful arrangements, and I have promised to be at Marino in four days. Signor Fabrizio being on his way to join me, I do not see that I can draw back with honour to my lord, as the thing is so far advanced, and was arranged with his consent. Your excellency need have no fear for my safety, when you learn that I first go to Marino, and then 'incognita' to Rome with Madonna Agnesina, to visit the churches ordained for this holy Jubilee, without showing myself or speaking to any person. I shall be lodged all the time I stay in Rome in the house of the Cardinal Savelli. This is situated as I would wish, in the middle of the Colonna quarter, but the greater part of my time I will return to Marino and stay there. Therefore your excellency need have no doubt or anxiety for my safety, though, if I were not already on my way, I would have given up my desire, to show my obedience to your excellency, not from dread of danger or difficulties. Yet since I am already so far advanced on my journey, I trust you will be contented with this letter, and I pray and supplicate you to write to me in Rome, to say that you are satisfied, so that I may be able to keep this Jubilee with a happy contented mind. Otherwise I shall be in continual distress and trouble; and to the good grace of your excellency I commit myself.

"DE LA S. V. MINORE SORELLA ELIZABETTA.

"ASSISIJ, xxi. Marti, 1500."

Having written this submissive letter, she continued her journey the following day, with a quiet mind. Everything seems to have passed off well, as she had expected, and she fulfilled the desire of her heart by spending Holy Week in Rome, and visiting the various churches, St. Peter's, the Tombs of the Apostles, and all other objects of her devout pilgrimage. She paid another visit before returning home, to the Colonna's Castle of Marino, in that gloomy walled city among the Alban hills, about twenty miles from Rome, near the Lake of Albano. Here she was first introduced to her little niece, the daughter of Madonna Agnesina, that Vittoria Colonna who, at the age of seven, had already been some years betrothed to the Marquis of Pescara. Elisabetta must have been much interested in the brilliant, intelligent child, who so much resembled her in character, and who was so distinguished in after years.

On her return to Urbino, the Duchess was much distressed to hear of the death of Antonio Gonzaga, a brave captain and near connection of her husband, whose wife, Emilia Pia, was one of the favourite ladies of her court. We shall find her constantly mentioned later, in the account of those famous "conversations" of the "Cortigiano," when she regained her old brightness, but at the time she was quite broken-hearted by the loss of her husband. Isabella d'Este sent her a kind letter in which she reminded her that "it was a journey on the which we all shall go . . . and that she must seek to submit to the will of God, that her prayers for the departed soul might be accepted by Him."

The next year, Elisabetta heard with dismay that a marriage was suggested between the daughter of Pope Alexander VI. and the son of Duke Ercole of Ferrara. After the death of her sister Maddelena, the widower, Giovanni Sforza, had married Lucrezia Borgia and been divorced by her, and her second husband had been murdered. An alliance with this lady did not seem desirable, but the Borgia family were all-powerful, and when all the other members of the family had accepted the inevitable, the Duchess of Urbino consented to receive the bride at Gubbio and bear her company as far as Ferrara. This journey has been fully described in the life of Lucrezia Borgia. The Pope was so grateful for the consent of Elisabetta, that he had a magnificent litter specially made, in which she and Lucrezia could be carried together, wherever the roads permitted of it.

It was a cruel blow that, after she had thus sacrificed her feelings and graced the wedding with her courtly presence—the very same year she and her husband should be victims of Cæsar Borgia's treachery. In the beginning of June, Lucrezia's brother set forth from

Rome in great force, and marched through the Umbrian plains, leaving terror and desolation behind him. He had written friendly letters to the Duke of Urbino, asking leave to pass through his State, with the declared intention of attacking Camerino. This had been readily granted, and when Cæsar reached Nocera, he sent an embassy to Guidobaldo, asking for the assistance of his artillery, and as many soldiers as he could furnish.

But when Cæsar Borgia arrived at Spoleto, he turned suddenly up the Furlo Pass—cut by Vespasian through the Apennines—hurried along the Flaminian Way, and through the valley to Urbino. As we are told by the chronicler of the dukes: "On the 20th day of June, Guidobaldo, himself the very soul of honour, and not suspecting disloyalty in others, rode out in the cool of a summer evening to a favourite resort of his, the gardens of the Zoccolanti convent, where he sat down to supper amid the orange groves, enjoying the peaceful rest and soft balmy air; supposing himself to be in absolute security." When a messenger was seen approaching in urgent haste, he only supposed that it was a letter from his wife, who was enjoying a visit at Mantua with her friend, after the wedding of Lucrezia Borgia. But what was his dismay, when he found the man had ridden hard from Cagli, to warn him that Cæsar Borgia was marching on Urbino with a large army, and was already outside the city walls. The passes of the Apennines were already in his possession, and it was rumoured that a reward was offered for the arrest of the Lord of Urbino.

Thus taken by surprise, the duke saw that resistance was hopeless, and with some difficulty he was persuaded to save his life by flight, in company with the young heir of Urbino, his nephew Francesco della Rovere. "Such ingratitude and treachery was never before known," he writes in natural indignation. "I have saved nothing but my life, my doublet and my shirt." Fortunately it was in the middle of summer, or he would never have lived to tell the tale; and so after many hair-breadth escapes and perilous adventures, he and his nephew arrived in safety at the palace of Porto, outside Mantua. Here Elisabetta was enjoying the peaceful seclusion of those exquisite gardens, with her books and her music, in the company of the Marchesa, when the terrible news arrived.

Isabella thus gives her impression of the event in a letter to her sister-in-law Chiara, the Duchess of Montpensier: "Here at Porto, in peace and content, we were taking much pleasure in the society of the Duchess of Urbino, who has remained with us since the carnival, and we needed but your presence to make our happiness complete, when there reached us tidings of the unlooked for and most perfidious taking of the duchy of Urbino. The duke arrived here himself with but four horsemen, having been of a sudden taken by surprise and attacked with so much treachery that he had a bare escape with his life. The blow has quite overwhelmed us, and we are so stunned and distressed that we scarce know where we are, and my pity for the duchess is so profound that I could have it in my heart to wish I had never known her."

And yet as we know, only three days later, the same Isabella could write to her brother, the Cardinal Ippolyto d'Este, at Rome, urging him to make any effort to secure for her certain treasures which she coveted, from the spoils of the matchless palace of

Urbino! But all this is more fully told in the life of the Marchesa.

The Duke of Valentino had entered the hill-city at daybreak on the morning of June 21, and taken possession of the duchy. It was too late for resistance, any vain opposition was checked by imprisonment or the dagger. Urbino was treated as a conquered city, and all the priceless treasures of that palace, the envy of the whole civilised world, were at the mercy of the Roman brigand. We are told that for some weeks, a constant train of mules might have been seen creeping down the steep hill side, laden with the stolen wealth of gold and silver plate, of rare tapestries, and statues, and bronzes, and paintings beyond all price. It is impossible to estimate the value of such unique works of art, but it must have been more than half a million of gold pieces.

When Lucrezia Borgia heard of her brother's treachery, we learn that she was greatly distressed, and quite miserable to think that the Duchess of Urbino, who had been so kind to her, should have been thus treated. "I would not have had this happen for all the world!" she exclaimed.

Meanwhile, the unfortunate fugitives at Mantua were not suffered to remain there long, for in self-preservation the marquis had to keep on good terms with Cæsar Borgia. In September, the duke and duchess left the hospitable roof of the Gonzagas, and found a refuge at Venice, where they were most kindly received by the Signoria, who placed at their service a villa at Canareggio and even allowed them a small pension, for they were absolutely destitute. It must have been a sore trial to be thus suddenly cast down from magnificence to real poverty; but Elisabetta's courage never failed her, and she refused with indignation the insulting offer of a large revenue from Cæsar, if she would suffer her marriage to be annulled, and her husband would renounce his duchy and take orders. Anne de Bretagne, the noble-hearted French queen, would gladly have received her, but nothing would induce her to leave Guidobaldo. Her devoted friend and companion, Emilia Pia, was a great comfort to her in those days of trial, and she had tokens of affection and sympathy from all her relations.

It was impossible for a man of the duke's courage and spirit to remain passively in exile, and he seized the first opportunity of asserting himself. The Duke of Romagna, as Cæsar now called himself, had entered into a new treaty with Louis XII., which caused much alarm to the Italian States in alliance with him. A diet was convoked at Perugia, when his conduct was fully discussed and blamed; the news spread, and the people of Urbino seized the fortress of that place, asserted their independence, and begged their duke to return. Guidobaldo set forth at once with eager hopes, although he had not been able to induce the Marchese of Mantua to give him any help. This was early in October, and meantime the wily Borgia had reassured his former allies and made a fresh league with them, so that the duke was compelled to fly a second time, but not before he had dismantled the fortresses within his States "to the end they might not be garrisoned by his enemies, to keep in subjection a people devoted to their rightful sovereign."

Guidobaldo escaped as far as Città di Castello, where he fell seriously ill, but was unable to send any tidings to his wife, who was in terrible anxiety about him. Her brother Sigismondo, the protonotary of the Pope, went to Venice at this time of trouble to give her all the help and comfort in his power, but it was not until the end of January that she was relieved by the arrival of her husband. There was more trouble in store for the poor lady that year, for in June her eldest sister Chiara, Duchess of Montpensier, died at Mantua. She felt this bereavement very keenly, as her touching words bear witness: "I have been deprived of high estate, of my home, and of fortune, and now I have lost the sister who has ever been to me as a mother."

But a change was at hand of wide-sweeping influence over the whole of Italy. On August 18 that same year, 1505, Pope Alexander VI. died suddenly, and his son's power fell like a house of cards. The good news spread with marvellous rapidity, and everywhere the exiled princes hastened back to claim their lost dominions. At Venice there was general satisfaction, and when the duke received the welcome message he set off at once for Urbino, where the people greeted him with the wildest acclamations of delight. Eye witnesses tell us that such rejoicings were never seen before. "The very stones seemed to rejoice and sing out with gladness." Elisabetta remained at Venice until all should have settled down quietly; and meantime Pope Pius III. having only survived his elevation a month, Giuliano della Rovere had succeeded him under the name of Julius II. The accession of a Pope of his own family was a splendid stroke of fortune for Guidobaldo, who was appointed captain-general of the Church, while his sister's son, Francesco della Rovere, who was also nephew to Julius, was publicly acknowledged heir to the duchy.

The duchess took a most courtly leave of the Doge and Senate, giving them public thanks for their hospitality, and then started for Urbino at the beginning of December. The following very interesting letter of her seneschal to Isabella has been preserved, describing her return.

"ILLUSTRISSIMA MADAMA,—I propose with all deference to give your highness a record of the entrance into Urbino of her Excellency the Madonna, but words cannot relate the disasters and mishaps which we endured from bad roads and bad hostels on the way from Venice to Urbino. At last, as we came within four miles of Urbino, all the city streamed forth to meet her, chanting Te Deums, bearing olive-branches in their hands, and crying: 'Gonzaga e Feltro!' When we arrived at Urbino a vast number of gentlemen and citizens waited at the gates, and came forth to greet her with the greatest joy, kissing and pressing her hand with tears of affection, in that it was nigh upon three hours ere Her Excellency could arrive at the Piazza. In face of the Vescovada she dismounted from her horse and entered the church, where all the ladies of Urbino were assembled, and there was brought to her an olive-branch with leaves of gold, and with one voice all proclaimed the name of Her Excellency, and with great joy embraced her. Upon this, Monsignore the Bishop, robed in his vestments, led forward Madonna the Duchess by the hand to the front of the high altar, where she knelt, and all the priests were there assembled, and the Te Deum Laudamus, and other devout prayers were sung. After the blessing had been spoken, they came forth from the church and entered the palace, in company with the Bishop and all the priests and a great multitude of people, who remained in the palace till after midnight. Every day and night has Her Excellency been greeted after this fashion. She is in good health, and commends herself to your illustrious highness, and, lowly as I am, I cast myself at your feet. . . .

"Humile servitor,

"ALEXANDER, SENESCHAL."

Thus was celebrated the return of the duke and duchess to their old home, where they were so much beloved by their people. But only by slow degrees did the dismantled palace regain its former magnificence, and the famous tapestries of the Trojan War were lost for ever. But most of the rare books and many of the art treasures were sent back by Cæsar Borgia, in his desire to win the favour of Pope Julius, and once more life was resumed in that far hill-city, with added splendour and culture.

For here, in this court of Urbino, we find ourselves of a sudden wafted into an enchanted land. The magician whose might has done this is the Count Baldassare Castiglione, to whom it occurred in a moment of inspiration that he would chronicle the "sweet conversation" of the noble personages who gathered round the peerless duchess, and that he would thus seek to crystallise for ever the evanescent charm of the spoken word.

It was in September 1504 that Castiglione came to Urbino, that "island of the blest, the abode of mirth and joy and high philosophy," and to those few years which followed, he looked back with tender memories all the rest of his life as to a golden age. In his "Cortigiano" he has embodied all the most brilliant qualities of Renaissance court life, and has brought vividly before us the fair ladies with their quick intelligence and ready sympathy, and the larger proportion of gallant knights, poets, men of learning, artists, and witty cardinals. Of these we may mention the Prince Giuliano dei Medici, third son of Lorenzo the Magnificent, who afterwards married Philiberta di Savoia, and so became Duc de Nemours. For him Michelangelo carved that marvellous tomb in Florence, with the figures of Day and Night.

The Signor Cesare Gonzaga, Knight of Jerusalem, "who excelled in letters, in martial prowess, and every worthy quality."

The noble Ottaviano Fregoso, who was afterwards Doge of Genoa, and his brother, Federigo Fregosa, made Archbishop of Salerno.

They were of a Genoese family, connected with the Duke of Urbino, and their sisters, Margherita and Constanza, were in attendance upon the duchess. Of Ottaviano it was said that he was "a man the most singularly magnanimous and religious of our day, full of goodness, genius, and courtesy, a true friend to honour and virtue."

Monsignore Bernardo Bibbiena, Cardinal of Santa Maria in Portico, "of pleasing society and charming conversation."

Monsignore Pietro Bembo, a Venetian noble, afterwards made cardinal, perhaps the most eloquent speaker of all. He was a relation of Caterina Cornaro,

Queen of Cyprus, and called his 'Asolani' after her abode at Asolo.

The Count Lodovico Canossa, a connection of Castiglione.

The Ladies Margherita and Ippolyta Gonzaga, related to the duchess, Signora Raffaella, and the Lady Emilia Pia, the beloved friend and companion of Elisabetta Gonzaga.

Amongst the other guests were Giulio Romano, the artist, Giovanni Cristofero, the sculptor, Gasparo Palavicino, Alessandro Trivulzio, captain of Florence, and Bernardo Ascolti, "Unico Aretino," a man of keen wit and trenchant satire.

They were a delightful company, and there is something engaging and attractive even preserved in their portraits, as, for instance, that of Castiglione himself, painted by Raphael, and now in the Louvre. Sometimes a great man, a scholar or artist, who chanced to be passing through, would be welcomed to the courtly circle, as when Pope Julius, on his return to Rome, took Urbino on his way, and was honourably and sumptuously received, some of his company being so attracted that they continued there many days.

Last of all, but best and brightest, was Elisabetta Gonzaga herself, the peerless duchess, sovereign lady of that galaxy of talent. "Such was the respect we bore the duchess that our very liberty was a bridle; our greatest delight was to please her, our bitterest grief to offend her." All who came into her presence were attuned to her gentle will and subject to her grave and virtuous majesty. Such sway as hers was only won by infinite talent, tact, and self-suppression. With instinctive subtlety she had to select choice spirits and congenial topics, and, with apparent unconsciousness, guide the course of conversation, always lightly holding the rein, that she might tighten it in a moment by a word, a gesture, or "flash of silence."

"At Urbino the discussions were broken by hunting, riding, and hawking parties, by dance and music, but all was refined with wit and intellect. In summer the brilliant reunion would often be held in the fair gardens, on a grassy lawn, under shady trees, sheltered from sun and breeze. At other times the meeting would have a splendid setting—in a fair palace hall, with hangings of silk and tapestry, or of rich cloth of gold decked out with a wonderful number of rare antiques in marble and bronze, most excellent paintings, and instruments of music. But the noblest ornament of all was the collection of rich and rare books in Greek, Latin, Hebrew, and the Tuscan tongue, with their choice bindings of gold and silver. If the hours of the day had been given up to tilt and tourney, to every device and pastime meet for noble gentlemen, when the evening came all drew together where the Duchess was with her ladies, for she was the chain which kept all linked harmoniously in pleasant converse, subtle imagination, and witty jests."

In this atmosphere of social ease there was no set programme, but the subjects were chosen in hearty good-fellowship, which could vary from perfect courtesy to affectionate familiarity. In this aristocracy of mind there was a sentiment of equality, of high-bred refinement without pretension or ambition; the absolute freedom of intimate friends who understood each other with a half-spoken word, and who could show a gay delicacy in playing on the surface—or striking boldly

COUNT BALDASSARE CASTIGLIONE

RAPHAEL

into the vast ocean of philosophy. Count Castiglione tells us that his purpose in writing "The Courtier" was "to make a portrait in painting of the Court of Urbino, not of Raphael or of Michelangelo, but of some unknown painter, who can but draw the chief lines, without setting forth the truth in beautiful colours, or with the art of perspective." The idea of setting forth various topics in the way of dramatic talk, was very popular in the time of the Renaissance, to whose spirit the "Dialogues" of Plato, on Love and Beauty, appealed so strongly. The "Decameron," the "Canterbury Tales," the "Heptameron" are alike in this; but when we compare the work of Boccaccio and others with the refined yet brilliant discussions of the "Cortigiano," we are amazed at the contrast, and can only attribute it to the influence of the beloved Duchess, Elisabetta.

The truths of philosophy, frozen in the mind of the lonely student, are brought out into the free open air, and take life and strength as they are tossed hither and thither in gay dalliance, with keen intelligence, humour, and quick sympathy. Old stories of classical and mediæval days become mellowed like half-faded figures in some rare tapestry. Many themes are lightly touched upon, but the main purpose of the book is indicated in the title—to draw the picture of a perfect Courtier, the Scholar Gentleman, the ideal Knight—henceforth a model for all the Courts of Europe, wherein our Sir Philip Sidney may well have beheld his own image. Milton had the "Cortigiano" in his mind when he said: "I call therefore a complete and generous education that which fits a man to perform justly, skilfully, and magnanimously all the offices both private and public, of peace and war."

Spenser declares that the aim of his book is the same: "to fashion a gentleman in noble person, in virtuous and gentle discipline." We might fill a volume with instances of the marvellous influence which the work of Castiglione had upon Elizabethan literature, as we hear it echoing through the Sonnets of Shakespeare, Spenser's Hymns "Of Heavenly Love," "Of Heavenly Beauty;" Ben Jonson, Marlowe, Burton, the poets and early dramatists, even the grave Ascham; and, amongst later writers, Shelley's "Hymn to Intellectual Beauty" is steeped in the same Italian Platonism.

In the conversations recorded of this polished Court of Urbino, the play of wit, the quick retort, the delicate irony, are inimitable; and the following extracts can do no more than give a faint shadow of its charm:

"When the evening came the company assembled where the Duchess was, each sitting at his will in a circle as it always chanced." One evening, when subjects for discussion were proposed, it was Monsignore Frederigo Fregoso who suggested that they should describe all the qualities which go to the making of a perfect courtier. Count Lodovico di Canossa was first called upon to speak, and he began thus:

"First, the courtier must be a gentleman born and bred, as more will be expected of him, and being of the nobler sort, he will desire to excel his ancestors; nobleness of birth, like a clear lamp, showing forth both good and evil. Our courtier will need to be born full of grace and comeliness, and all qualities of mind and body ; and he must have good bringing-up in his youth."

Then Signor Gasparo Pallavacino objects that nobleness of birth is not indispensable for a courtier, if a man is born fortunate, with the highest gifts of nature. But Count Lodovico replies that for the perfect courtier noble birth is most desirable, for he is in high estimation at once, and so much is taken for granted, which he has not to prove and display, as a man of low birth would need to do. Men are apt to love and hate without sufficient cause. "The courtier's chief profession is arms, and herein he must excel, yet we would not have him boastful. . . For unto such may well apply the saying of a fair lady,* who courteously desired a certain knight, who shall be nameless, to dance with her, and on his refusal offered him music and other entertainments, but he declared that such trifles were not his profession. At last she asked him : "What then is your profession, signor ?"

With a frown, he replied : "To fight." Then said the lady :

"Seeing that you are not now in war, nor in any place to fight, I marvel that you do not have yourself and your harness greased, and hung up with other implements of war in an armoury, lest you should become even more rusty than you are." There was much mirth at this story, but Signor Gasparo maintained that few men who excel in anything whatsoever, abstain from praising themselves ; and on this subject there was more general conversation.

Then Count Lodovico pointed out that the courtier must be a perfect horseman, and distinguish himself

* Said to be Caterina Sforza.

in all manly sports; hunting, swimming, wrestling, running, leaping, and also in games such as tennis, which requires so great quickness and nimbleness. But in all his actions, the one essential point is that all be done with a certain grace, which cannot be learnt, but must come by nature. "Chi ha gratia, quello è grato." (Whoso hath grace, findeth grace.) Then follows a fine speech on this "Sprezzatura," an untranslatable word, meaning a negligence or apparent unconsciousness of his own merit; a grace beyond the reach of art, and not to be acquired. Only by magnanimity can he attain unto it, and no education can raise a petty soul, nor bestow upon him that crowning virtue. "Perhaps I may be able to tell you what a perfect courtier should be, but I cannot teach you how you may become one."

Even with the best natural disposition, great study and diligence is required to excel; and the instance is given of Messer Galeazzo Sanseverino, who, besides his natural advantages, had always excellent men about him, and learnt from each, that in which he was most admirable. Over preciseness must be avoided, for it offends against simplicity, and the crown of art is to hide all art, and suffer it to seem like nature.

A very slight matter betokens knowledge, such as the way of taking the weapon in hand, certain first notes in singing, or an unstudied line in drawing, or a simple graceful movement in dancing.

The courtier must speak and write well in his own language, not seeking out curious and obsolete words; and that he may do this rightly he must have knowledge, and so have somewhat worthy to say. A good voice is to be desired in speaking, not too soft and subtle as in a woman, nor yet boisterous and rough, but clear and sweet with good pronunciation and expression, set forth with fit gestures in accord with the words.

"If this courtier speak with such fineness and gravity, I doubt whether all will understand him," was objected.

"Nay, every one shall understand him," answered the count. "He will not be always grave, but will speak lightly and pleasantly, with merry conceits, and jests when occasion serves. On certain subjects he will speak with dignity and vehemence, using figures of speech with striking words to arouse and stir the mind of his hearers; yet ever with such ease, that the listener may think it an easy matter to do likewise." Then followed a discussion upon the various dialects of Italy, and on great speakers and writers. After a while, Count Lodovico remarked that in "letters is the true glory. Noble courage is inflamed by reading the deeds of famous captains and great men; for who doth not prefer the getting of that perpetual fame, before this poor life that lasteth but a day or two?"

The courtier should be a scholar, learned in history, in oratory, in poetry, and yet modest withal. Monsignore Pietro quotes that sonnet of Petrarch, CLIV.:

Giunto Alessandro alla famosa tomba
Del fero Achille, sospirando disse:
'O Fortunato, che si chiara tromba
Trovasti, e chi di te si alta scrisse!

If Alexander envied not Achilles for his deeds, but for his fortune in being sung by Homer, we see that he esteemed the words of the poet more than the arms of the soldier. Poetry was the supreme art, for with one stroke the poet paints soul and body.

Vocal music represents the speech of soul to soul. "The courtier should be a musician," continued the count, "and should have skill on sundry instruments." But the Signor Gasparo thought not so; for such delicacies would make him womanish, and bring him to dread death.

"Speak it not!" cried the Count Lodovico. "For I would give high praise to music, which has always been renowned; wise philosophers say the world is made of music, and the heavens in their moving make a melody. Socrates played the harp, and the stern Lycurgus permitted music; and the great Achilles learnt it of Chiron; and many great men and warriors have loved it well. We see it used in holy temples to laud and praise God; and labouring folk beguile their toil with song, and prisoners in adversity; and babes are hushed to sleep with it. Music is the charm of life; its light, its sunny grace. No art responds thus to the needs of our nature, none brings us such vivid and varied emotions. It softens, calms, penetrates us; it raises us to heaven with the quick eager beating of its wings."

Then the Prince Giuliano said: "I believe that music is not only an ornament, but is needful for a courtier. . . ." and there was much talk in praise of it. Presently the count continued:

"I would also have him to learn the art of drawing, which beside being of itself most noble and worthy, is of great use in war, to draw countries, rivers, bridges, fortresses, and such like."

The Lady Emilia, turning to Messer Cristofero

Romano, asked of him: "How think you? Is painting of greater worth than carving?"

He answered: "To my mind carving is of more labour, art and dignity than painting. . . ." But the count still upholding painting, Cristofero replies that surely he has Raphael in his mind; the artificer rather than the art. . . . but is interrupted by a burst of eloquence in praise of painting: "The sculptor cannot show the colour of golden hair, and the delicate flesh, nor the brightness of the eye, nor the glistening of armour, nor a dark night, nor a sea tempest, nor the burning of a city, nor the rising of the morning, in the colour of roses, with beams of purple and gold. It alone can discourse of Nature, reproduce for us the starry skies, hills and woods, gardens and rivers and cities."

Much more was said on that topic, when of a sudden, there was heard a sound of many footsteps on the floor, and a tumult of voices, and turning they saw at the chamber door a great light of torches; and presently there entered, with a great and noble train, the Lord General, who returned from accompanying the Pope a part of the way towards Rome. He joined awhile in the discourse with much pleasure; then, as it grew late, the Duchess desired the Lady Margherita and the Lady Costanza Fregosa to show them a dance, which they did, hand in hand, to the sound of sweet music. Then the Duchess arose, and every man taking his leave reverently of her, departed to his rest.

The last evening was the crown and flower of all. The first subject of discussion was the duty of a perfect courtier towards his prince, whom he must guide into ways of wisdom and nobleness. We are told that "we need a kingship in the world, for which justice and intellectual beauty are the qualifications, and which is thus more real and of divine right than any other. The love of gold, the love of power and pleasure can only reign in a world of night, when we have eyes, but cannot see;" when we have lost our enthusiasm and are dead to all higher things.

As music, sports, pastimes, and other pleasant fashions are the flower of courtliness, so the training of the prince to goodness is the fruit of it. Then followed an eloquent description of the ideal prince, whereupon one of the company protested: "But a ruler with all the qualities the Prince Giuliano would bestow upon him is, I fear, like the Commonwealth of Plato, and we shall never see such, unless it be in heaven."

The Lord Ottaviano answered that truly it was rare for the heavens to bring forth so excellent a prince, and yet he did not despair, as for his own part he had great hope of Duke Guidobaldo's nephew and heir.

Upon this the Duchess gracefully remarks: "You have gathered together so much, my lord, and so well, concerning courtliness, that we may truly say that you are not only the perfect courtier whom we seek, but also it may be the good prince yourself, which should not be without great profit to your country."

We who look back on the story of the past, are interested to find the gracious prophecy fulfilled—as the gallant Signor Ottaviano Fregoso became Doge of Genoa, in 1513.

As the book of the "Courtier" draws to an end, Baldassare Castiglione makes a supreme effort, and suddenly launches forth into a rapt exposition of the Platonism of the Renaissance; those "solemn harmonies of unearthly music." The subject of the courtier as a lover, he assigns to Pietro Bembo, who had already written, in high Platonic strain, a book of dialogues on the miseries and joys of lovers, called "Gli Asolani"; and who now pours forth his impassioned outburst.

Beginning with a masterly exposition of Platonic views on love and beauty, "a little discourse to declare what love is, and wherein consists the happiness of lovers," he earnestly declares that beauty is a holy thing, and that we may not be so profane and wicked as to speak ill of it, and thereby draw down upon us the wrath of God. Love is a desire of beauty, and heavenly love is the soul's desire for ideal beauty.

What eyes cannot see with the rays of celestial light? Of a truth, for the sake of the beloved one, the lover deserts parents and brothers and friends; he despiseth all those riches and honours of the world which he valued before, seeking the heavenly part rather than the earthly. He desireth only the brightness of divine majesty, which filleth his soul with wonder. And this is Love. . . . The "influsso" of divine beauty shines on all the created world. It rests like a ray of light on a fair face, "with marvellous grace and glistening like the beams of the sun, striking on precious fine-wrought gold, set with precious gems," adding to its beauty, shining through it and delighting the soul. "Let us therefore turn to this most holy light which showeth the way to heaven; let us climb up the steep stairs to the high place where the heavenly beauty dwelleth, and there shall we find a most happy rest, and a sure haven in the troublesome storms of the tempestuous sea of this life."

At the end, the devout Platonist breaks out into a rapturous invocation, of which this is but a fragment: "Oh! most holy love, who can praise thee aright? Most beautiful, most good, most wise, that comest from divine wisdom and returnest thither! Thou sweetest bond of unity, bringing discords into harmony, changing foes into friends, giving fruit to the earth, calm to the sea, and to heaven its light of life!

"Vouchsafe to lighten our darkness with the brightness of thy most holy fire, and show us the right way, thou who art the beginning and end of all goodness. Give us to hear thy heavenly harmony, that the discord of passion may have no more place in us. With the shining beams of thy light, purge our eyes from misty ignorance, that they be no more set on mortal beauty. Burn our souls in the living and cleansing fire, that they be sundered from the body, and joined with a most sweet and everlasting bond to the heavenly beauty! So shall we be raised from earth and admitted to join the feast of angels on high. . ."

As the speaker came to an end, he was so ravished with the images which he had called up, that he stood unconscious of all around him, until the Lady Emilia touched him and said:

"Take heed lest these thoughts draw not your soul to forsake the body, Monsignore Pietro."

"Madonna," he replied, "it would not have been the first miracle that love hath wrought in me."

The conversation, which continued for a while after this, had so entranced the listeners that they took no note of time until they were startled by the coming of daylight. "When the windows were thrown open on that side of the palace which looks towards the lofty crest of Mount Catari, they found the east aglow with rosy dawn, and the stars faded away save only Venus, the sweet ruler of the heaven, who keepeth the bounds of day and night. From thence came a soft breeze which awoke the song of birds amid the wooded groves of the hillside.

"Whereupon they all took leave with reverence of the Duchess, and departed homeward without torches, the light of day sufficing." *

It is with somewhat of the same feeling that, after this fair Platonic vision, we return to the light of common day. But such moments of high enthusiasm cannot long endure, and the golden years of Castiglione all too soon came to an end with the death of Duke Guidobaldo in April 1508.

Too often in this life, if we but turn over the page of our story, all is changed. In the allusion to the Duke's illness, we have already a foreboding of coming disaster in this interesting letter written by the Duchess to her friend, Isabella d'Este, in 1507.

"It is a month since I received the letter of your signoria, with joy and delight beyond words, and if I would

* "Il Cortigiano" was translated into English in 1552 by Sir Thomas Hoby, and became the delight of Elizabethan writers, to whom Italy was a land of Arcadia. It was the Bible of Platonism and a code of æsthetics for all Europe, and may be looked upon as an epitome of the moral and social ideas of the Renaissance. It was translated into Spanish by Boscan in 1540, and into French by Jacques Colin, secretary to King François I., in 1538. Castiglione was a favourite name in the circle of Marguerite of France. His influence still lasted in England in the days of Dr. Johnson, who remarks: "The best book that ever was written upon good breeding, 'Il Cortigiano,' by Castiglione grew up at the little Court of Urbino, and you should read it."

speak or write the joy and content I take in reading your eagerly looked-for and valued letters, it would take me an eternity. Yet if you but understood the happiness they give, I know you would give your secretary more frequent labour. . . . Though your excellency would raise my jealousy by reciting all the great and splendid things you have seen at Milan, I make answer that I feel no envy whatever. What sight can out-do that of Rome? I beheld that city, now and ever the first in the world, with all its wonderful treasures of ancient and modern times, to my unceasing amazement and delight. I saw the Pope representing God on earth, with around him the whole Roman court, second to no other. I own that your signoria has seen splendid sights, but had you beheld these, you would count them less. Of one matter I can make my boast with more cause than your excellency, which is that if I have visited Rome but once, yet Rome and the Roman court has come hither to visit me at Urbino, not once but twice at Urbino. . . . My lord duke has made a good recovery from his illness. I am in good health, and trust to hear that you are likewise. "Your sister,

"ELISABETTA, Duchess of Urbino.

"URBINO, *September* 7, 1507."

That winter was very severe at Urbino, and Guidobaldo, who had been seriously out of health for years, became steadily worse, and died on April 11 the next spring, at the age of thirty-six. "During his long and painful illness he had studied his complaint and watched the slow-paced approach of death, knowing perfectly that neither the pleasant climate of Urbino nor the most assiduous attentions would retard by an hour. And yet, even under the burden of his last anguish, he retained full possession of his intellect, with its charm and flame and serenity. His friends pretended not to have given up hope; 'why envy me so desirable a blessing?' he said to them gently. 'To be freed from this load of terrible suffering—tell me, is it not a blessing?' At the very last he turned to Castiglione and recited to him one of the finest passages in Virgil. Thus with noble colloquies, men lulled even pain asleep." *

Guidobaldo, the "Good Duke," was laid to rest by the side of his father, in the convent of the Zoccolanti friars, standing in the midst of his favourite gardens and orange groves. A solemn requiem mass was held in the cathedral, and his old tutor spoke his funeral oration with touching sympathy. As for Elisabetta, she was broken-hearted, and prostrate with exhaustion, for she had nursed her husband with the most devoted affection. The diplomatic agent sent from Mantua with condolences, thus reports his interview with her:

"I found this illustrious Madonna in her room among her ladies, all in black, the shutters closed, and only one torch placed upon the floor. She was seated upon a cushion, a black veil upon her head, . . . and I could scarcely see. She held out her hand and burst into tears; a moment passed before her sobs and mine permitted us to speak. . . .

"The funeral ceremonies, as Signor Giovanni has told you, were sumptuous. There were 825 mourners, wearing long cloaks with trains and hoods. All the

* De Maulde.

friars and priests of the State and five bishops were present, and stood round the catafalque, with an infinite number of lighted torches. . . . The universal grief and lamentation here is beyond words to describe."

The widowed Duchess appears to have behaved with admirable wisdom in her new position, and to have so managed the affair of Urbino that her husband's nephew Francesco Maria della Rovere succeeded peacefully to his inheritance. Her youngest brother Giovanni, who was devoted to her, came to be with her at this time, and he writes: "There was never so wise and prudent a Madonna, she is indeed to be praised in all she does."

She remained at the court, where she was treated with reverence and affection, and in the following year we find her going to Mantua to fetch the bride of the new Duke; Leonora Violante, the young daughter of her friend Isabella d'Este, who was extremely anxious by this marriage to win the favour of the Pope. At this time, her husband, Duke Francesco, was in a Venetian prison, and she had sore need of every powerful friend. This is how she alludes to the matter:

"We have been here entertaining the Duchess of Urbino, and a large and honourable company at large expense, but with much gladness. In a few days she will take back our young Duchess, whom we gladly send with her, trusting that his Holiness will now show us still more favour, and all the more as we hear that his Beatitude wishes her and the duke to come to Rome for the pontifical celebration of their marriage." The Pope had shown his interest by sending a splendid litter for the bride, of cloth of silver with gold cords, carried by two handsome pages in liveries to match, and also a fine dapple-grey horse with rich trappings.

Once more we have the account of a wedding journey in winter, with the doleful tale of hardships and misadventures. There was so thick a marsh fog when they left Mantua that before they reached their first resting place they lost their way and wandered about for hours in the dark. When at length they arrived as far as Modena and Bologna, they were hospitably received with banquets and dances; but as they rode on towards Faenza, the Santerno was in flood, and they were nearly drowned in crossing a mountain tributary. The stream was so full, and the rush of water had been so sudden, that a chariot with two ladies of honour and their luggage actually floated for some distance, the oxen who drew it being swept off their feet by the violence of the current. The rest of the journey was after the same fashion, through heavy rain and the worst of roads. Yet every precaution had been taken, but "the astrologer who fixed the date and hour of departure must certainly have made a false calculation," as Isabella wisely remarks.

At length the hill of Urbino was reached in safety, and the duke rode out to meet and welcome his bride and his aunt Elisabetta, and escorted them to the palace, which was splendidly prepared for them. The elder lady seems to have been very much attached to Leonora, whom she treated like her own daughter, with the image of the dearly-loved mother ever before her. It must have been a new link between the two friends of so many years. Early the next spring, when the Duke of Urbino took his wife to Rome, Elisabetta was included in the Pope's invitation, and the two ladies used every effort to induce Julius II. to obtain the freedom of the Duke of Mantua. He would reply with gracious good temper: "Have a little patience, my children;" but it was not until the following July that Leonora was gladdened by her father's liberty.

This was in 1511, and for a few years the ducal family lived in peace and happiness. A little son was born to the young Duchess in 1514, and baptized Guidobaldo, after the late duke; but already there were storms on the horizon, since the death of Pope Julius II. and the accession of the Medici Pope, Leo X. In 1515 the Duke of Urbino was deprived of his office of Gonfaloniere of the Church, and in vain Elisabetta went to Rome to plead his cause. He was excommunicated and deprived of his estates. After a vain resistance he cast his guns into the river, and fled with the two duchesses to Pesaro, from whence they embarked to travel by sea to Mantua. After a terribly stormy passage, in which they were almost driven on to the Slavonian shore, they at length reached the little village of Pietole, which became for some time the refuge of the unfortunate exiles, until the ladies were permitted to occupy rooms in the Castello of Mantua.

The following year, Francesco Maria made a vain but gallant attempt to regain his duchy, and after eight months was compelled to make terms with the Pope, who paid the arrears due to his army, and gave him leave to take his guns and his precious library of books to Mantua. He also carried with him fifty-six banners, a barren honour when they were in such great straits of poverty; for the stolen dowries of the two ladies were never restored to them, and they had to melt down all that remained to them of gold and silver plate. The Marquis of Mantua showed them much kindness, and made them a yearly allowance of 6000 ducats, which he also continued to them by his will when he died in 1519. His sister and his daughter, the two exiled Duchesses of Urbino, were present at his death-bed, and he took an affectionate leave of them.

Their long and sad exile continued until the death of Pope Leo X. in 1522, when without delay the Duke of Urbino set out once more to recover his dominions; his people rose in arms against the papal governor, and greeted him with the old cry: "Feltre! Feltre!" It must indeed have been a glad return for Elisabetta and Leonora.

We next hear of a visit paid to them at Pesaro by Isabella d'Este on her way to Rome, three years later. On this occasion, it was her young grandson Guidobaldo who rode forth beyond the gates to meet her, while the ladies awaited her coming at the great staircase of the lovely palace of the Sforzi. The dowager Duchess was already in failing health, and this was their last meeting, for early in January the next year, just after the shock of losing her beloved brother, Cardinal Sigismondo, she passed away from a world where she had so nobly played her part, and which would ever remain the poorer for her loss.

In his Prefatory Epistle to the "Cortigiano," it is with a sudden cry of grief that Baldassare Castiglione alludes to the death of his peerless lady, Elisabetta Gonzaga. "But that which cannot be spoken without tears is that the Duchess, she also is dead. And if my mind be troubled with the loss of so many friends . . .

that have left me in this life, as it were in a wilderness full of sorrow, yet with how much more grief do I bear the affliction of my dear lady's death, than of all the rest; since she was more worthy than all, and I more bounden to her."

His great work was partly written as a memorial of his "most excellent lady," who remained all his life highly enshrined in his soul.

Pietro Bembo never forgot his happy life at her court, and he says of the Duchess: "I have seen many excellent and noble women, and have heard of some who were as illustrious for certain qualities, but in her alone among women, all virtues were united and brought together.

"I have never seen or heard of any one who was her equal, and know very few who have even come near her."

INDEX

INDEX

INDEX

INDEX

INDEX

INDEX

INDEX

INDEX

INDEX

INDEX

INDEX

INDEX

INDEX

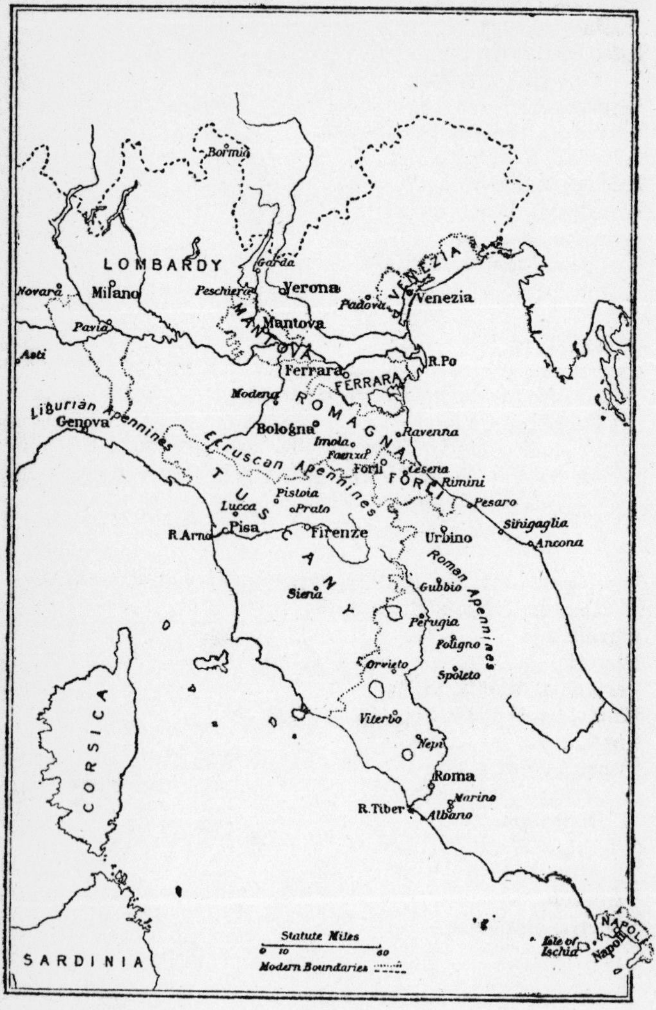

Bormio
LOMBARDY
Garda
Novara
Milano
Peschiera
Verona
Padova
VENEZIA
Venezia
Pavia
MANTOVA
Mantova
Asti
R.Po
Ferrara
FERRARA
Modena
ROMAGNA
Liburian Apennines
Genova
Bologna
Ravenna
Imola
Faenza
Etruscan Apennines
Forli
Cesena
FORLI
Rimini
TUSCANY
Pistoia
Lucca
Prato
Pesaro
Sinigaglia
Pisa
R.Arno
Firenze
Urbino
Ancona
Roman Apennines
Gubbio
Siena
Perugia
Foligno
Orvieto
Spoleto
CORSICA
Viterbo
Nepi
Roma
Marino
R.Tiber
Albano
Statute Miles
0 10 60
Modern Boundaries
Isle of Ischia
NAPOLI
Napoli
SARDINIA